Issues in Religious Education

Religious Education in schools continues to b... ...
cially topical in our multicultural and multifaith society. This book is designed
to give student and newly-qualified teachers a contextual and theoretical background to this subject, by exploring and challenging assumptions about the
place of religion in education.

The book is divided into three sections:

- Section 1 sets out the context for Religious Education in the curriculum. It
  looks at political, social and religious influences on legislation, particularly
  in faith schools, and raises questions about assessment and inspection.
- Section 2 focuses on Religious Education in the classroom, exploring our
  understanding of religion and the concept of development in Religious
  Education. It also looks at teaching Religious Education to pupils with
  special educational needs.
- Section 3 examines Religious Education as a whole-school issue, considering its relationship to literacy, citizenship, collective worship and
  spiritual, ethical and moral development.

Issues in Religious Education Teaching will be important reading for student
teachers at all levels, and will also provide a useful refresher for experienced
teachers.

Lynne Broadbent is Director of the British and Foreign School Society
National Religious Education Centre at Brunel University.

Alan Brown is an educational consultant, advisor and writer.

Issues in Subject Teaching Series
Series edited by Susan Capel, Jon Davison, James Arthur
and John Moss

Issues in English Teaching
Edited by Jon Davison and John Moss

Issues in Geography Teaching
Edited by Chris Fisher and Tony Binns

Issues in History Teaching
Edited by James Arthur and Robert Phillips

Issues in Physical Education Teaching
Edited by Sue Capel and Sue Pietrowski

Issues in Mathematics Teaching
Edited by Peter Gates

Issues in Modern Foreign Language Teaching
Edited by Kit Field

Issues in Music Teaching
Edited by Chris Philpott and Charles Plummeridge

Issues in Science Teaching
Edited by John Sears and Pete Sorensen

Issues in Teaching using ICT
Edited by Marilyn Leask

Issues in Design and Technology Teaching
Edited by Bob Barnes, Jim Morley and Su Sayers

Issues in Religious Education
Edited by Lynne Broadbent and Alan Brown

Issues in Religious Education

Edited by Lynne Broadbent and
Alan Brown

London and New York

First published 2002
by RoutledgeFalmer
11 New Fetter Lane, London EC4P 4EE

Simultaneously published in the USA and Canada
by RoutledgeFalmer
29 West 35th Street, New York, NY 10001

RoutledgeFalmer is an imprint of the Taylor & Francis Group

Typeset in Goudy by Taylor & Francis Books Ltd
Printed and bound in Great Britain by MPG Books, Bodmin

British Library Cataloguing in Publication Data
A catalogue record for this book is available from the British Library

Library of Congress Cataloging in Publication Data
Issues in Religious Education / edited by Lynne Broadbent and Alan
Brown.
p. cm. – (Issues in Subject Teaching)
Includes bibliographical references and index
1. Religious Education. I. Broadbent, Lynne, 1949– II. Brown, Alan,
1944– III. Series
BL42.I87 2002
379.2'8'0941–dc21

ISBN 0–415–26252–6 (hbk)
ISBN 0–415–26253–4 (pbk)

Contents

Notes on contributors   viii
Abbreviations   xi
Preface   xiii

PART I
The nature of Religious Education within the school curriculum   1

1   The statutory requirements for Religious Education 1988 – 2001:
    religious, political and social influences   3
    ALAN BROWN

2   A rationale for Religious Education   16
    LYNNE BROADBENT

3   Religious Education in Church schools   27
    JOHN BAILEY

4   Commitment and indoctrination: a dilemma for Religious
    Education?   44
    TREVOR COOLING

5   Issues in the teaching of Religious Education: assessing
    achievement in RE from early years to 'A' Level   56
    JOHN KEAST

6   Inspecting Religious Education: can inspections improve
    Religious Education?   71
    JAN THOMPSON

7 Religious Education in the European context   86
   PETER SCHREINER

PART II
Religious Education in the classroom   99

 8 How far do Programmes for RE relate to the Social and
    Psychological Development of Pupils?
    Development through Religious Education.   101
    BRIAN GATES

 9 Ethnography and Religious Education   111
    ELEANOR NESBITT

10 Not 'either-or', more a case of 'both-and': towards an inclusive
    gender strategy for Religious Education   123
    DINAH HANLON

11 Religious Education and pupils with special needs: a dialogue 136
    LYNNE BROADBENT AND ALAN BROWN

12 The birth of a new Religious Studies at post-16   150
    ARTHUR GILES

PART III
Religious Education and the wider curriculum   163

13 The contribution of Religious Education to whole school
    initiatives   165
    LYNNE BROADBENT

14 Is Religious Education and ethical and moral debate a contradiction? 178
    PETER VARDY

15 Embodying the spirit: realising RE's potential in the spiritual
    dimension of the curriculum   189
    JOHN HAMMOND

16 **Religious Education and Collective Worship: bedfellows or just good friends?** 201

GEOFF MARSHALL-TAYLOR

17 **World religions: the boundaries of belief and unbelief** 210

JOHN BOWKER

Bibliography 218
Index 228

Contributors

John Bailey taught RE in Kent and the ILEA, was RE Adviser for Lincolnshire in the 1970s, a District Inspector in Manchester and County Chief Inspector for Bedfordshire in the 1980s. He came to Lincoln Diocese as Schools Officer in 1991 and was appointed Diocesan Director of Education in 1995. John has written and edited a wide range of books on RE and Collective Worship, the most recent being *Cultural Development* (The National Society 1997) and *Worship! Making Primary School Worship Come Alive* (The National Society 1999).

John Bowker was formally Professor of Religious Studies at Lancaster University and Fellow of Trinity College, Cambridge. He is an Honorary Canon of Canterbury Cathedral. He is the author of numerous books including *Is God a Virus? Genes, Culture and Religion* (1995) and *The Meanings of Death* (awarded the HarperCollins Religious Book Award in 1993) and was editor of the *Oxford Dictionary of World Religions* (1999). His latest book is *God: A Brief History* (Dorling Kindersley 2002).

Lynne Broadbent is Director of the British and Foreign Schools Society's National Religious Education Centre at Brunel University. She is course tutor for PGCE secondary and primary courses in Religious Education, an RE Consultant to two LEAs, an INSET provider and an OFSTED and Section 23 inspector. She has written on the contribution of Religious Education to the primary curriculum, to Values and Citizenship Education, and to pupils' spiritual, moral, social and cultural development. Her research interest is in the relationship between subject knowledge and pedagogy.

Alan Brown is a freelance education consultant with a wide experience of teaching, writing and advising on Religious Education, Collective Worship and Spiritual and Moral Development. He was Schools' Officer (RE) for the Church of England's Board of Education and Director of The National Society's RE Centre in London. He has been Chair and Secretary of the Shap Working Party and currently edits the Shap Journal. He was President of the Intereuropean Commission on Church and Schools for six years. His latest publication is a series for Key Stages 1 and 2 Encounter Christianity CHP (2001/2002).

Trevor Cooling is Director of the Stapleford Centre, a charity which offers resources and training for teaching Christianity in school RE. He is also a Special Lecturer in the School of Education at the University of Nottingham and is course leader for the distance learning courses in RE validated by the University.

Brian Gates is Professor of Religious and Moral Education in the Department of Religion and Ethics at St Martin's College, Lancaster. His interests include staffing and ICT resource provision in this curriculum area, the interface between faith and health, and religious development across the lifespan. He is vice-chair of the RE Council of England and Wales.

Arthur Giles was head of RS at Barnstaple Grammar and Garrett Green School. He lectured at Borough Road College, which is now part of Brunel University, and has been Head of RS and Head of Humanities. He has been an 'A' Level examiner for about thirty years, including AQA, and is Chief Examiner for Edexcel.

John Hammond studied for a degree in Religious Studies with Ninian Smart at Lancaster. He then taught RE at high schools in London and Preston. Following a break for an MA he joined St Martin's College to run the PGCE in RE, teach Religious Studies and work in Performing Arts courses in Drama and Myth. As well as occasional articles and reviews in RE journals he co-authored *Christian Belief and Practice*, a GCSE textbook, and *New Methods in RE*, a teachers' handbook. Recently retired from St Martin's, he is now engaged in consultancy work, mainly in Lancashire and Cumbria and the Roman Catholic Diocese of Lancaster, and is working on another hand-book for teachers that emphasises the communal and embodied dimensions of religion and RE.

Dinah Hanlon is Senior Lecturer and Subject Leader for Religious Education on the primary BA and PGCE courses in the Faculty of Education, University of Central England, Birmingham. She has extensive experience of teaching, lecturing, advising and inspecting both RE and Equal Opportunities in school, HEI and LEA contexts.

John Keast works for QCA as Principal Manager for RE, Citizenship and PSHE. From 1989 to 1996 he was a County Adviser and Inspector for RE and PSE. He has been a teacher since 1974 in comprehensive schools, Deputy in a Sixth Form Centre, an Ofsted inspector and an examiner for Religious Studies.

Geoff Marshall-Taylor was until recently Executive Producer, BBC Education, responsible for School Radio Collective Worship programmes on School Television RE programmes. A former teacher in both primary and secondary phases, he is an Associate Fellow of the Warwick University Institute of Education and an INSET provider. In addition to articles on RE and Collective Worship, his publications include *Come and Praise* (BBC), *Let's* *pray Together* (Collins), *The Children's Bible* (Octopus) and the *Dorling Kindersley Children's Bible*. A lay reader in the Church of England, he is now an educational consultant and programme producer.

Eleanor Nesbitt is Senior Lecturer in Religions and Education in the Institute of Education, University of Warwick. She has published widely on religious socialisation in UK Sikh, Hindu and Christian communities. She co-edits the *International Journal of Punjab Studies* and *Guru Nanak*, co-authored with Gopinder Kaur, received the Shap award 2000.

Peter Schreiner is educational researcher (Diplom-Pädagoge) and works at the Comenius-Institut in Germany, a centre for research and development in education of the Protestant churches and Protestant teachers' associations in Germany. He is doing research in comparative religious education in Europe and ecumenical learning. As General Secretary he is involved with the Intereuropean Commission on Church and School (ICCS).

Jan Thompson studied theology at King's College, London and has a Masters Degree in education. She taught Religious Education in secondary schools before becoming RE adviser for Bromley LEA in 1987, and qualified as an OFSTED inspector in 1997. She has many publications to her name, having written RE textbooks and teachers' handbooks since 1979. She has recently become Assistant Director of Education (Schools) for the Diocese of Rochester where she organises the Section 23 inspections of church schools.

Peter Vardy is Vice-Principal of Heythrop College, the specialist theology and philosophy College of the University of London. He is a former chair of the board of Theological Studies of the University, author of the best selling 'Puzzle' series of books on God, Evil, Ethics, The Gospels and Sex which have been translated into six languages, founding editor of 'Dialogue Australia' and was theological adviser to the recent BBC series on *Sex and Religion*. He runs conferences for sixth-form students and teachers throughout England and Australia on ethics, philosophy of religion, science and religion and the Hebrew and Christian scriptures. His latest book, *What is Truth?* is published by the University of New South Wales.

Abbreviations

A2 - Advanced Level GCE
ACAC - Curriculum and Assessment Authority for Wales
AEA - Advanced Extension Award
AQA - Assessment and Qualifications Alliance
AREAIC - Association of RE Advisers Inspectors and Consultants
AS - Advanced Subsidiary
AT - Attainment Target
CCEA - Council for the Curriculum, Examinations and Assessment in Northern Ireland
CPD - continued professional development
CSE - Certificate of Secondary Education
DES - Department for Education and Skills
DfEE - Department for Education
DfES - Department for Education and Science
EFs - Evidence Forms
EFTRE - European Forum for Teachers of Religious Education
ERA - Education Reform Act
FARE - Forms of Assessment in RE
FE - Further Education
GCSE - General Certificate of Secondary Education
GNVQ - General National Vocational Qualification
HMI - Her Majesty's Inspector
HND - Higher National Diploma
ICCS - Intereuropean Commission on Church and School
ICT - Information
ID - identification (cards)
INSET - In-service Training
ISKCON - International Society for Krishna Consciousness
IT - Information technology
KS - Key Stage
KUE - Knowledge, Understanding and Evaluation
LEA - Local Education Authority
MA -Master of Arts

NASACRE - National Association of SACREs
NBRIA - National Board for Religious Inspectors and Advisers
NC - National Curriculum
NCC -National Curriculum Council
OCR - Oxford, Cambridge and RSA Examinations
OFSTED - Office for Standards in Education
PcfRE - Professional Council for RE
PE - Physical Education
PGCE - Post Graduate Certificate of Education
PHSE - Personal, Health and Social Education
PSE - Personal and Social Education
RE - Religious Education
RS - Religious Studies
QCA - Qualifications and Curriculum Authority
SACRE - Standing Advisory Councils for Religious Education
SCAA - School Curriculum and Assessment Authority
SEN - Special educational needs
SLD - Severe Learning Difficulties
SMSC - Spiritual, Moral, Social and Cultural Development
TTA - Teacher Training Agency
UCAS - Universities and Colleges Admissions Services
UNESCO - United Nations Educational, Scientific and Cultural Organisation
WCC - World Council of Churches
WRERU - Warwick Religions and Education Research Unit

Preface

Religion is a challenging and dangerous phenomenon encompassing the beliefs and commitments at the heart of the individual and a public and political image frequently associated with violence and war. Both its intensely personal and its public images can lie uncomfortably with the teaching of Religious Education in schools: for many trainee teachers there can remain an ambiguity between personal belief and professional activity, while the controversial nature of the subject can prove daunting for experienced practitioners. For many pupils, but thankfully not all, the challenging and dynamic nature of religion is left at the school gate and Religious Education lessons become a technically well-managed yet vacuous description of religious practice rather than a vigorous, exciting and relevant process of learning.

This book has been compiled during a period of heated debate about the role of religion in schools, specifically in the proposed increase in 'faith schools'. The book aims to help the reader place the development of Religious Education in an historical and education context. It seeks to address the issues that influence the inclusion of Religious Education within the school curriculum and the impact of Religious Education upon the curriculum and upon the intellectual and personal development of pupils.

The book falls into three sections. Part I sets the context for Religious Education in the curriculum. It explores the political, social and religious influences which affect national legislation and local syllabus construction. It addresses the teaching of religion in schools with a religious affiliation, a pertinent concern at a time when government initiatives focus on extending the number of faith schools. This, in turn, raises once again questions about the relationship between personal faith stance and the professional process of teaching about religion in schools. Issues of assessment and inspection have featured strongly in public discourse since the Education Reform Act of 1988. The section concludes with a reflection on legislation and pedagogy relating to Religious Education within European countries.

Part II focuses on the issues posed when teaching Religious Education in the classroom. One chapter explores the whole concept of 'development' when applied to the teaching of RE, while another explores the influence of ethnographic research on our understanding of the nature of 'religion' itself, scattering any conveniently structured approach to the study of religion to the winds! Further contributions address the perceived tendency for Religious Education to appeal to girls rather than boys, the relevance of Religious Education at 16-plus and the principles and practices of teaching Religious Education to pupils with special educational needs.

Part III adopts a broader frame of reference to consider the contribution of Religious Education to whole school issues. It includes consideration of recent government initiatives related to literacy and citizenship, to the spiritual dimension of the curriculum, to collective worship and to developing pupils' skills in ethical and moral debate. Finally, a chapter by John Bowker raises the subject of religion in an international context and sounds a warning note to those tempted to underplay or even dismiss the significance of Religious Education in contemporary society.

We would like to acknowledge the enthusiasm and co-operation of the contributing authors who have given so generously of their time, energy and insight. Thanks is also due to those who have lent their IT skills to the final compilation of the text and to Pat Hughes for her considerable secretarial support throughout the project.

Lynne Broadbent
Alan Brown

Part I

The nature of Religious Education within the school curriculum

1 The statutory requirements for Religious Education 1988–2001

Religious, political and social influences

Alan Brown

The curriculum for a maintained school satisfies the requirements of this section if it is a balanced and broadly based curriculum which –

(a) promotes the spiritual, moral, cultural, mental and physical development of pupils at the school and of society; and

(b) prepares such pupils for the opportunities, responsibilities and experiences of adult life.

(Education Reform Act 1988 chapter 40 part 1 Section 1:2)

Any Agreed Syllabus...Shall reflect the fact that the religious traditions in Great Britain are in the main Christian whilst taking account of teaching and practices of the other principal religions represented in Great Britain.

(Education Reform Act 1988 chapter 40 Section 8:3)

These two extracts from ERA, now incorporated into the Education Act (1996), represent the axiom upon which the balance of RE has rested for the last two decades. Prior to 1988 there was no clear guidance in law as to the content of Religious Education (or as it was then called, 'Religious Instruction'); the words 'Religious Education' being reserved in the defining Education Act of 1944 for the twin foci of ' Religious Instruction' and 'Collective Worship'.

RI, RE or RS

What is generally not well known was that in 1987 there was a brief discussion between the then Secretary of State for Education and representatives from the Church of England whether RI could be changed, not to RE, but to Religious Studies. The reason was that many teachers of RE in secondary schools were already adopting an approach which allowed them to stand back from the truth claims of the various religions in order to study them more 'objectively'. The emphasis was very much on the study of religion and educating pupils through that strategic approach rather than educating them 'into' religion. There was already a 'Religious Studies' style of teaching very much in line with the influential views of Professor Ninian Smart and his phenomenological approach outlined in the Schools' Council Working Paper 36 and promoted through the activities of the *Shap Working Party on World Religions in Education* (1999/2000). It was felt that 'RE' was as much as Members of Parliament could cope with at the time; to make a more significant change would be likely to affect any other changes already in the pipeline – so RE it remained. The political advice was well judged as the debates on RE in the House of Lords demonstrated. In retrospect, of course, the subject is now called RS at Key Stage 4 and at post-16 education, so the suggested change has happened almost by default.

The Education Reform Act 1988

There have, of course, been interpretations of the wording of the 1988 Education Reform Act (ERA) since its enactment, notably by the then DES in its Circular 3/89 on Religious Education and School Collective Worship and, more controversially some years later, in its subsequent Circular 1/94. The controversy that raged in the world of RE and amongst some religious groups was primarily concerned with those paragraphs in the Circular 1/94 that related to Collective Worship. Circular 3/89 had been regarded as generally helpful and supportive to those teaching RE and to the organisers of Collective Worship. The 1988 ERA had, for the first time, defined the basic content of RE (see ERA Ch. 40:8:3). It was really quite remarkable, given the tetchy quality of the debates in the House of Lords, that the teaching of the principal faiths in Great Britain should have been included in primary legislation and not just the teaching of Christianity (though the legislation did in fact reflect common practice, particularly in secondary schools). This situation may seem dated, almost neolithic in the early twenty-first century, but a cursory glance through the debates in Hansard catches the flavour of the deep feelings expressed. The openness and enabling character of the legislation owed much to Kenneth Baker, then Secretary of State, and the Bishop of London, Dr Graham Leonard. As the bill proceeded through the Lords it became clear that the members did not distinguish between RE and Collective Worship; in fact, many did not distinguish between school education and church Sunday School education. As a consequence there began to emerge an agreement that as long as Christianity was mentioned in such a way that it was given pre-eminence there would be an acceptance of the proposed wording for RE. There would, however, need to be a 'fudge' regarding Collective Worship. The wording on Collective Worship was obscure and complex and is not the main concern of this chapter: what is important to note is that many teachers and others continue not to make a clear distinction between what the law required for RE and what it required for Collective Worship: that confusion still surfaces today.

The ERA did, however, focus people's minds on what Religious Education should be about. The writer remembers having lunch in the 1980s with the Parliamentary Private Secretary to Keith Joseph, then the Secretary of State for

Education. She observed that RE was an unimportant subject in the curriculum and the influence of the religious lobby on education was minimal. Within a very few years the initial two lines on RE and Collective Worship in the Education Reform Bill had burgeoned to several pages and in Hansard there are more pages devoted to RE and school Collective Worship than to any other single topic in that major Bill.

New syllabuses emerged, as did the legal requirement for every LEA to convene a Standing Advisory Council on RE (SACRE). This body, convened under different regulations from the Syllabus Conference, was intended to support and provide guidance for the teaching of RE in each LEA. It would report annually to the central government curriculum agency, now called QCA. Today, with the greater financial pressure on LEAs, SACREs function variously; some are clearly excellent and provide very good guidance for teachers of RE and a supportive advisory system; others take their responsibilities more lightly. This has led some to call for a national syllabus for RE but there is little support for it in the LEAs. It would be a further centralisation of the curriculum, taking away more autonomy from the local authorities. The Model Syllabuses have, to some extent, provided a basic formula for new RE syllabuses, particularly as they are now a requirement in initial teacher training. Unfortunately they are now dated and in urgent need of revision.

Circular 3/89 and after

The Circular 3/89 was generally believed to support RE teaching and teachers. It was an 'enabling' Circular, supportive of the contemporary situation, intended to bring order and calm after the tensions of the 1988 legislation. A small though influential group, however, worked hard to influence the Secretary of State in order to 'protect' Christianity in the classroom; a view seen as quite unnecessary by the vast majority of those teaching RE and by those involved in the 1988 ERA. Christianity was the central theme of every syllabus, especially every new syllabus, so did this group have another more subversive agenda? In general, the argument concerned *what* should be taught, to *whom* and *how much* time should be given to the teaching of Christianity. In the main, the vociferous, traditionalist Christian group were quite content for Jews, Muslims, Hindus and other faith groups to be given a religious education in their respective faiths, but everyone else, Christian and others (those who were not positively of another faith), had to receive the appropriate dosage of Christianity and a Christianity that was taught as true. It was, in effect, a reaction against the phenomenological approach that had been so influential – no matter that its originator and promoter was a Scottish Episcopalian! This, crudely, meant, 'we teach the Christian religion to everyone who isn't anything else; the other faiths can teach their own pupils but they too will need to know something of Christianity because of its influence on culture, literature, politics et cetera'. The study of religion, therefore, as an academic subject with its own intellectual integrity came under considerable threat. Was this the real agenda:

Christianity, when taught, had to be taught as true, not as a religion that claimed to *be* true and have a truth to share?

It may be noted in passing that the current government policy on religious schools could be seen as a derivation of this view. The teaching of Religious Education will be important in these schools but will it always be taught as if the religion on which the school is founded is true and will the Religious Education taught encourage pupils to look at the beliefs and practices of other faiths? Will teachers be able, and will they want, to teach in the classroom the truths of those faiths not recognised in the foundation of the school? Will the result be that RE *will* be taught in the religious schools but slip quietly into the background in the community schools? It would be, unfortunately, a failure to recognise the integrity of Religious Education as an academic study worthy of study for its own sake and that is the criterion for its inclusion in the school curriculum. It is not clear at the time of writing whether the churches and other religious groups are prepared to intercede on behalf of the study of religion in *all* schools as opposed to the promotion of their own distinctive understanding of what RE should contain in their own schools. It may be that the Christian traditionalists have lost a battle or two but will win the war!

Circular 1/94 and all that

In a letter to Chief Education Officers on 18 March 1991 the then Secretary of State, Kenneth Clarke, offered guidance regarding the format and content of RE Agreed Syllabuses. Whatever advice emerges, from the DES, DofE, DfEE or DfES, it is based on legal advice on how the law may be interpreted and, therefore, can only be advisory. This letter appeared to be much more prescriptive than the law required. The letter marked the beginning of the end of what might be called 'aims and objectives' syllabuses. The trend had developed for RE syllabuses to contain little detailed content (this would be incorporated into an accompanying Handbook) and would contain a list of aims and objectives for each age range and programme of study. The Syllabus itself would only be a few pages long; the advisory Handbook would be much more substantial. This approach was never popular among the more conservative Christian lobby because it allowed LEAs and schools far too much freedom to teach aspects of religion other than Christianity. Clarke's ill-timed and ill-considered intervention meant that syllabuses would have to be much more content-laden so that parents and gimlet-eyed Christians would know *what* was being taught and *when* to pupils and for *how long*: they would be able to measure how much time was being devoted to each religion. The dis-ease caused by the letter and the discontent felt by some evangelical Christian groups led five years later to the production of another Circular superseding Circular 3/89 though still based on the ERA.

The controversial aspect of the Circular on RE and School Collective Worship (1/94) arose directly out of dissatisfaction with Kenneth Clarke's letter, and essentially concerned Collective Worship (which is addressed below). For some reason the RE profession, ill-advisedly, allowed itself to be drawn into the debate even though the responsibility for the organisation of Collective Worship lies not with the RE teacher, it lies with the head teacher. What Circular 1/94 did *not* do was decide the detailed content of RE, that was now relatively uncontroversial, leaving the RE profession with some integrity, so why did they feel the need to become embroiled in the debate on Collective Worship?

There was a concerted lobbying of the Secretary of State for Education by some Christian groups to require him to offer an interpretation of the Law which would allow less flexibility for the LEAs who were writing their new RE syllabuses. This was resisted and the section of the 1988 Education Reform Act relating specifically to Religious Education has largely been unchallenged except by one or two Christian evangelical groups who appear to regard the wording as a sell-out to the multifaith, multicultural lobby, inhibiting their approach.

RE and Collective Worship

It is worth noting that while RE specialists, particularly those teaching at Key Stages 3, 4 and 5, generally wish to make a sharp distinction between RE and school collective worship, that distinction is by no means so clear to the general public, nor to many pupils, nor to teachers in primary schools. If one wished to be controversial, one could make a case for the RE profession never really defining their subject sufficiently in subject-oriented, educational terms. There still exists a large group teaching RE for whom RE remains a confessional subject, having strong links with Collective Worship, and an endemic Christian morality as opposed to any other moral view, religious or humanist. The linking of RE and Collective Worship has historic overtones and has, in many ways, become a burden around the neck of those who wish to promote RE as a systemic, distinctive subject. Their argument is strengthened by the fact that in most schools, particularly the non-religious schools, school worship bears no relation whatsoever to worship as carried out by followers of any particular faith. School worship, therefore, does not illuminate the teaching about worship in the faith communities that takes place in curriculum RE.

Pre-1988: an overview

Religious Education has always been attached to controversy. The inter-denominational wrangling between the various Christian groups prior to the 1944 Education Act resulted in central government distancing itself from the content of RE. The legal requirement to establish Syllabus Conferences to determine the content of RE in each LEA gave a special place among the religious groups, in England, to the established church, the Church of England. The assumption was that RE was essentially to do with biblical knowledge (because all Christians agreed the Bible was important) and moral teaching and the Church would be the guardian of such basic truths. Such assumptions die hard outside the parameters of those concerned professionally with the teaching of RE. Politicians and others tend to perceive RE as having the major aim of inculcating faith and providing moral fibre. A swift survey of the development of RE since the 1940s illustrates the point.

In the 1940s until the early 1960s most agreed syllabuses were little more than lists of content relating to the Old Testament, New Testament and some periods of church history. The assumption was that 'Biblical teaching based on a Christian interpretation was Religious Instruction'. Pupils at school during this period would have received an unvarying diet of Bible stories largely unrelated to Christian beliefs, rites and practices. Indeed, in many schools it was called 'Divinity' or 'Scripture' – a custom that has not entirely disappeared.

In the 1960s there was a move, encouraged by the work of Ronald Goldman (1964) and also Harold Loukes (1961), to interpret Religious Instruction in a more relevant manner which would relate in some existential way to the lives of the pupils. Such initiative received a patchy response and it was really the West Riding Syllabus for RE of the late 1960s which tried to put this into effect. The move was perhaps a belated reflection on the changing society of the 1960s but reflected the way in which educational philosophy was changing. 'Relevance' appeared to be of central concern to curriculum planners and RE sought to respond. The period remains important because, perhaps for the first time, Religious Education as a curriculum subject was prepared to be closely associated with moral education and personal and social education. This developing relationship continues to be attractive to some, mainly on the Christian right, who appear to see a direct link between RE, moral behaviour and violence at football matches. One MP and ex-teacher, very supportive of RE, announced at an RE conference, 'if there was more RE in schools there would be less violence at Chelsea football matches'. The relationship is difficult to sustain on many levels, not least religion's own violent history.

More seriously, however, the era of the 1960s did create a platform with which RE constantly struggles; is it an academic subject in its own right and therefore has a body of knowledge worthy of in-depth study; or is it a collection of personal attitudes, behaviours and the like? Does it regard its curricular strength as taking into itself aspects of every other subject, particularly those lying at the perimeter of the curriculum? The tension has not been resolved as any glance at the new examinations specifications (2001) in Religious Studies reveals. ERA defined RE as being part of the 'basic curriculum' but the phrase fell rapidly into disuse.

Internecine warfare

The 1970s and 1980s witnessed a further shift. This time those concerned with a 'world religions' approach to RE really did lock horns with the conservative conventionalists who saw the predominance (and perhaps the truth) of Christianity being threatened in the classrooms of England and Wales. The highlight of this period was the process through which the Birmingham LEA arrived at a new RE syllabus in the mid-1970s where the study of Humanism and

Communism as religions were in, then out. In fact, during the 1970s and 1980s (including the vitriolic debates during the progress of the Education Reform Bill through the House of Lords in 1987/8) the rigour of debate was largely between Christians themselves rather than between educators and Christians, or between members of other religions and Christians. It is too easy and truly simplistic to regard the debates on RE in the 1970s and 1980s as gladiatorial, though at times it seemed to be certain evangelical Christians versus liberal Christians in the Coliseum of Westminster (though it must be said that Dr Leonard, who proposed the ammendments that passed into law, was not normally considered to be the most liberal bishop in the Church of England). It was, in reality, much more like the 'Christians versus Christians' on the streets of Constantinople at the time of the Crusades where Christians were far more interested in landing blows on other Christians than on other faiths (or none).

The academic integrity of religion

An important criticism of the 'world religions' approach made by its opponents was that some promoters of the approach argued from the premise that as Britain was 'now' a multifaith, multicultural society, that should be reflected in the syllabus content of RE. The weakness lies in statistics, as even today (2002) the percentage of people in the United Kingdom who are members of a religion other than Christianity is probably about 5–6 per cent (though the 2001 census may amend that slightly). The presence of people from an Afro-Caribbean background increased the percentage of 'other religions' only minimally as many have strong links with the Christian faith. In that sense, therefore, the United Kingdom, nationally, is barely *multi*-faith or even *multi*-cultural. (This ignores the internationalism that the global village has made available and the density of religious and ethnic groups in some urban areas). The willingness of some people to see 'multifaith' and 'multicultural' as a tautological does not help.

RE and SMSC

The recent trends in Religious Education have been affected significantly by the first of the two quotations from the ERA at the beginning of this chapter. In 1992 the School Inspection Act required the creation of OFSTED and a new model of inspection. One area that now required inspection (in accordance with rigorous, if ill-defined criteria) was Spiritual, Moral, Social and Cultural Development (SMSC). Nearly sixty years ago the Education Act of 1944 had used 'spiritual' as being less definitive and more inclusive than 'religious' and the practical meaning of the term in the school context had lain dormant. Now, however, it was given new life, but unfortunately, no one knew quite what it meant. Admittedly, worthy and knowledgeable civil servants, OFSTED inspectors and the religious hordes gave voice to a definition, but all appeared to have little sensitivity to a word which has all the guile of the *via negativa*. RE (or more precisely some within RE) spied a bandwagon on which to jump. One could side step the phenomenology of the 'world religions' approach and engage more directly with an experiential understanding of religion (never actually excluded at all by the phenomenologists). As a result, syllabuses, resource books and in-service training began to link spiritual development and RE.

The problem with this approach was twofold. First, it was very difficult to arrive at an agreed definition of spirituality, so to link it so firmly to religion was a hard task. 'Spirituality' is not a word that lends itself easily to definition. 'Fluffy' appears to epitomise this approach, for while religions are indeed concerned with spiritual values and spiritual development, it is impossible to assess spiritual development as if it were just another curriculum subject; spirituality is an evasive word that can mean what one wants it to mean. Teachers can, and unfortunately some do, teach religion as if it were simply a collection of moral codes, rules and threats to humanity. They transfer information as if there were no spiritual content in religion at all. One can assess some of the skills and attitudes needed in the exploration of spirituality and religion but spirituality is so determined by the affective, one can never assess progress and understanding with confidence and clarity.

Second, there was a concern that Religious Education should be 'doing something' with and to pupils above and beyond the call of general education provision. Of course the study of every subject should have an effect on the pupils' whole development, but why do those who link RE and spirituality look for significant change in pupils? This is a Platonic-style reflection of the confessionalism and neo-confessionalism of the 1940s–1970s (still alive and well) which might be termed pseudo-confessionalism because teachers 'pretend' not to want to change pupils' points of view but actually seek to do so and judge success by the pupils' response.

The Values Forum and citizenship

The late 1990s and early 2000s held out another tempting morsel to those who wished RE to hang onto the coat tails of other curriculum subjects. In the mid-1990s it was pointed out to the government curriculum agency, SCAA, that in the reduced National Curriculum produced at the time, all reference to spirituality had been erased, inadvertently of course. In response the Values Forum was created. One hundred and fifty people, the great and the good, were called together to produce a statement of values which would reflect the concerns of society and give a clear message to schools. A number of seminar papers were written for this first meeting, some being of excellent quality but they were barely used and were certainly never published, what in OFSTED speak might be called a 'missed opportunity'. The final statement emerged, a collection of worthy ideals which would, and should, be supported by people of goodwill even though some are contradictory and there is a fragrant odour of truth, justice and American pie! The product of the Values Forum became one of the bases for the move to include citizenship in the school curriculum. The other basis was the more influential report produced by Bernard Crick on *Citizenship* (1998).

To the outside observer there was an interesting battle between Crick and SCAA over which report would have the most effect. As might have been expected, the decision was a political one and little is now heard of the Values Forum.

The RE professionals continue to be split in two by the initiative on citizenship. On the one hand there is much that RE can genuinely contribute to citizenship. The citizenship documents do, however, tend to perceive the contribution of the study of religion and the religious communities as a sociological exercise encouraging harmony, deeper understanding, tolerance and respect for each other in a multicultural, multifaith society (the track record of religion in promoting such values appeared to have been conveniently set to one side). On the other hand, citizenship was requiring 5 per cent of curriculum time, and where was that curriculum time to come from?

Remember from decades earlier, those who regarded RE as a form of moral education and Personal Social Education (PSE)? They and their descendants emerged, metaphorically speaking dressed in skins and clutching clubs and spears, prepared to encourage RE to associate closely with citizenship because the teaching of (citizenship) RE would deliver better citizens more willing to contribute to a respectful harmonious society; people who would behave better and create no waves – just like the great founders and prophets! There is, of course, no evidence to suggest that people who are well-informed about religion make better or worse citizens, but the argument has an emotional convenience and continues to be used.

Model syllabuses

The government's curriculum agency, SCAA (previously called the National Curriculum Council (NCC)), called together representatives from a selection of religions and denominations within religions with the aim of determining what each religion would find acceptable content to be in classrooms. It would also offer advice as to which religions would be taught when and how much time would be allocated to the teaching of each religion. The blue paper was lit and tense discussions began. This amorphous and rather self-conscious group eventually produced the 'model syllabuses', two to be precise, with two attainment targets, normally referred to now as 'learning about' (AT1) and 'learning from' (AT2) religion. At the time the exercise appeared fruitful and to have been a valid activity, not least because however unrepresentative the groups were, and however much weighted the exercise was towards the Christian majority, at least people were talking to each other! Thunderclouds were, however, gathering.

Hindsight is the greatest teacher, but the model syllabuses are too content driven. Every religion was desperate to ensure pupils were taught about their faith – but all in less than 5 per cent of curriculum time? Nevertheless, huge amounts of content were lifted into place to please (appease) everyone. It should be said that the Christianity section is the worst example of this reflecting the vested interests of the various Christian groups.

The attainment targets, particularly AT2, would allow, some years later, RE to fall gracefully and uncomplaining into the Personal, Health and Social Education (PHSE) and citizenship camp. There should have been *one* AT requiring pupils to 'understand religion'. 'Learning about' and 'learning from' could have become secondary or subsidiary aims; as it is they have become a means of moving the focus of RE away from intellectual study so that it continues to serve the 'moral education' school of pupil morality. What continues to be of concern is that these syllabuses, which were never intended to be used wholesale by LEAs (although they were by a few) have now become a compulsory element in initial teacher education. Unlike LEA RE syllabuses, which are required to be reviewed every five years, there has been no review at the time of writing (2002) nor is one planned. This is quite appalling, given the acknowledged weaknesses and flaws in the syllabuses, and an indictment of QCA and OFSTED; for neither is pressing for a major review – no doubt for political and personal reasons. Syllabuses that were intended to be enabling have become set in stone and some who at the time recognised their flaws and temporality now argue for their permanence.

RE as part of the National Curriculum

The model syllabuses, together with Schemes of Work for Key Stages 1–3 (published in 2000), are the closest RE has come to occupying a centralised place in curriculum planning. Whatever their merits they have had an enormous effect on LEA agreed syllabuses particularly with respect to the two attainment targets, which, although only advisory, have become authoritative. Very few LEA RE syllabuses ignore the model syllabuses, which is unfortunate; to accept their contribution to RE as tablets of stone, set firm forever, could result in an ossification of the development of RE.

There has been a long discussion regarding the place of RE in relation to the National Curriculum. It was rejected (in 1987–8) on the grounds of how would denominational schools fit into a national system. Their approach to teaching would have different aims from the conventional wisdom in county (now community) schools; and there was a value in allowing such a sensitive subject to be determined locally. Certainly one can see why central government would want any controversy settled locally.

Since then arguments have ebbed and flowed over whether RE should be in the National Curriculum. Would it have more financial resources made available? Who would decide what would be taught? What educational, philosophical or theological rationale would there be? Would it improve the quality of RE? Who would control the subject, the DfES, OFSTED, or QCA? The argument is finely balanced and at the beginning of the twenty-first century there is no doubt that OFSTED and QCA want greater centralisation of the RE curriculum. The argument for a national syllabus has some force, particularly while some of the 150 or so LEAs have weak syllabuses and refuse to invest properly in advisory support and guidance. Some LEAs, however, have produced excellent syllabuses; and teachers, particularly non-specialist teachers of RE, have been able to respond; these initiatives would be more difficult to sustain under any centralising body. Since 1944 local representatives have had a significant contribution to make to RE. If their powers were to be removed who would write the national syllabus for RE? Whom would the government choose? What lobby groups would emerge? The model syllabus experience suggests there would be great problems. Who wants a national syllabus? Support is very thin on the ground with the initiative coming from OFSTED and QCA, but not from anywhere else, certainly not from those who become involved in creating syllabuses. The politics of such a situation would be difficult, with all types of religious and professional pressure groups wanting to influence central thinking.

The publication of *Schemes of Work in RE* by QCA in 2000 has, in effect, become a centralisation by stealth because as soon as they are adopted by the Syllabus Conference as part of the LEAs, RE syllabus, they become statutory. This is unfortunate as the Schemes of Work:

(a) vary significantly in quality;
(b) are not designed for general acceptance straight into a syllabus;
(c) do not cover (m)any of the topics in some syllabuses.

There continues to be a view among RE teachers that says 'whatever central government agencies produce, be it QCA or OFSTED, then we must accept it wholesale'. History is, sadly, littered with stark occasions when the 'people' simply accepted what governments say; education should, by its very nature, *encourage* critical evaluation and *discourage* mindless acceptance. Is that not a distinctive quality of the 'good citizen'?

The nearest there has been to a national RE syllabus is the introduction of the short course in RE at GCSE Level. In 2001 60 per cent of all pupils sitting GCSE took a full or short course GCSE in Religious Studies (all GCSE, AS and A2 courses are now called Religious Studies). This has had a tremendous effect upon the subject, providing a sense of purpose for Years 10 and 11 and for those teaching them. While some schools have dropped the full course, others, ironically, have taken it up owing to the popularity of the short course. It would not have been thought possible ten years ago for such statistics to emerge regarding GCSE RS courses.

In 2000 the new modular syllabuses (or specifications) in Religious Studies were introduced at post-16 level. It is too early to comment on these as yet, but there is some anecdotal evidence that some of the modules examined in Year 12 do not allow students to demonstrate the development of the maturity of their thinking. It is early days and, as with all new initiatives, there are likely to be teething problems. It may be that syllabuses will need to be re-designed to match the style and modes of assessment more effectively.

If anything has been controversial in RE/RS in the 1990s, it has been assessment. Given that the two attainment targets have now become almost universally adopted (in spite of their obvious weaknesses), how are pupils to be assessed? How does a teacher assess what a pupil has 'learned from' a religion (or from the religion being taught) as opposed to what has been learned anywhere else? There have been different, and helpful models of assessment developed over the last decade that are dealt with elsewhere in this book.

Is RE different from other subjects?

What makes RE slightly different from other subjects is both the attitude of parents and the religious communities who watch what is taught. Both groups are far too sensitive, so much so that the religion being taught is often presented in an anodyne, banal manner. The idealistic terms presented to pupils mean it is simply not representative of the average worshipper in the street. The subject 'protects' pupils from the religious, theological, philosophical and social challenges of this new century. Certainly some Christian pupils will learn things they would be unlikely to learn in church, but, on the other hand, they may not be allowed to discuss openly religious attitudes to controversial theological and moral problems in case they arrive at the 'wrong' answer. RE teachers, quite understandably, find it very difficult to take on the religious conservatives of any faith – and why should they? One reason should be that religion is nothing if not controversial. Virtually every religious leader or prophet was, and is, challenging the contemporary world. Religion is often taught as if it were the bastion of conservatism when, in fact, the reverse is the case. Religion is subversive and constantly involved in change, otherwise it dies. But parents and faith communities want their children to be brought up in quiescent acceptance of eternal verities that never change: and the syllabuses and schools collude with this view, ignoring the 'disagreed' RE syllabus that brings excitement to the study of religion. In the eyes of most pupils the religious conflicts of the world are brought into their homes by television: religion appears to be caught up in violence and bigotry, but where does this appear on the curriculum?

Religious Studies/Religious Education are fascinating subjects for study. They are, however, like other subjects, likely to suffer from trends in education and the latest fashion in social engineering. Many parents, of whichever faith, prefer their children not to learn about 'other religions', fearing a challenge to their family structures and authority. This is the current dilemma for RE. Does the teacher present each religion to all the pupils as the religion would want to be presented; or is it presented in a manner that invites critical evaluation, the latter a very European model of Christian thinking which would not be wholly endorsed by all? The alternative is to present religion not as a list of rules, social order, conventions etc., that produce punishment when not adhered to, but as a means of coping with the dilemmas, problems and pain of life. The latter may be tendentious but is likely to be more interesting and certainly more challenging to pupils who, in their vast majority, have no religious affiliation at all.

The lesson of the last fifty years in RE is that the study of religion should not be in the hands, solely, of the religions; there are political, social and, most important, educational considerations to hold in place. 'Creative tension' describes Religious Education as it currently survives – once creativity is lost, the tension goes too, debate ceases and RE loses all integrity.

Questions

1 Are political considerations always a central part of determining the RE curriculum?
2 Would Religious Studies be a more appropriate title for the subject than Religious Education?
3 How would Religious Education benefit if it were part of the National Curriculum? Would such benefits outweigh the benefits of local control within a national framework?

2   A rationale for Religious Education

Lynne Broadbent

Introduction

The 1988 Education Reform Act which legislated for a national framework for teaching and learning has, in recent years, determined discussion about the curriculum. The Act established the National Curriculum with its core and foundation subjects, identified the requirement for schemes of work and for assessment and reporting procedures. Religious Education retained the statutory position within the curriculum which it had held since 1944, and, together with the National Curriculum, it became the 'basic curriculum' for all schools.

The rationale for this new framework for teaching and learning was brief; it simply required that the curriculum should be 'balanced and broadly based', should 'promote the spiritual, moral, cultural, mental and physical development of pupils and of society' and prepare pupils for the opportunities, responsibilities and experiences of adult life (HMSO 1988). The need to debate the purposes of the curriculum and to seek a rationale for the inclusion of each subject became superseded by the simple need to fulfil government policy. This is not to say that the formation of a National Curriculum did not have positive features; indeed it has provided a clear structure for raising achievement, but effectively it has quashed discussion on curriculum issues and has polarised discourse among educationalists, with those based in universities and training institutions seeing education as a matter for continued open debate, while those working as local authority inspectors and advisors, members of government quangos such as the Qualifications and Curriculum Authority (QCA) and HMI inspectors hold as their prime concern the implementation of government policy. The former fertile discussions between HMI, schools and teachers which often resulted in ground breaking reports have in recent years been curtailed.

For newly-qualified teachers entering the profession, the process of Religious Education is defined by its two attainment targets, 'learning about' and 'learning from religion' and the content of teaching determined by their LEA agreed syllabus, in most cases heavily influenced by the model syllabuses (SCAA 1994). Rarely will teachers find themselves in a forum which seeks to formulate a rationale for teaching Religious Education. Where questions of validity are raised it is usually by recalcitrant Year 8 pupils who demand 'Why do I have to do RE? I don't want to be a vicar or a nun' or by teachers of social science who helpfully suggest that religion would be better taught under the history, sociology or philosophy banner. So is there an argument for including Religious Education within the school curriculum and if so, what sort of a subject should it be?

Towards a rationale

Writing five years before the Education Reform Act about the problems and possibilities for Religious Education, Edwin Cox suggested that for Religious Education to be universally accepted, it would have to meet certain criteria:

> it would have to be attempting something that everyone agrees is enlight-ening and enlarging pupils' minds and outlooks...which will relate to some of the accepted disciplines in the academic world. In practice, it will have to use material which is thought worthwhile in the present culture and with which pupils can feel able to respond with warmth and interest, and in its outcome it will need to convey some knowledge or insight which will enable them to understand better other people's belief systems and clarify their own beliefs.
>
> (Cox 1983: 130)

Cox's thesis seems to suggest three broad criteria by which the inclusion of Religious Education within the curriculum might be justified. First, it would have to be justifiable within an accepted academic framework. Second, it would need to be seen as worthwhile in terms of the current cultural and thus social context. Third, it would need to be effective in stimulating pupils' interest, and develop them educationally by enlarging their outlooks, and practically, by helping them to understand the beliefs of others and clarify, or begin to clarify, their own beliefs: 'it would have to be attempting something...which will relate to some of the accepted disciplines in the academic world'.

In Cox's writing there are strong echoes of the work of the educational philosopher Paul Hirst, who asserted that a liberal education is a 'deliberate, purposeful activity directed to the development of individuals and particularly with the development of mind' (Hirst 1974: 32, 41). He identified eight 'distinct disciplines' or forms of knowledge, one being religion, the others being mathematics, physical sciences, human sciences, history, literature and the fine arts and philosophy and claimed (1974: 44) that these forms of knowledge constitute the ways in which our experience of the world is structured. Each form of knowledge has four distinguishing features, namely central concepts particular to itself, a distinctive logical structure, distinctive expressions or statements and particular techniques and skills for exploring experience. For religion, Hirst suggested God and sin as examples of central concepts, but these could also include the concepts of faith and worship. The logical structure of religion might be perceived in more than one way: it might be studied through the consequences of its central concepts; for example, the consequences of a belief in a Creator God would render all aspects of the world as part of a created universe with humans having responsibility as caretakers of that universe: or, religion might be studied phenomenologically through the dimensions of religion identified in the work of Smart (Smart 1998), namely, through its ritual (worship, prayers), mythology (the stories of the faith traditions), doctrines (beliefs and teaching), ethics (codes of ethical behaviour), society (communal organisations), the experiential dimension (the experience of both key figures and individual adherents) and the material dimension, and the way in which these dimensions relate to each other in religious discourse. In its credal statements, rituals for daily life and for individual and communal worship, religion is abundant in distinctive statements and expressions, while particular techniques and skills for exploring experience may be found in the practice of prayer and meditation, the measuring of one's life experience against the life and teachings of key figures. For Hirst, the purpose of an education based on these forms of knowledge would not be focused on learning about minute details, of knowing all there is to know, but rather on 'coming to look at things in a certain way' (1974: 47). Pupils would therefore need 'sufficient immersion in the concepts, logic and criteria of the discipline for a person to come to know the distinctive way in which it "works"' (1974: 47).

The proposition of religion as an accepted academic discipline, yet one whose content for educational purposes is specifically selected and limited, was explored by another educational philosopher, Philip H. Phenix. Phenix saw human beings as 'creatures who have the power to experience meanings' and education as 'the process of engendering essential meanings' (Phenix 1964: 5). He analysed the nature of meaning and mapped six interrelated and complementary 'realms of meaning' or distinctive modes of human understanding, these realms being symbolics, empirics, aesthetics, synnoetics (from the Greek for meditative thought), ethics and synoptics which included history, religion and philosophy, disciplines which Phenix suggested integrated all the other meanings into a coherent whole. Nevertheless, Phenix considered that there were various threats to meaning, one being the volume of knowledge to be learnt. He identified four principles for the selection of curriculum content: first, it should be taken from a specialist field of enquiry; second, it should be representative of that field with a relatively small volume of knowledge being effective in developing understanding; third, the chosen content should exemplify the methods of enquiry to enable the pupil to become a skilled and independent learner; and fourth, it should arouse the imagination of the learner.

What implications do the writings of Hirst and Phenix have for religious educators, with Hirst's concern with knowledge and Phenix's concern with realms of meaning? Certainly, from both perspectives we can see religion being justified within an academic framework, a form of knowledge which develops the mind and the individual's capacity to structure their experience and as one means of making sense of the world. However, it is apparent that for this development to take place and for meaning to be made, what is required is not a vast body of knowledge but a clear focus on central concepts, distinctive features and representative methods of enquiry. And a further point is apparent: for Hirst and Phenix it is 'religion' itself rather than 'religions' which is the focus of study. All this is very much at odds with the current practice in schools. A glance at any local agreed syllabus for Religious Education will indicate a curriculum focused on the acquisition of knowledge of the six principal religions represented in Great Britain rather than a curriculum based upon central concepts. And while in some syllabuses there is a recommendation to include only Christianity and two other religions at any one Key Stage, other syllabuses require pupils to encounter the six faith traditions at each Key Stage. Weighted towards content as syllabuses appear to be, it is questionable whether Religious Education can indeed contribute to a process of meaning making. This raises the question as to whether our intentions in teaching religion should lie in enabling pupils to 'come to know the way it works', or in contributing to the 'process of engendering essential meanings', or in the acquisition of knowledge about religions rather than religion. This is not a criticism of any one intention but to raise the question of clarity in relation to curriculum design. It is at this point that we need to address the second area identified by Cox. In practice, it will have to use material which is thought worthwhile in the present culture.

There are perhaps four aspects of the present culture which might serve to justify an education within religion, namely the nature of multifaith Britain itself, the significant reporting of religious issues in the media, the recent phenomena of religious ritual in response to public disasters and the evidence of religious or spiritual experience within the population at large.

Britain as a multifaith and multicultural society

That Great Britain has been for centuries a multifaith and multicultural society is incontrovertible. There has been a significant Jewish presence in the country since Norman times, while one of the oldest mosques at Woking, Surrey, dates from the late nineteenth century and a visit to Osborne House on the Isle of Wight confirms the presence of Muslim and Sikh courtiers in the household of Queen Victoria. Today, almost all major cities and many larger towns testify to the range of local faith communities through the presence of churches, mosques, synagogues, gurdwaras and mandirs, kosher and halal food shops and a diversity of religious and cultural dress. These features have served to heighten public consciousness of the influence of religious commitment on the lives of individuals and communities, resulting in a common, yet probably false, perception that faith communities other than Christian communities demonstrate a stronger commitment to their religious beliefs. Furthermore, there is a realisation that it is religion that becomes the means by which a person identifies him/herself as a member of a local, national and international community.

It would be difficult to argue that any form of education should not concern itself with 'enlarging minds and outlooks' by developing a knowledge and understanding of those aspects of culture which are encountered in daily life. It stands to reason then that pupils in schools will require some form of education in matters of religion in order to understand the physical features of their local areas and the motivating and defining identities of the people with whom they share their classrooms and streets. However, there may be a further agenda for such an education for it has long been claimed that education can have a significant influence upon society, both the current society and the society to be created for future generations.

The contribution of Religious Education to a multifaith and multicultural society

The White Paper which preceded the 1944 Education Act suggested that the education system, and specifically a programme of Religious Education, could be effective in reviving 'the spiritual and personal values in our society' (HMSO 1943: 11). Some years later, the Swann Report (DES 1985) identified the contribution of Religious Education 'in preparing all pupils for life in today's multi-racial Britain' (Swann 1985: 518) and its significant role in 'challenging and countering the influence of racism in our society'. More recently, the Macpherson Report (1999), which followed the death of the black teenager Stephen Lawrence, called for amendments to be made in the National Curriculum 'aimed at valuing cultural diversity and preventing racism, in order to better reflect the needs of a diverse society' (Macpherson 1999: 334), and reports following race riots in Bradford and Burnley in 2001 have reiterated the need for schools to become increasingly involved in addressing issues of diversity and race. The new guidance for citizenship education reflects the need to include reference to diversity within local communities. Such issues must be addressed by the education system as a whole and cannot be the sole concern of Religious Education, however, Religious Education would seem to have a significant contribution to make. Provision for learning about the six principal faith traditions represented in Great Britain is identified as an aim in each and every local agreed syllabus for Religious Education, and implementation of the syllabus should inevitably bring encounters with members of faith communities. The assumption that this in itself would bring about change in community relations is questionable. Nevertheless, the power of knowledge and personal encounters to influence attitudes should not be underestimated, while we continue to consider what would be sufficient and necessary to bring about that change in community relations and just how far programmes of Religious Education might contribute to it.

Religion in the media

Grace Davie identifies religious broadcasting as 'believing without belonging par excellence' for she suggests it seems to encourage 'a rather self-indulgent form of armchair religiosity' (Davie 1994: 13). This may indeed be so, but the range of religious broadcasting can provide an indicator of financial commitment on the part of programme commissioners and makers to public interests. In the year of writing, the television media has broadcast a wide variety of programmes focused on the Hindu, Christian and Muslim traditions. There was daily coverage from India on the Hindu festival of Kumbh Mela, when millions of pilgrims, including the rich and famous such as Madonna and Richard Gere, were expected to bathe in the River Ganges near Allahabad in anticipation that their sins would be washed away and they would be closer to *nirvana*. A documentary series about the life of Jesus entitled 'Son of God' used sophisticated technology to explore first-century Jerusalem and the possible physical characteristics of Jesus. Further programmes included a lengthy series on the Apostles and one on the effects of the Alpha course on the lives of a small group of Christian 'initiates', as well as the long-established Songs of Praise and Sunday morning religious broadcasts. BBC television devoted a week to an exploration of Islam, its historical development and its practice in Britain, while a radio series explored the boundaries of faith and unbelief and a popular soap ran storylines based on religious responses to euthanasia, raising a huge public response. In the print media, the case of the Roman Catholic parents who, despite doctors' advice, refused permission for an operation to separate their conjoined twins aroused lengthy public debate about religious and professional commitment and responsibility when the case was referred to the courts. The reporting of the bombing of the World Trade Centre and the subsequent war in Afghanistan has demanded a clear distinction between religious belief and fundamentalist attitudes which manifest themselves in terrorism. All this is indicative of a 'present culture' where the media is infused by religion, whether from an historical or moral perspective, or by the reporting of current perspectives or events in the national and international communities. Young people therefore will need opportunities, such as those presented by programmes of Religious Education, to develop skills to discuss these public issues presented in the media. But more than this, if pupils are receiving through the media an abundance of information and opinion on religious issues, they will also need to develop the skills of discrimination in order that they might challenge and refute limited and frequently biased representations to which they are unwittingly exposed.

A further factor which seems to support the inclusion of Religious Education within the curriculum relates to the fact that religion has become an increasingly social phenomenon, particularly at times of public disasters. Davie notes that these disasters provoke out of the ordinary behaviour and 'particular moments...when the sacred becomes an acceptable topic of conversation' (Davie 1994: 88). She cites the tragedy at the Hillsborough stadium in 1989 when Liverpool played Nottingham Forest and ninety-four Liverpool supporters were killed in a crush at the perimeter fence. Shocked Liverpool fans, or pilgrims as they became called, flocked to their stadium at Anfield to place football scarves and caps, mascots and rattles amongst flowers, cards and wreaths. Davie refers to the Anfield phenomenon as a 'curious mixture of common and conventional religiosity that continues to pervade British society'. A similar explosion of public grief followed the death of Diana, Princess of Wales. The rituals of mourning were religious; large crowds gathering together for comfort in their disbelief, remembering Diana's life and trying to find meaning both in her life and in her death, the field of flowers in Kensington Gardens, pictures of Diana surrounded by candles, flowers and words of remembrance almost like shrines. It would appear that religious ritual has become an accepted means by which ordinary women and men respond to public yet personally experienced disasters and find in the ritual of religion a language for their grief. This is perhaps a surprising shift from the postwar privatising of religious practice to a culture where rituals and questions of meaning become part of public discourse.

It may be that these events have little to do with formal religion, and it might be argued that not all social phenomena should find space within the curriculum. However, it is part of the culture in which pupils are living and an exploration of the whole context of belief and values, rituals and questions of meaning, whether or not they are specifically religious, might serve to convey knowledge or insight which will enable pupils 'to understand better other people's belief systems and clarify their own beliefs' (Cox 1983: 130). This broad exploration of religious and non-religious belief and ritual might be a far more realistic approach to classroom discussion than the assumption, often totally disbelieved by pupils, that the population as a whole holds any kind of religious affiliation to a synagogue, mosque or gurdwara.

There has been a long tradition of research into the area of spiritual experience and considerable evidence of personal spiritual experience within the population at large might be further confirmation of the need for a religious education which provides a forum to address religious and spiritual questions. Perhaps most well known to those engaged in Religious Education is the work of David Hay. Hay's research, reported in *Exploring Inner Space* (1982), was conducted in Nottingham and based on the question: have you ever been aware of or influenced by a presence or power, whether you call it God or not, which is different from your everyday self? Of those questioned, a very significant proportion claimed to have had an experience of this kind. The experiences themselves were diverse and included an awareness of a sacred presence in nature, a patterning of events in personal life and a sensing that, in nature, all things are one. Often, the experiences had a significant and life changing effect on the individual although many reported that they were frequently not shared with others for fear of ridicule, leading Hay to suggest that: 'society...will not permit them to own the significance of their inner perceptions' (Hay 1982: 165). The frequency of positive responses in Hay's findings challenges and expands notions of what it means to be human. They suggest that human beings are not defined purely in physical, intellectual and social terms but may have other experiences, described as religious or spiritual, which are a significant influence in life and may run counter to a public view of the world which is founded upon a scientific or technological world view. These experiences or 'inner perceptions', often occurring in childhood, (see Robinson 1977) are a significant part of development for almost two-thirds of the population and thus has implications for Religious Education.

it would have to use material...with which pupils can feel able to respond with warmth and interest, and in its outcome it will need to convey some knowledge or insight which will enable them to understand better other people's belief systems and clarify their own beliefs.

Attempts to match programmes of Religious Education to pupils' psychological development are not new. Ronald Goldman (1964) attempted an investigation into how far the development of religious thinking in children followed the pattern of psychological development described by Piaget in the 1920s. Goldman described three main stages in religious thinking which corresponded to Piaget's ages and stages theory, namely the intuitive, concrete and abstract stages. Goldman's research methodology has been questioned in recent years, but it is interesting to note his conclusions that teaching should not be based upon a list of facts to be learnt but upon the understanding of religious concepts.

A further model of development was presented by Erikson, namely his 'Eight Ages of Man' (Erikson 1956). In each of the eight stages there is a tension between the fundamental emotions or themes that people contend with in and between themselves. The task of resolving these tensions is a life-task, for while these themes are progressive they are also re-worked at different stages of development, so the themes of early childhood are re-worked during adolescence. The themes are as follows:

1   basic trust versus basic mistrust
2   autonomy versus shame and doubt
3   initiative versus guilt
4   industry versus inferiority
5   identity versus role confusion
6   intimacy versus isolation
7   generativity versus stagnation
8   ego integrity versus despair

Chris Arthur reviews Erikson's model in an attempt to 'tease out from Erikson's developmental theory a framework of possible goals in relation to which our conception of religious education might be radically expanded' (Arthur 1990: 149). Arthur notes that Erikson's model provides a theory of continuous human growth, unrestricted to notions of maturity at puberty, and that this is consonant with an education in religion. Furthermore, he considers that to disregard patterns of psychological development renders any justification of Religious Education in the curriculum difficult. He suggests that a religious education related to Erikson's model might be beneficial on three counts: first, it would broaden the context of encounter with religion; second, it would integrate religious, moral and social education; and third, the themes of trust, autonomy and initiative might facilitate the selection of both content and methodology which renders teaching in Religious Education intrinsically worthwhile from the developmental point of view of pupils.

Although it would be a challenge to develop schemes of work, most of the above themes could be easily tracked through religious stories, rituals and celebrations from across the faith traditions; through the accounts of personal, family and community experiences. However, if these themes are those which, by virtue of our humanity, we all share, then it might be helpful to refer to the ultimate questions identified by the theologian Hans Kung as 'ultimate and yet immediate perennial questions of human life' which arise in personal and social life (Kung 1978: 75). These ultimate questions relate to questions of truth ('What can I know?'), questions of norms and behaviour ('What ought I to do?') and questions of meaning ('What may I hope?'). Kung presents the questions as follows:

> What can we know? Why is there anything at all? Why not nothing? Where does man come from and where does he go? Why is the world as it is? What is the ultimate reason and meaning of all reality?
>
> What ought we to do? Why do what we do? Why and to whom are we finally responsible? What deserves forthright contempt and what love? What is the point of loyalty and friendship, but also what is the point of suffering and sin? What really matters for man?
>
> What may we hope? Why are we here? What is it all about? What is there left for us: death, making everything pointless at the end? What will give us courage for life and what courage for death?
>
> (Kung 1978: 75)

These are challenging and controversial questions with a strong moral imperative. There may be a range of responses to the questions and pupils will need to fine tune their skills of analysis, interpretation and expression to explore and evaluate potential responses to discover which, if any, best fits their own standpoint, or to identify a standpoint to which they wish to subscribe. If these are the questions which resonate with human experience and if some, or many, of these responses are related to religious belief and practice, then a forum is required to enable pupils to confront this aspect of maturity.

In 1980, *Hampshire Education Authority* identified Kung's questions in its handbook, *Paths to Understanding*, stating that 'to ask questions about the meaning and purpose of existence – an activity typical of mature human beings – is educationally more proper than to ignore such questions', and suggested that these issues would provide the 'life-blood' of Religious Education (Hampshire Education Authority 1980: 62). Here, it is not just the content of Religious Education which is being directed at the maturing of pupils but also the promotion of skills, skills of raising questions and thinking, creatively and rigorously about possible answers. Both content and skills are required as preparation for mature adult life. There have been attempts to engage pupils in responding thoughtfully within Religious Education through the second of the two attainment targets, 'learning from religion'. However, while a recent QCA guidance document (QCA: 2000) identified 'learning from religion' as being 'about the concepts in religion(s)' there is a tendency for it to be associated with pupils' experiences of specific rituals, such as rites of passage, or symbols rather than being based in the 'bigger', ultimate questions cited above. Furthermore, QCA monitoring and OFSTED inspection reports indicate that teachers lack confidence in promoting 'learning from religion', finding the first attainment target, 'learning about religions' more factually based and less ambiguous.

Currently, decisions about the content of Religious Education at both LEA and school level are dominated by a perceived need to teach pupils the 'facts' about individual religions. When, in 1994, members of faith communities gathered to agree what should be taught about their religion at each of the four Key Stages, the concern was to adequately represent the religions in line with adherents' requests. The resulting model syllabuses for Religious Education (SCAA 1994) are therefore structured lists of religious content unrelated in any educational way to the developmental stages and interests of pupils. As 'models' for the construction of LEA syllabuses, they have been highly influential, for in the main, those constructing the LEA syllabuses have been reluctant to break away from the closely structured approach of the models. Perhaps this reticence relates to a concern that to integrate a 'pupil centred' or 'developmental approach' alongside teaching about religious traditions would undermine educational credibility, but it seems unbelievable that in planning programmes of Religious Education for pupils between the ages of five to sixteen or eighteen years, there can be at present, such a disregard of the developmental stages and interests of the 'consumers'.

So, what kind of Religious Education?

What kind of Religious Education would best satisfy the above rationale? First, we would need to clarify whether our intentions in teaching religion were to focus on enabling pupils to 'come to know the distinctive way in which it [religion] works', or to contribute to the 'process of engendering meanings' or to the acquisition of knowledge about religions. It may be that all of these aspects would be important for Religious Education in schools but the balance between these intentions would need to be specified and related to both content and methodologies.

Second, any programme of Religious Education would, without doubt, be based upon a body of knowledge which rendered it an accepted academic discipline. However, the territory for learning and teaching in Religious Education would not be formed from the extensive, 'raw' content which is identified in current syllabuses and presented under headings such as 'beliefs' and 'leaders'; rather there would be an identification of the central concepts distinctive of each religion, and the selection of stories, rituals and celebrations, from history and from current practice, which serve to illustrate these central concepts. Thus, a relatively small body of knowledge would serve to develop understanding. Such a process would imply a review and revision of the model syllabuses in order that they might better serve the Local Education Authorities in devising agreed syllabuses.

Third, Religious Education would need to be relevant to the cultural context of the pupils. It would therefore need to develop their knowledge and understanding of the religious communities present in their local area and those represented nationally and internationally. However, given Phenix's caution that an abundance of information mitigates against the process of engendering meaning, the way in which pupils' knowledge and understanding was to be developed would require stringent review. Discourse about beliefs, values and rituals, both religious and secular, would need to be set in a much broader framework than currently exists in agreed syllabuses. Not all syllabuses allow for the inclusion of humanism let alone the exploration and analysis of Davie's 'curious mixture of common and conventional religiosity that continues to pervade contemporary British society' (Davie 1994: 91).

Fourth, Religious Education would need to be more strongly skills-based. This would enable pupils to engage in discourse about beliefs and values as outlined above and to engage in meaningful encounters with members of faith communities. While language skills might predominate, pupils would need to develop skills of discernment and discrimination in order to challenge and refute the frequently biased reporting of religious issues in the media.

Fifth, Religious Education would need to take cognisance of pupils' psychological development and interests. This would not mean limiting areas of content in a misplaced attempt at age-appropriateness. Rather it would mean an acknowledgement that pupils, in their process of maturation, are concerned with the 'big' or ultimate questions of life and need a forum where these questions might be addressed and where they might bring their personal perceptions to bear upon the very human issues of identity, loyalty, suffering, death and hope.

Religious Education has the potential to enlighten and enlarge pupils' minds; it can make reference to material which is worthwhile in the present culture and it can contribute to the development of knowledge and insight which will enable pupils to understand others' belief systems and to clarify their own. Arguments for the inclusion of Religious Education within the curriculum touch on historical, sociological, philosophical and spiritual elements. It is the unique combination of these elements which secures the place of Religious Education in the school curriculum and validates its role in preparing pupils for life in a multifaith society.

Questions

1 How far do you consider that current syllabuses for Religious Education address the understanding of central concepts?
2 How might a Head of Department or Subject Leader make links between curriculum content and pupils' psychological development?
3 How far can Religious Education make a contribution to a multifaith society and what factors influence that contribution?

3 Religious Education in Church schools

John Bailey

In considering the topic of Religious Education in Church schools, this chapter will be restricted in the main to Roman Catholic schools and Church of England schools. Some years ago the National Society published guidance for Church of England schools entitled *Mission, Management, Appraisal*, which suggested that in considering its mission statement a Church school should consider where the school stood on the continuum of 'serving members of the Church', at one end of the spectrum, to 'serving the local community' at the other end of the spectrum. By and large, Roman Catholic schools, virtually all of which are voluntary aided, are at the 'serving members of the Church' end of the spectrum. By contrast Church of England schools, a majority of which are Voluntary Controlled, tend to be at the 'serving the local community' end of the spectrum. There is also a marked difference between voluntary aided and voluntary controlled Anglican schools; Voluntary Aided schools follow a syllabus for religious education which is determined by the governors of the school and which often involves using a diocesan syllabus or guidelines, whereas Voluntary Controlled schools will normally follow the local authority's agreed syllabus for Religious Education (which is dealt with elsewhere in this volume).

This chapter will deal with three main areas: first the provision of Religious Education in Roman Catholic Voluntary Aided schools; secondly, Religious Education in Church of England Voluntary Aided schools; and thirdly, Religious Education in Church of England Voluntary Controlled schools.

Religious Education in Roman Catholic aided schools

In Catholic schools Religious Education is determined by the Bishop's Conference for Religious Education. The first aim for Roman Catholic schools is still 'a Catholic education for a Catholic child'. In some areas, Roman Catholic schools are still filled by Catholic children. For example, in Leicester in 1999, in one Roman Catholic primary school, there were 57 applications from Catholic parents for 40 places, and of these 57, 55 were for Catholic children. In other areas by contrast, Roman Catholic numbers are relatively low but the Church still tries to keep a Roman Catholic presence. Where numbers are sufficient to justify the existence of a Roman Catholic school, then the policy is to fill the school with Catholic children. Where the numbers are not sufficient the numbers may be made up by non-Catholic children. The policy will still however be for the religious education in these schools to be Catholic education, and furthermore, such Religious Education will be primarily a study of Catholic Christianity from within. The assumption is that the purpose of Religious Education is to deepen and strengthen the faith of an already committed individual. It is not so much education about religion or even education about Christianity, but nurture in the Catholic faith.

The 1996 publication of the Bishops' Conference of England and Wales, *Religious Education, Curriculum Directory for Catholic Schools*, begins by speaking of the task of 'handing on the faith to future generations', and clearly sees this as being the meaning of Religious Education. It defines evangelisation, catechesis and Religious Education and states that in the living and sharing of faith, these three, evangelisation, catechesis and Religious Education, are always intertwined: 'Religious education given to children and young people in Catholic schools must always deepen their understanding of Catholic belief and will contribute to their education in and to Catholic faith. Furthermore, the life and ethos of the Catholic school must provide the witness and the community which enables this understanding to develop as a response to God in faith.' This document states that the aims of Religious Education in Catholic schools are to promote knowledge and understanding of Catholic faith and life; knowledge and understanding of the response of faith to the ultimate questions about human life, its origin and purpose; and the skills required to engage in examination of and reflection upon religious belief and practice. More specifically, the objectives of curriculum Religious Education in Catholic schools are said to be to develop knowledge and understanding of the mystery of God and of Jesus Christ, of the Church and of the central beliefs which Catholics hold; to develop awareness and appreciation of Catholic belief, understanding of its impact on personal and social behaviour and of the vital relationship between faith and life, life and faith; to encourage study, investigation and reflection by the pupils; to develop appropriate skills, for example, ability to listen, to think critically, spiritually, ethically and theologically; to acquire knowledge and organise it effectively, to make informed judgements; to foster appropriate attitudes, for example, respect for truth, respect for the views of others, awareness of the spiritual, of moral responsibility, of the demands of religious commitment in everyday life, and especially the challenge of living in a multicultural, multifaith society. This emphasis on the promotion of the Catholic faith is reflected in what the document has to say about methodology. For example, it states that Religious Education learns from evangelisation and catechesis, that learning and growth in matters of faith involve active participation and response. Teaching in Religious Education will introduce 'those formulas which develop young people's understanding of Catholic belief, the tradition of the Church in maintaining, practising and professing the faith that has been handed on, values, formulas which provide a common language that all may use'. Such formulas will include texts from the Bible, the liturgy and the traditional prayers of Christian faith, such as the Creed, Our Father and Hail Mary.

This emphasis is reflected in the details of the areas of study, which are Revelation, Church, Celebration and Life in Christ. The first area of study, Revelation, breaks down into Trinity, Creation, Scriptures, Jesus Christ, Son of God and the Holy Spirit. The second area of study, Church, has five components: Church, One and Holy, Catholic, Apostolic and Mission. The third area of study, Celebration, covers Liturgy, Sacraments, Baptism, Confirmation and the Eucharist, Reconciliation and the Anointing of the Sick, Holy Orders and Matrimony and Prayer. Area of study four, Life in Christ, consists of the Dignity of the Human Person, Freedom/Responsibility/Conscience, Law/Grace/Sin, the Human Community, Love of God and Love of Neighbour. These sub-divisions of the areas of study apply across all four key stages in each case.

The way this programme for Religious Education works out in practice in primary schools is based on a programme entitled *Here I Am: A Religious Education Programme for Primary Schools*. This is a thematic approach, but despite the apparent similarity between these and similar-sounding themes in Agreed Syllabuses, this is a confessional rather than an educational approach; the aim is the confession of faith, rather than education about religion. The themes are topics such as Myself, Invitations, Birthdays, Journeys, Communion, Growing, Good News, Choices, Neighbours, Beginnings, Friends, Preparations, Special People, Meals, Good and Evil, Messengers, Change, Treasures, Babies, Initiation, Gifts, Books, Memories, Death and New Life, etc. The programme is immensely detailed and notes are provided for each lesson all the way through each of the four Key Stages. Although the topics sound very broad, in practice they are very closed. For example, the topic of Journeys for Years 5 and 6: in this topic the children explore their experience of life as a journey. They hear about Christian life as the Church family journeying with Jesus. A key skill would be to identify and describe the practice and faith of a community. A key attitude to be fostered would be respect and reverence for faith and tradition. This is the first of three themes that focus on the basic question, 'who am I?', and the Church's response of faith in the incarnation: 'In the person of Jesus God became one of us, the word was made flesh, he lived among us' (John 1.14). The learning outcome for early years would be that children know that people journey to church on a Sunday. For Year 1, the outcome would be that the parish family journeys to church on Sunday and the Holy Family journeyed to the temple. For Year 2, children would know that as the parish family journeys to church for different reasons, the Holy Family journeyed to the temple. For Years 3 and 4, they would have learned that the liturgical year is the Christian family's journey with Jesus, and for Years 5 and 6, that Christian life is a journey with Jesus.

In secondary schools a new programme has been published from the year 2000 entitled *Icons*, again with the full approval of the Bishop's Conference of England and Wales. This programme provides materials for ages 11–14 and is rooted in the catechism of the Catholic Church. It is intended to implement the *Religious Education Curriculum Directory* referred to earlier. For each year *Icons* provides three units with clearly stated aims and learning outcomes. The structure of the units is shaped by the questions concerning the foundations of human and Christian life, identity, purpose and fulfilment. Each unit has five sections: Jesus Christ, the Church, the Human Person, the Sacraments and the Liturgical Year. There is also a small amount of material on other faiths. The approach to other faiths however, is not an objective one. In approaching Judaism for example, the approach is that Christianity is the fulfilment of Judaism and the full revelation is Catholicism.

There is however, some indication that Religious Education in Catholic schools is beginning to approach world religions with a greater attitude of respect for other people's honestly held beliefs, even if they are wrong! This probably reflects the fact that it is less likely nowadays that all teachers in Catholic schools will have been products of a Catholic school themselves and have been trained in a Catholic college of education. The Catholic Teachers' Certificate has now changed to become the Catholic Certificate in Religious Studies, which includes a module on other faiths (one out of ten modules). The Roman Catholic Church is clearly at the beginning of a transitional stage in its approach to Religious Education. A minority of Catholic religious educators is spearheading a more liberal approach to Religious Education, a more open view. This group would wish to move to an approach to RE which is closer to that of agreed syllabuses but will still centre upon the Catholic experience; a kind of open-ended approach into a closed answer. It would still be faith nurture at the end of the day. Other faiths will be referred to as examples to help understand one's own faith and practice better as well as to develop respect for other faiths. This move towards a change in approach to RE is provoking something of a backlash, however. Those opposing these changes would say that if the new educational approach is so good, why has attendance at Mass declined? This debate clearly will run and run.

Religious Education in Church of England aided schools

One of the difficulties in writing in general terms about religious education in Church of England schools is the enormous variety of theory and practice across the different Anglican dioceses of England and Wales, and the consequent difficulty of saying what is generally accepted as Anglican. By contrast with the approach in Roman Catholic schools, RE in Church of England voluntary aided schools is not determined by a National Conference of Bishops. Instead, each diocese is free to develop its own approach to Religious Education or syllabus for Religious Education with the approval of the Diocesan Board of Education, which may issue a diocesan syllabus or guidelines on RE to the aided schools in the diocese. Even then, governors of aided schools are responsible for their own RE policy; diocesan guidelines are purely advisory, even if endorsed by the Diocesan bishop. Three very influential diocesan syllabuses for Religious Education in Church of England voluntary aided schools are the *Durham Diocesan Syllabus* (1993), the Winchester and Salisbury guidelines for Religious Education, entitled *Inspire* (Weatherley and Harris 1996), and the Manchester Diocesan Board of Education *Syllabus* (1995).

The *Durham Diocesan Syllabus* begins by explaining the denominational character of Religious Education in Voluntary Aided schools as follows: 'The content and approach to Religious Education have to be determined by the governors in accordance with the trust deed of the school or if this is lost, RE has to be in accordance with the beliefs and traditions of the Church of England. The governing body as a whole is responsible for determining the nature of Religious Education provided in its school, but it has to be in accordance with the trust deed.' It explains therefore that this diocesan syllabus can only be advisory until a governing body adopts it either in whole or in part and adds that governing bodies are of course free to adopt another syllabus or to draw up their own. Durham offers the following three aims for Religious Education in Church schools: (1) helping pupils to develop a knowledge and understanding of religion and faith; (2) furthering pupils' personal growth and development through the study of the beliefs and values of Christianity and other faiths; and (3) contributing towards pupils' experience of Christianity as a living faith.

The first aim, *developing a knowledge and understanding of religion and faith*, is said to be concerned with a general knowledge of Christianity, its key figures and central beliefs; some knowledge about and an appropriate understanding of some of the beliefs of other major world faiths; an understanding of what it means to think about experience in a religious way and an appreciation of the effect religious belief has on values and behaviour.

The second aim, *furthering pupils' personal growth and development through a study of Christianity and other faiths*, is concerned with pupils' ability to relate belief to experience of life, pupils' own search for meaning and purpose, pupils' spiritual development, attitudes of care and concern for others, exploration of religious questions about life and so on. Pupils are invited to reflect upon the relevance of Christianity for themselves and to explore their own religious beliefs and insights.

The third aim, *contributing towards pupils' experience of Christianity as a living faith*, is concerned with studying Christianity within a faith setting, experiencing a Christian ethos, experiencing church life through contact with the local church, taking part in the yearly cycle of Christian festivals and taking part in a daily pattern of prayer and worship.

It can immediately be seen that Religious Education following this pattern is an educational activity with the task of helping children to think about faith, but also that this is taking place in the context of a school which is a Christian foundation. The educational aspect involves children bringing their critical faculties to bear on analysis of and reflection on faith and religion. The fact that the school is a Christian foundation means that the context for this educational activity is that of nurturing as part of an understanding of the Christian faith. The Durham Diocesan Board of Education sees these two aspects of Religious Education as complementary.

On the question of the balance between teaching about Christianity and teaching about other faiths, the advice of the Durham Syllabus is that at least 80 per cent of RE teaching time should be devoted to Christianity, though schools might properly devote more time than this. However, when another faith is studied the syllabus suggests that sufficient time should be allocated for such study to be worthwhile and meaningful. This implies that the equivalent of at least two and not more than eight half-terms should be devoted to other faiths in years 1 to 6; that is, between 5 and 20 per cent of RE teaching in this period. The study of other faiths is seen as important; it should not be trivialised, and other faiths are not to be taught as in some way inferior or subservient to Christianity.

The Syllabus is divided into four sections: Christian Foundations (the Bible, Jesus, God and Prayer); Christian Practice (Church Life and Worship; the Church's Year; Followers of Jesus); Exploring Faith through the Experiences of Life (subdivided into The Natural World, Ultimate Questions and Self and Others) and fourthly, Other Faiths, which provides units on five other major world faiths, giving an introduction to the essentials of each faith and offering suggestions for curriculum work.

The Winchester and Salisbury guidelines, *Inspire* (Weatherley and Harris 1996), are intended to complement the local agreed syllabuses for RE, to explore Christianity in accordance with the principles of the Church of England but with reference to other denominations and faiths. Some two-thirds of this document are devoted to the Trinity, exploring God, Jesus and the Holy Spirit. Each section begins with an outline of the attributes of the Three Persons of the Trinity, and within each section the Three Persons of the Trinity are explored, for example, Where is God?, God as Creator, God as Father, the Annunciation, Advent, The Birth, The Holy Spirit at Work and so on. Remaining sections explore baptism, confirmation, Eucharist, marriage, reconciliation, ordination and the Anointing of the Sick. The Eucharist is examined in some depth. As the introduction states, *Inspire* is essentially guidance for exploring Christianity in accordance with the principles of the Church of England. Reference is made to other Christian denominations and faiths to enable teachers to make relevant links to the agreed syllabus requirements if they wish so to do.

As an illustration of the broad approach to a study of Christianity exemplified by this syllabus, see the Key Stage 1 unit of work on the Temptations of Jesus. This starts with a colour photograph of a desert and invites children to think about what life would be like in this sort of wilderness, asking them to describe what they can see in the picture, thinking about what sort of place it is and how they would feel in such a place, particularly how they would feel if they were alone with no food and no drink. It asks them to think why Jesus might have gone to such a place and suggests that the story of Jesus's Temptation be read to them from a suitable children's version. Teachers should then make a 'thinking space' in the classroom for children to be alone if they wish to have time for themselves or their own thoughts. Next, dramatise the story of Jesus's Temptation and make up scenes of people being tempted today and discuss how these situations could be resolved. Finally, it suggests that questions of right and wrong behaviour be discussed, and pupils make some posters for the school encouraging right behaviour. It is immediately clear that this is a very broad approach with an attempt to understand, at the children's own level, something of what the Temptations meant to Jesus.

For Key Stage 2 the same topic is expanded to include a study of different versions of the story in the Gospels, thinking about a time when the children may feel they have done something wrong and trying to imagine that they could have been tempted by 'a little devil' and creating a picture to show what this little devil might look like. This is followed by a discussion of the hymn, *Forty Days and Forty Nights* (nineteenth century), telling the story of Jesus in the Wilderness and going on to other work on Lent, fasting in other faiths, prayer and meditation, and so on. These units of work are clearly educational; although based upon Christianity, they invite reflection, and they are not narrowly indoctrinatory, although they do lead into a study of Christian belief and practice.

Similarly, the Manchester Diocesan *Syllabus* (1995) states that the principal aim of Religious Education, to aid pupils on their spiritual journey, will in aided schools offer pupils a firm grounding in the principles and practices of Christianity, especially as represented in the Church of England, but also in recognition of the society in which all children are growing up, pupils should be offered the opportunity to explore the other faiths represented in Britain today. The expectation of this syllabus is that in most aided schools about 66 per cent of the RE time would be spent on studying Christianity. However, no doubt reflecting the pattern of attendance at aided schools in Manchester Diocese, it is suggested that in some schools, notably those with significant numbers of pupils from faith backgrounds other than Christianity, it may be more appropriate to spend only 50 per cent of the available RE time studying Christianity. It suggests that where schools wish to devote more time to Christianity, it is not possible to pay proper attention to a world faith component in less that 25 per cent of the time available to RE.

In all these diocesan syllabuses for Church of England Voluntary Aided schools there is a feeling that one should be careful not to confuse the children by attempting to study too many other faiths. Manchester, for instance, suggests that especially at Key Stage 1 and 2, pupils should not attempt to study more than two faiths in depth in addition to Christianity. This is a maximum provision: schools may choose to offer fewer than two other faiths. However, by contrast with the Catholic syllabuses, Manchester is quite clear that the Board of Education feels that Church schools have an obligation to introduce pupils to the religious experience of the multitude of people in Britain and worldwide who belong to faiths other than Christianity. This is partly just to enable pupils to understand their fellow citizens in the hope that greater understanding will lead to more respect and harmony. The syllabus emphasises however, that this teaching of other faiths should be done in a way that takes seriously both their religious premise and each faith's own understanding of itself.

The Manchester *Syllabus* suggests five units of work on aspects of Christianity for Key Stage 1, the Bible, Jesus Christ, the Church, Festivals and

Christian Living. It also offers introductory units on Hinduism, Judaism, Islam and Sikhism. At Key Stage 2 there are again five units on Christianity with the same titles and four core primary units on world faiths (Hinduism, Judaism, Islam and Sikhism). The balance between Christianity and other faiths in diocesan syllabuses for Church of England voluntary aided schools, while reflecting the differences between dioceses with largely rural, mainly Christian or post-Christian backgrounds and those which are more urban and multicultural, nevertheless emphasises the need for Religious Education to include both teaching about Christianity and other faiths and also to empha-sise the context in which such education takes place, i.e. a Christian foundation.

However, the ethos of most Church of England Voluntary Aided schools, in contrast to Catholic ones, is much more towards the 'serving the community' end of the spectrum described earlier. Church of England Voluntary Aided schools are usually community schools in the sense that they draw all children from a particular neighbourhood, parish or village. This is particularly true of primary schools; perhaps less so of the smaller number of Church of England Voluntary Aided secondary schools in urban areas where there is some possi-bility of parental choice and where in order to obtain a place at a popular and successful school, parents have to obtain a Certificate of Church Attendance from their local parish Church. Even in these circumstances, however, there can be no assumption made that the children are themselves committed to Christianity, and by and large the Religious Education provision in such schools makes no such assumption. The Christian nurture, if such there be, is much more to do with the context in which the Religious Education is offered, rather than the actual content of the Religious Education.

In contrast to the Roman Catholic voluntary aided sector, there is a signifi-cant imbalance in Church of England schools between primary and secondary provision. In 2000, there were 774,000 places in Church of England primary schools, but only 150,000 secondary places. Consequently only one in five chil-dren in a Church primary school can be offered a place in a Church secondary school. This means that it is very difficult for parents to find Anglican educa-tion for their children throughout the age range 4–18. The recent report of the Archbishop's Council Review Group on the future of Church of England schools, *The Way Ahead* (commonly referred to as the Dearing Report, after its chairman) highlights this point and recommends that over the next five to eight years, the Church should seek to provide some 100 more Church of England secondary schools. Should the Church succeed in this somewhat daunting task, this will pose a considerable challenge for the supply of profes-sionally qualified, secondary trained RE teachers who are committed to the ethos of Church of England schools.

It is interesting to note that a significant number of Anglican dioceses are now recommending to governors of Voluntary Aided schools that they should give serious consideration to adopting the LEA Agreed Syllabus for RE, in whole or in part. This is perhaps not surprising, given the leading role that

Anglicans (often the Diocesan Director of Education and/or Diocesan RE Adviser) nowadays play on LEA Standing Advisory Councils for RE and agreed syllabus conferences. If the Church of England, as a constituent member of an LEA agreed syllabus conference is 'agreeing' to a new RE syllabus for community and controlled schools, it can be argued that the syllabus should be appropriate for Voluntary Aided schools too – indeed, that such provision is every child's entitlement. This position is open to the objection that it would erode the distinction between aided and controlled schools, but as controlled schools have in many other ways been rediscovering their Christian foundation and ethos in recent years, perhaps this distinction is disappearing anyway.

Religious Education in Church of England voluntary controlled schools

The legal situation is clear and explained elsewhere in this publication. Religious Education in voluntary controlled schools is in accordance with the local authority agreed syllabus, unless the parent requests denominational education. In this case there should be at least one 'reserved teacher' on the staff of the school who is able to teach Religious Education of the type that would be offered in an aided school, i.e., in accordance with the tenets of the Church of England. In practice nowadays this kind of request very rarely takes place, and the system of reserved teachers for denominational RE has fallen into abeyance in many dioceses. Most Church of England Voluntary Controlled schools happily follow the local authority agreed syllabus, although they may in practice emphasise the Christian content of such syllabuses to a greater extent in writing their own scheme of work than perhaps would be the case in some community schools.

There is also a very interesting tendency in recently published agreed syllabuses for RE, such as the 2000 *Lincolnshire Agreed Syllabus for RE*, for the pendulum to swing back from the type of syllabus of the late 1980s and early 1990s, where objectivity and fairness in the study of religions tended to lead to Christianity being seen as just one religion among many and expected to be accorded an equal amount of study time to other faiths, towards the kind of approach which emphasises teaching about Christianity as being the form of religious observance which pupils are most likely to encounter, particularly in rural areas, with less time devoted to other faiths. Such syllabuses also tend to offer less on other faiths in Key Stage 1 and 2, leaving the more detailed study of other faiths to Key Stages 3 and 4, partly on the grounds that specialist teachers with a degree of knowledge and expertise are more likely to be found in this stage of education in the secondary school, and partly because of the danger of primary school pupils being confused by 'too much being taught too soon'. The 2000 *Lincolnshire Agreed Syllabus for RE*, for example, has only two compulsory units of work for Key Stage 1, one on Celebrations for Christians and one on celebrations for members of another world religion (chosen from Judaism, Islam, Hinduism, Sikhism and Buddhism). Examples are given of other units of work which might be followed in this Key Stage, including The Good Earth, Belonging to a Christian Community, Belonging to a Jewish Community and Talking about God. At Key Stage 2, again there are three compulsory units, one on Christian belief and lifestyle and two on belief and lifestyle from another faith. Further study units suggested include Christian Journeys; Beautiful World, Wonderful God?; Symbolism in Worship in the Cathedral and/or the Mosque; Christmas and Diwali; Religion in the Neighbourhood; What made People Want to Follow Jesus; What is Special about the Bible; What can We Learn from People of Faith Today; What can We Learn from the Life of Muhammad; Where did the Christian Bible Come From; How do Christians Try to Live Out Their Beliefs About God; What do the Easter Celebrations Mean for Christians; and What is Special About Hindu Family Life? The emphasis upon Christianity in primary school RE in this agreed syllabus is strongly evident and reflects the structure of society in Lincolnshire. It is also no doubt influenced by the difficulty for schools in this area to visit places of worship other than Christian, the difficulty of getting visitors into the school from other faiths and the need to start from where the pupils are. However, there is clearly a willingness in such a syllabus to move from the present and the immediate towards a study of other faiths, and the approach is clearly educational and not indoctrinatory or nurturing. But syllabuses such as these are being welcomed by teachers in Church of England schools, partly because non-specialist teachers of RE in primary schools find them easier to use, and partly because such an approach to Religious Education is easier to relate to the ethos of a Church of England voluntary controlled school. Voluntary Controlled schools walk a tightrope. On the one hand they are community schools that draw all the children from a particular neighbourhood. On the other hand they are clearly Christian foundations, their worship has to be specifically Christian and their links with the local church are usually quite strong. An agreed syllabus with a balance and approach such as that of Lincolnshire lends itself to such an ethos well and is generally welcomed by such schools.

An excellent example of a way in which a Church of England Voluntary Controlled school can walk this tightrope in respect of its provision for RE can be found in the booklet *Religious Education in the Primary School*, by Alan and Erica Brown (1996). Although it has no official status and makes no claim to be the official voice of the Church of England on this subject, the fact that it is published by the National Society (Church of England) for Promoting Religious Education does give this slim volume considerable authority, as an Anglican view on RE in the agreed syllabus. It complements and supports the approach taken to RE in both the Manchester Diocesan *Syllabus* (1995) and the *Lincolnshire Agreed Syllabus for RE* (2000). It emphasises the need for pupils to learn *about* religion as well as *from* religion. It makes a clear distinction between inculcation *into* a religion, and study *of* religion, and contains the following Church of England Board of Education guidelines for teaching Christianity:

The Bible

Key Stage 1

Pupils should be able to:

- identify some stories from the Bible;
- recognise Christmas and Easter stories;
- demonstrate awareness that the Bible is a special book for Christians;
- know why Christians read and listen to the Bible;
- respond imaginatively to stories from the Bible.

Key Stage 2

Pupils should be able to:

- demonstrate some awareness of how the Bible grew;
- look up references in the Bible;
- demonstrate knowledge and understanding of some key material from the Old and New Testaments;
- demonstrate a knowledge of some of the ways Christians use the Bible in life and worship;
- reflect on and respond imaginatively to Biblical material.

Jesus

Key Stage 1

Pupils should be able to:

- demonstrate knowledge of key events in the life of Jesus;
- give an example of a story Jesus told;
- demonstrate awareness of the effect Jesus had on the people who met him;
- explain how Christians remember Jesus in worship;
- recognise the cross and crucifix as Christian symbols;
- be able to offer an opinion about an aspect of Jesus's teaching.

Key Stage 2

Pupils should be able to:

- demonstrate familiarity with the life of Jesus as outlined in St Mark's or St Luke's Gospels;
- explain the connection between key events in the life of Jesus and major Christian festivals;
- demonstrate some understanding of key ideas about Jesus held by Christians;

- demonstrate an ability to reflect on the teaching of Jesus;
- demonstrate some understanding of the importance of Jesus for Christians;
- recognise and name important Christian symbols and give a simple explanation of their meaning;
- explain some of the ways in which Christians remember Jesus in worship.

The Church

Key Stage 1

Pupils should be able to:

- name correctly some essential features of a church building and explain their use;
- identify why a church is a special place for Christians;
- begin to understand that the Church is a collection of people and not just a building;
- identify connections between the building and the activities which take place there;
- respond imaginatively to the building.

Key Stage 2

Pupils should be able to:

- recognise some differences and similarities between two different places of Christian worship;
- show understanding of the relationship between the worship and the form of the building;
- demonstrate understanding of how Christians in the Church see themselves as members of a community;
- reflect on the need for believers to have a special place of worship;
- show understanding of how members of the Christian Church community feel about their building, and why.

Christian festivals

Key Stage 1

Pupils should be able to:

- demonstrate familiarity with stories relating to Christmas and Easter;
- respond imaginatively to stories of Christmas and Easter;
- demonstrate an awareness of how Christians celebrate Christmas and Easter;

- identify key features of at least two other Christian special times, e.g. Advent, Mothering Sunday, Pentecost, Ascension.

Key Stage 2

Pupils should be able to:

- identify the major festivals and other special times of the Christian year; their relation to each other; their celebration and significance for Christians;
- know and comment on the symbols connected with those festivals;
- demonstrate an awareness of the different ways in which different groups of Christians may celebrate the same festival.

Christian worship

Key Stage 1

Pupils should be able to:

- demonstrate knowledge of some significant features of worship;
- recognise and identify some well-known Christian prayers and hymns;
- make some connections between belief in God and worship;
- recognise that Jesus is the focal point of Christian worship.

Key Stage 2

Pupils should be able to:

- demonstrate understanding of the basic form and importance of the Eucharist;
- demonstrate awareness of forms of worship used to mark rites of passage;
- demonstrate understanding and some knowledge of ritual;
- demonstrate an understanding of the use of symbols in worship;
- identify and recognise responses of joy, sadness, thanksgiving, penitence and reconciliation;
- recognise some well-known prayers, including the Lord's Prayer.

Belief, faith and values

Key Stage 1

Pupils should be able to:

- comment on the events and characters in some of the parables;
- demonstrate a knowledge of the lives of some of the famous Christians;
- demonstrate an awareness of the importance of forgiveness;
- identify the moral in a simple Biblical and/or Christian story.

Key Stage 2

Pupils should be able to:

- identify the importance of morality in the teaching of the Bible;
- comment on the importance of Jesus in the lives of Christian believers;
- demonstrate knowledge of how and why Christians communicate their faith;
- demonstrate the diversity of views among Christians on some moral issues;
- give examples of the ways in which people show that their faith is important to them;
- give examples of ways in which Christian belief has made a profound difference to the lives of individuals.

These are bare bones or, if you prefer, a scaffolding upon which to build and support RE and the teaching of Christianity. If pupils leave a primary school with this sort of understanding of Christianity then they will have been involved in a lively and informative teaching programme.

Many recent LEA Agreed Syllabuses recommend a specific allocation of time for RE in the school curriculum: most recommend a minimum of 5 per cent of curriculum time as being necessary to deliver the content of the syllabus. OFSTED and Section 23 Inspections indicate that this is sometimes difficult to verify in primary schools where RE is integrated with other subjects, but where it is taught as a discrete subject this target is usually achieved in Church primary schools and in Key Stage 3 in secondary schools. The picture is not so rosy in Key Stage 4, even in Church schools where students not taking Religious Studies as a GCSE option have often received minimal provision of basic RE. The advent of short course GCSE, however, and its rapid growth as Religious Studies provision in Key Stage 4, is transforming this situation.

The provision of resources for RE is also changing rapidly. A wide range of excellent, accurate and attractive textbooks for RE is now available, and other resources (videos, IT software) are continually appearing in a rapidly changing market. These are not cheap, however, and RE subject leaders often have to fight hard for an equitable share of the school's capitation, even in Church schools.

Of greater concern is the supply of professionally trained specialist teachers of RE, in both primary and secondary schools. RE does not feature on DfES official lists as a 'shortage subject' – perhaps because many teachers with an RE qualification are elsewhere in the system as managers and heads, and not as classroom practitioners – but the everyday experience of those in the field is that when seeking to appoint an RE subject leader in a primary school or specialist teacher in the secondary sector, the market is extremely thin. It is to be hoped that the recommendations of the Dearing Report (*The Way Ahead: Church of England Schools in the New Millennium*, Church Schools Review Group 2001) and in particular, its recommendations to Church colleges, will begin to ameliorate this situation.

A realignment of community based education: extending provision for religious schools

Editors' note

In recent months, the proposal for an increase in the provision for religious schools has elicited heated debate in the British press. The Government's Green Paper, *Schools: Building on Success* (DfES 2001), supported the development of greater diversity in education and made it clear that the government would welcome more state funded schools provided by the churches and other religious groups. Lord Dearing's report for the Church of England, *The Way Ahead: Church of England Schools in the New Millennium* (Church Schools Review Group 2001) indicated: 'perhaps as never before in 50 years, the Church has a great opportunity to pursue and develop its mission to the nation through its schools' (ibid. 2001: 5). One of the aims of the Report is to establish 100 new Church of England Voluntary Aided secondary schools in the next five years, an ambitious aim. It also says: 'no Church school can be considered as part of the Church's mission unless it is distinctively Christian' (ibid. 2001: 3), and, 'the purpose of the church in education is not simply to provide the basic education needed for human dignity. That purpose is to offer a spiritual dimension to the lives of young people, within the traditions of the Church of England, in an increasingly secular world' (ibid. 2001: 3).

The Government's Green Paper and the Dearing Report raise two fundamental questions; first, the reasons for continued, maybe even a growing, interest in a faith-based education on the part of parents and government; and second, the question of the fairness of provision and the implications of this for a multifaith and multicultural society.

Parental interest in religious schools might be focused on religious or social reasons. Some religious families will seek a school which affirms their child in the faith practised in the home. This could offer a strong level of coherence between the values and attitudes of the home and school, with the curriculum itself possibly being interpreted in the light of religious teaching that underpins the foundation of the school. For pupils, this would serve to minimise tension between their experiences within the home and their experiences of the outside world. It can, however, create a tension between the requirements of the National Curriculum and the school's interpretation of its *raison d'être*. Some parents from minority groups might favour a religious school, whether or not that school reflects their personal religious affiliation, for social reasons. This was apparent in an inner city area where the local imam was happy to send his children to a Church of England primary school believing that the strong sense of community based around religious values would foster a strong sense of social bonding. He would take care of his children's nurture and growth into Islam, the faith of the home. For other parents, a religious school might be perceived as having a strong moral ethos. This too might be located in a generalised acceptance of common moral values rather than in specifically religious teaching, for religions can share certain moral values but for very different ideological reasons.

Government preference for an increase in a faith-based education appears to hinge on parental choice and recognising the achievements of the current religious schools. There is also an argument built on 'fairness': if the Roman Catholics and the Anglicans can have so many schools surely those opportunities should be open to all religious groups. The current Secretary of State, Estelle Morris, and her predecessor, David Blunkett, have both used the image of wishing to 'bottle' the ethos of a Church school so it might be released in other schools because the ethos in Church schools is so good.

Unfortunately the metaphor also conjures up cans of 'Lakeland' air costing tourists money but being full of nothing! In fact Church schools are very different with the vast majority of Church of England primary schools accepting pupils who live nearby, and of those primary schools over half, about 2,500, are in the control of the local authority and accept pupils on the same basis as community schools. So the Church of England statistics need to be interpreted with care and not regarded in a straight comparison with the statistics for Roman Catholic schools. It is an unusual aspect of contemporary society, which is claimed to be increasingly secular, that the Government wants to increase the number of religious schools. Will this merely increase existing divisions? Would the Government want to create religious schools if there were none? Is the drive for more religious schools taking place on the back of an historical provision that is now out of date?

However committed parents and Government might be to faith-based education, it can be argued that such a position challenges notions of fairness and equality, particularly in relation to a multifaith and multicultural society. First, while more religious schools might be regarded as increasing parental choice, this will not be true in all cases and in all parts of the country. Religious schools operate, as do all schools, an admissions criteria. Voluntary Aided schools have an admissions policy taking the form of a sliding scale which normally favours those from the local worshipping community, members of the same faith tradition who worship elsewhere, siblings of existing pupils, local pupils with health issues which prohibit travel and only then other local pupils (one needs to remember that of the 5,000 Church of England schools only 204 are secondary schools with only 146 of those being Voluntary Aided. So relatively few Anglican schools apply admissions criteria; most primary schools take pupils on application though they too will have admissions criteria). There is therefore little or no choice for parents who are not members of the religion or those who are not prepared to attend worship in the period prior to admission! A second argument, linked to the selection process, suggests that parents are willing to run the gauntlet of the selection process results in schools with strong parental support so securing a sound environment for raising standards of achievement. Denominational schools tend to have a reputation for being 'good schools', although there may be some evidence to suggest that they do not extend pupils as much as might be expected.

The strongest argument against denominational education relates to accusations of creating cultural ghettos which do not then prepare pupils for life within a multifaith and multicultural society. A significant issue is the question of how Religious Education is taught and will be taught in this increasing number of schools. Will the teaching be related solely to the teaching of one religious tradition, or, if other faiths are included, from what perspective will they be taught? Will the syllabuses for such schools be monitored, and, if so, by whom? If the aims for Religious Education cited in the model syllabuses (SCAA 1994), namely that Religious Education should (i) enable pupils to 'develop their knowledge and understanding about Christianity and other principal religions', and (ii) enable them 'to develop a positive attitude towards other people, respecting their right to hold different beliefs from their own', are sound aims for an education in religion in the twenty-first century, what does this mean for pupils attending religious schools? Why should one set of aims be appropriate for some pupils but not others? Surely the teaching of different faiths has a much stronger basis within a religious school where the whole ethos will be indicative of that faith. Will pupils in such schools be allowed to side step the educational importance of understanding about the other religions in Great Britain as envisaged in the Education Reform Act of 1988?

There are strong arguments against the extension of religious schools. The possibility of creating more religious schools, particularly from those faiths other than Christianity, must be considered in the light of the current context. There are 6,926 publicly funded schools from the Christian tradition and a very few publicly funded schools run by faith traditions other than Christianity.

Furthermore, there is the secular position to consider: why should the State, in the form of the taxpayer, subsidise the religious requirements of parents? Of course parents have a right to bring their children up within their own faith tradition, but why should the State fund the exercise? Some also argue that children, too, have rights not to be indoctrinated into a particular faith when they are in their formative years. Could there be Humanist schools which would not be required to keep to the law regarding RE, not teach RE at all and be absolved from daily Collective Worship? The next decade in education looks to be full of incident!

Questions

1 What do you think should be the main aims of RE in Church schools?
2 What do you think would be an appropriate balance between Christianity and other faiths in an RE syllabus for Voluntary Aided schools? Does the answer depend on the racial/cultural/religious nature of the area?
3 Recent Diocesan Syllabuses for Church of England Voluntary Aided schools seem to be similar in philosophy and approach to LEA Agreed Syllabuses. Should there be a distinction? Does it matter if the RE offered in Voluntary Aided schools becomes more or less the same as in Voluntary Controlled schools?

4 Commitment and indoctrination: a dilemma for Religious Education?

Trevor Cooling

Are you sitting comfortably?

It was a really strange sensation. One moment I was standing talking to a colleague in a room full of people. The next it was as if I was on my own in a railway station, with the noise and rush of air of an express train tearing past the platform.

This was a Friday evening in September 1988 and was, for me, one of those life-forming events. I was hosting a weekend for RE teachers at the conference centre where I was employed. We had just finished the session and, as usual, I had prepared the drinks in the kitchen. But that evening we broke the routine. Instead of bringing the conference participants down to the kitchen, we had, following the chance suggestion of one of the teachers on the weekend, taken the drinks through to the conference room. This was about twenty yards from the kitchen, behind a set of doors. About a minute after leaving the kitchen, I had my strange sensation. I cannot tell you how long it lasted, probably barely a second, but it finished with my becoming aware of a screaming engine and a blaring horn. I rushed out through the doors and there, in the kitchen right where I had been standing just one minute before, was a car!

The story is that a young man, worse the wear for drink, had a minor collision about 300 yards down the road from our premises. Instead of stopping, he had attempted a getaway by driving at great speed through the petrol station forecourt right next to our building. In his drunken state, he had forgotten that there was no exit that side. Instead he had driven right through our kitchen wall at 60 mph. My 'really strange sensation' was caused by the pressure wave that had gone through the building as a result of the impact. He and his passengers survived because the wall was weak and gave way. Hence the car's appearance in the kitchen (sitting on top of the washing machine!). However the room looked like a bomb had gone off. Where the wall had been, was a huge hole. Most of the bricks had hit the opposite wall ten feet away, making dents an inch or more deep. It was obvious that anyone in that kitchen would have been killed outright in an explosion of bricks and mortar. Anyone in its vicinity might easily have been injured or killed, or even died of fright!

Stories in RE

It is possible that my story may have caught your attention. One of the major emphases in RE has always been the importance of story. Religious communities use stories to express their faith and communicate their worldview. Individuals develop their own self-understanding through identification with other people's stories and through telling their own stories arising from personal life-experiences. However the word story is used at two levels. The first is the individual story, like Jesus's parable of the Good Samaritan or my experience with the car. The second is story with a capital S, those big ideas, sometimes referred to as meta-narratives, which express our whole understanding of the world and help people to make sense of their lives. For example, for Christians the meta-narrative of creation by God, rebellion by human beings, redemption through the coming of Jesus Christ and the hope of eternal life provides the framework for their whole understanding of life and the world. These two levels of story feed each other and both are important in RE.

The stories that others tell us and which resonate with our own experience and the stories we tell to others about our own life experiences are incredibly important shaping influences on who we are and on the commitments we make. For example, my story from 1988 is not just a useful party piece for social occasions. Rather, when I tell it to other people, I am telling them something very important about me and am bearing witness to something that is very important to me. I am an evangelical Christian. I believe in the providence of God. In telling the story of that evening in September 1988, I am sharing a deeply held belief that, in some way that I do not fully understand, there was a divine intervention which prevented the carnage that would inevitably have followed our usual routine of 'drinks in the kitchen'. I interpret the facts of this story in a way that resonates with the meta-narrative which shapes my life. Other people may be uncomfortable with my interpretation of my story, because they do not believe in an interventionist God. So 'my story' and 'their story' are different, and even conflict with each other, despite the fact that we do not dispute the actual events. However I cannot do other than bear witness to my story because it is an incredibly important element in my life. Abandon my interpretation of this story and my whole life changes because my God changes. These are not *just stories*. They convey what we each believe to be the truth.[1]

In a very significant article (1997), John Hick, the renowned professor and influential philosopher of religion, shared some of his life experience. His story is of an evangelical Christian background which was shaken by the experience of being a conscientious objector and service in the Friends Ambulance Unit during the Second World War. Of this he says, 'My earlier views seemed a little naive in some ways – intellectually closed, in a way that began to jar with my on-going philosophical training' (1997: 4). He also tells the story of another shaping experience, which was of growing inter-faith contacts through work in community relations in Birmingham from 1975. Of this he writes:

I often found myself in synagogues, gurdwaras, mandirs and mosques, as well as churches. Something struck me which had profound implications. Although all the externals of dress, posture, language, symbol and so on are very different, as are the mythology and beliefs, it seems clear to me that at the deeper level the same thing is going on.

(Hick 1997: 4)

As Hick grappled with the story of his life experience, he increasingly felt that it did not concur with the interpretation offered from the meta-narrative of his evangelical Christianity, namely that Jesus Christ is the only way of salvation. So his meta-narrative changed to one which he calls religious pluralism. He describes this as 'the view that the great world religions constitute different ways of conceiving the ultimate reality, and therefore different ways of experiencing that reality, and therefore different ways of responding in life to that reality' (Hick 1997: 4).

But this new story is not *just a story* for Hick. It is truth in the sense that he thinks it is extremely important for everyone. In this article, through the story of his life, Hick is commending the meta-narrative of religious pluralism to all RE teachers, and presumably to their pupils. He describes what happened to him, and the resultant change in his story, as growing in faith. As far as Hick is concerned, this is so important that he expends a lot of energy on seeking to persuade others to share his meta-narrative, as is evidenced by his impressive list of publications.

Across the other side of the world, another professor and philosopher, this time of education, tells a different story. Brian Hill was Professor of Education at Murdoch University in Perth, Australia for over two decades. He is a prolific writer and many of his publications are influential in Britain. As a young man, he was quietly persuaded to move from scepticism to Christian faith by leaders in the Inter Schools Christian Fellowship, now known as Scripture Union, an evangelical Christian body set up to share the Christian gospel with young people. He makes no secret of the fact that this evangelical Christian commitment has remained central to his life ever since (Hill 1999a, 1999b).

Like Hick, Hill's evangelical meta-narrative was challenged by encounters with religious pluralism. In particular, a visit to India led him to reflect at length on the management of values education in a secular state (Hill 1985). He encountered the raw pluralism that leaves no sensitive visitor to that country untouched. Another formative experience was addressing a conference in Manila on the education of the children of Christian missionaries, where the discipline of reflecting on the growth of Christian faith in the midst of a cross-cultural experience provoked yet more life-changing thinking (Hill 1986). Both experiences shaped his meta-narrative and, like Hick, led to reflection on and questioning of his evangelical background. However, unlike Hick, his evangelical faith was refined, not consumed, in this fire and he emerged advocating an understanding of religion which was in direct conflict with the relativistic models advocated by Hick and others in their response to the experience of pluralism (Hill 1990). For Hill, the nature of religion is to proclaim truth. There is a choice that has to be made between the truth of the different religions. The freedom to proclaim the uniqueness of Jesus Christ in the school setting is a fundamental freedom in a plural democracy. He is clear, however, that the freedom to proclaim their story is not just the right of Christians, but a right that all faith groups in society have.

These two influential professors illustrate an important point about all of us. They each have stories to tell from their own experiences which have shaped the meta-narratives that are the foundations of their lives and academic work. These stories are not *just stories*, rather they define for each of them something so important that both are passionately committed to their view. They want to persuade others of the importance and truth of what they write. There is no 'take it or leave it' attitude in either of them. They are both very anxious to influence how we, as RE teachers, think and therefore how our pupils think. It is for the reader to make their own judgement, but I make no secret of my agreement with Hill and of my conviction that Hick is wrong on this issue. But for the moment that is not the point. My purpose in citing these two professors is simply to show how we are all shaped by the stories of our life experiences. How we interpret these stories contributes to the meta-narrative which makes each of us who we are. These meta-narratives are a central commitment in our life. They matter so much that we believe them to be true in the sense that we think they are not just for us but for everyone. They are held in what might be described as a *religious* manner.

A second significant point that our two professors teach us is that it is not so much which religion we are committed to that is important in the context of the debates about RE, but what our meta-narrative has to say about the nature of religion. Hick is convinced that the true purpose of religion is to make us less self-centred. It is not primarily telling us truths about the nature of reality out there.[2] Hill, in contrast, is very much concerned with the truth or otherwise of the message of the religions. For him, the purpose of a religion is to help us know the truth about God and the world. In many ways this difference between two Christians is much more fundamental than the differences between people of the different world religions. Michael Grimmitt has argued that this debate between realist and non-realist views of religion cannot be side-stepped in RE. He, rightly in my view, says that this is 'essentially about the credibility of religious faith in a postmodern age' (Grimmitt 2000: 47). However this debate is still going on, as is reflected in the different positions taken by Hick and Hill in their response to the fact of religious pluralism. It is part of the landscape of controversiality that RE has to cope with, albeit probably one of the most significant parts. The widespread concern about evangelical Christian and Muslim attitudes to commitment on the part of many religious educators reflects the difference of opinion between those of a more non-realist persuasion and those who adopt a more realist approach.[3]

Religious education and commitment

I remember once attending a meeting to discuss the need to recruit more RE teachers for schools. Everyone was in agreement that a major priority should be to find young people from the faith communities. At that point I made a chance remark which evoked an embarrassed silence. I suggested that if religious people were to be persuaded to teach RE they had to be given a *religious* reason for doing so. In other words I was suggesting that RE teaching has to be a *religious* activity for people whose meta-narrative is a religious one. Otherwise why do it?

The silence I triggered reflects a deep anxiety that has been prevalent for many years in the debates about RE in school. There is a fear that if people teach RE because of their religious faith commitment, their primary loyalty will be to the propagation of their own views rather than to the educational aims of the subject. In other words there is a deep concern that RE will be hijacked (or domesticated as some express it) by religion, dogma will rule in the classroom and indoctrination rather than education will be the result. This fear has been particularly focussed on evangelical Christianity and Islam, which are widely viewed as two religions with propagating agendas. So, down the years, teachers have been exhorted to make their primary commitment to RE as a subject and to put their own faith commitment in second place.[4] On this view, RE ought not to be a *religious* activity.

For many years, this was interpreted as meaning that teachers should be neutral. In other words they were expected to leave their religious commitment at the school gate. Teachers, and indeed pupils, were encouraged to *bracket out* their own beliefs when studying religion.[5] The model was of detached academia, which in the universities was exemplified in the new Religious Studies departments. Even theology was not to be viewed as a *religious* activity. However it is now widely accepted, at least within the world of RE, that this is a cul-de-sac strategy.[6] A classic illustration of its inadequacy is found in the following attempt to define the spiritual in a neutral way.

> The term needs to be seen as applying to something fundamental in the human condition…It has to do with relationships with other people and for believers with God. It has to do with the universal search for individual identity – with our responses to challenging experiences such as death, suffering, beauty and encounters with good and evil. It is to do with the search for meaning and purpose in life and for values by which to live.
>
> (NCC 1993: 2)

On 21 April 1999, two teenage boys walked into Columbine High School in Colorado and systematically massacred twelve of their fellow students and one teacher before turning their guns on themselves. They called themselves the 'trench-coat mafia' and were known for their distinctive clothing and their strong sense of personal identity, which was fed by neo-Nazi websites and literature. They defined their self-identity through their relationships with others, and through their rejection of God. They created the ultimate challenging experiences of death and suffering. They had a very clear sense of meaning and purpose in life and of the values by which to live. According to our neutral definition above, they were spiritual. The problem was that their spirituality was perverted. Clearly no teacher would want to be neutral in relation to this meta-narrative.

The inadequacy of a neutral approach follows from what I have already argued about the importance of a meta-narrative in everyone's life. We are all shaped by stories which are not *just stories*. To leave them at the school gate is to leave an essential part of who I am behind. That is why it is impossible, even dishonest, on the one hand to want to recruit committed RE teachers from faith communities, but on the other hand to demand that they should not view their RE teaching as a *religious* activity. The effect is to secularise these teachers' beliefs by banishing them to the private domain of an individual's life.[7]

In response to the collapse of the neutrality strategy, more recently the importance of teachers finding a harmony between their personal meta-narrative and their professional responsibilities as religious educators has been recognised. There is great damage done to the quality of RE, if teachers behave as though they are neutral when they patently are not. So some authors are arguing that what teachers have to do is to find a meta-narrative that is appropriate to the professional responsibility of RE teaching. In other words it is accepted that there is a real sense in which RE is a *religious* activity. However an important question then becomes will *any form* of meta-narrative do?

The emerging consensus appears to be that the sort of religious activity that is appropriate for an RE teacher is what John Hull, an influential commentator on this subject, has called anti-religionist (1998). Hull defines religionism as follows:

> The identity which is fostered by religionism depends upon rejection and exclusion. We are better than they. We are orthodox; they are infidel. We are believers; they are unbelievers. We are right; they are wrong. The other is identified as pagan, the heathen, the alien, the stranger, the invader, the one who threatens us and our way of life.
>
> (Hull 1998: 55–6)

Religionism is regarded as a disaster for a plural society because it is perceived as providing no basis for co-existence and co-operation between members of different faiths and as leading to indoctrination. Anti-religionist RE requires teachers who do not hold religionist views, in other words teachers who share John Hick's commitment to religious pluralism.

The idea that RE may not be the place for religionists is explored by Michael Grimmitt, an influential university lecturer and trainer of RE teachers. He is particularly critical of the influence of faith communities in the drawing up of the SCAA Model Syllabuses during the 1990s, which are still used as important framework documents. He views the faith community input to that process as the taking captive of RE by self-interested religionists (Grimmitt 2000: 14–15), a captivity from which the subject needs liberating.

Grimmitt implies that the preferred type of religious support for RE should derive its inspiration from liberal/radical Christianity (2000: 30) and take a non-realist approach as its framework (2000: 46–7). This takes what he terms an *instrumental* view of religion, by which he means that the function of religion within education is primarily the promotion of healthy human development. So religion is not about, to put it somewhat crudely, discovering the truth about a God or an objective reality outside of ourselves, but it is rather about promoting the inner being of the human person, or as Hick would put it becoming less self-centred. Other influential writers[8] offer a similar analysis which draws on a view of religion which is largely relativist in approach and emphasises the subjective inner-world of the believer rather than the objective reality of God.

At this point I wish to make a somewhat provocative observation. I can see no difference between this approach and the (generally perceived to be) problematic approach traditionally associated with evangelical Christianity and Islam. One vocal exponent of the evangelical Christian view is Penny Thompson who, citing Basil Mitchell, adopts a simple logic, namely that Christianity is true and therefore it ought to be taught as such (Thompson 2000: 7). In many ways I agree absolutely with Thompson. I share her evangelical Christian convictions about the truth of the uniqueness of Christ, his resurrection and the authority of the Bible. But the difficulty with this straightforward position is that it cannot cope with others who similarly argue that their truth should also be taught as true. The classroom is reduced to the counter claims of the pantomime with each faith group shouting 'oh yes it is' about their truth and 'oh no it isn't' about other people's truths. It is unclear how this approach prepares pupils for the demands of living in a religiously plural world where they have to make judgements of their own as to the validity or otherwise of a variety of commitments, while respecting the rights of people whose beliefs differ from their own.

However, exactly the same criticism applies to what I have described as the anti-religionist approach. It certainly starts with the intention of avoiding indoctrination. However, it has finished with the active promotion of a particular approach to religion, which is treated as normative even though it draws its inspiration from one strand of Christian theology. In terms of our meta-narratives above, this favours Hick's view over and above Hill's view of the nature of religion. What possible justification can there be for such a strategy in a plural democracy? What difference is there between this and the more familiar (and overt) style of indoctrination classically associated with evangelical Christians and Muslims? How does it prepare pupils to live in a plural society if a form of religion (liberal/radical Christianity) is propagated through RE, when that same form is deeply offensive to many religious communities? Have we not here, a classic example of discrimination in the cause of non-discrimination, of indoctrination in the cause of non-indoctrination, of religionism in the cause of anti-religionism?

The problem is this. As I have already argued, we are all shaped by our personal stories. Of particular importance for RE teachers is the fact that these will have shaped our meta-narrative, which define our view of the nature of religion. And, if we are honest, we are convinced that our meta-narrative is right for everyone. For some, like Brian Hill, Penny Thompson and myself, this personal story leads to the conviction that evangelical Christianity, with its realist view of religion (which we share with Muslims), is true. For others, like John Hick, John Hull, Clive Erricker and Michael Grimmitt, their life experiences lead to the conviction that more radical/liberal approaches, with their non-realist leanings, are 'true', in the sense of being the way forward for society as a whole in its approach to religion. And both sides argue their positions with the passion appropriate to the conviction of their truth. However these two approaches are directly contradictory and cannot be held together. If either is imposed in the classroom, the other group feels excluded. So how do we move beyond this seeming impasse?

An Alternative Model[9]

I suggest that the way forward involves the honest admission that every teacher comes to RE with a meta-narrative which defines for them what is the nature and importance of religion. This meta-narrative will be held with conviction and passion, because that is the nature of a meta-narrative. There will be an understandable desire to propagate this view, in the sense that there will be the hope that others will come to share it. In that sense, RE will therefore be a *religious* activity for all teachers. If a teacher denies this fact, I suspect it will either be because they really do not care that much about religion, in which case they will not be a very good RE teacher, or because they have not recognised the partisan nature of their own meta-narrative. It is all too easy to be blinded by the seeming common sense of our own commitments.

So given that we are all prepared to admit the strength of commitment we have to our own meta-narrative and our, legitimate, desire to propagate it, how can we avoid indoctrination in the classroom? I suggest there are three principles to be adopted.

The level playing field

This is the point at which I probably part company with some of my fellow evangelical Christians. In their view, if something is true it should be taught as such in school. The difficulty with that is that, although I agree with their assessment of the truth of Christianity, not everyone in our plural, and increasingly secular, democracy agrees with it. The same could be said of some of the anti-religionists who seem to feel that their liberal/radical view of religion is unproblematic, because it is the enlightened approach in the (post)modern world which offers decaying, old-style religion a new credibility. In the state-funded schools of a plural democracy, it seems to me that it is inappropriate for the state to adjudicate on matters where there is legitimate controversy. On such matters, the job then becomes to educate our pupils to make sound choices and decisions of their own. And this cannot happen if students are only exposed to one meta-narrative as 'the truth'.[10]

A simple illustration will suffice to make the point. In a meeting an RE teacher stood up and said, 'I always tell my pupils that there are no right or wrong answers in RE'. This sounds very tolerant, but is, in fact, indoctrination into a relativistic and anti-realist approach to religion. This teacher was not creating a level playing field. If he had revised his statement to 'I always tell my students that, in RE, there is no final agreement on what the right or wrong answers are', the effect is totally different. This leaves open the debate about realism and non-realism and recognises the importance of students making their own judgements. The subtle change of language has created the required level playing field by recognising the controversial nature of religion but without pre-determining the pupils' response.

What I have written here will attract certain rejoinders, which I want to deny straight away. In no sense at all is the admission of legitimate controversy in matters of religion the same as embracing relativism, the notion that there are many different, equally legitimate truths. Rather it is to accept that, given the fact of the existence in society of many different claims to 'the truth', the educational task is to equip pupils with the skills and knowledge necessary for making judgements themselves as to the nature of that truth. This is to embrace not the philosophy of relativism, but that of critical realism and the educational task of promoting religious literacy.[11]

Furthermore this is not a neutral approach where all religions, worldviews and meta-narratives are treated as equally legitimate, with no judgements being made. Exactly the opposite is true because the educational task is to equip pupils to make such judgements and the effective teacher will be a role model of how this is done. The task is to decide which is true, not to persuade pupils that they are all true or are all merely myths. And with certain meta-narratives, the school community as a whole will decide that they cannot be treated as legitimate players in this process, usually because of their total unacceptability in a society which values respect for each and every human being. To take an extreme example, the meta-narrative of neo-Nazism will not find a welcome place on this level playing field.

Finally this approach does not require that every single meta-narrative that has a legitimate claim to be taught in schools will be taught. This would be to overload pupils with information and be totally counter-productive in the effort to achieve the key skill of making informed judgements about truth. Selection will have to be made on some such grounds as, say, comparative significance in the social context of the school.

The rejection of indoctrination

Believing our meta-narrative is true and wanting others to share it does not amount to condoning indoctrination. By indoctrination I mean adopting teaching strategies which are designed to ensure that pupils come to share your views.[12] These can include, for example, excluding alternatives, mis-representing other views and abusing one's authority as a teacher by treating a controversial issue as non-controversial. Indoctrination is unacceptable for a number of reasons. First it is an assault on the integrity and human rights of our pupils, which in my Christian language is to fail to treat other people as image-bearers of God. Second it is unjust in the context of a plural society, because it illegitimately favours one way of life over another. Third, in the context of state-funded education, it is an abuse of the power of the State. Finally, it does not equip students with the necessary skills and attitudes for harmonious living in a plural world. Indoctrination is a definite no-no!

The embracing of shared goals

When we teach RE in a school that is not faith-based, it is important to realise that we are embracing goals that are different from those of a faith community. Faith communities quite rightly want to nurture the pupils' personal faith through their educational activities. This is not the same as indoctrination and is not to be confused with it. In other types of school, faith-nurturing is not possible since the school community itself will not share one faith.

However, the teaching of RE in non-faith schools can still be based on shared goals which can be supported by teachers who have very different personal meta-narratives. For example, there is widespread agreement that a key skill in the modern world is to learn how to live and work harmoniously alongside people who have very different commitments from our own. This will entail navigating some very controversial matters, such as attitudes to the role of women in society. One of the shared goals of RE teaching can therefore be the promotion of key abilities like learning to listen to and to hear others, expressing one's own convictions in a sensitive and non-offensive manner and negotiating ways forward in situations of disagreement. Another shared goal might be the promotion of religious literacy, in other words the development in pupils of the ability to make informed and sound judgements about truth.

It will of course be essential that the shared goals are not in conflict with one's own meta-narrative, otherwise we will be personally compromised, which is a deeply uncomfortable experience. That is why each RE teacher must ultimately teach for *religious* reasons and be able to see the shared goals as *religious* goals, in other words as justified by and derived from their own meta-narrative. It is entirely counter-productive for anyone to attempt to impose a single meta-narrative on everyone else in the coalition, be that a liberal/radical or evangelical one. Ultimately, there will be some teachers who will not be able to embrace the widely shared goals, in which case RE teaching in non-faith schools is not for them. This is no shame on them, but it does mean that another vocation, perhaps in ministry within their own faith community, will be more appropriate.

What I am suggesting is that we have to commit ourselves to what we might call 'the coalition of RE teachers', where the partners have shared goals but not shared meta-narratives. This requires the willingness to exercise restraint. By this, I mean that, on some occasions, one may decide not to speak out for what you believe to be the best because of other reasons. This is not the same as excluding the personal commitment of the teacher from the classroom or treating it as inherently problematic 'like a recalcitrant child that has to be constantly reined in' (Thompson 2000: 6). It is, rather, to accept that in some contexts my first and immediate response should not be to lead with a faith-based right hook. An illustration may help. As a parent one's greatest wish is to protect one's children from the pain of mistakes. An easy way to do this is to make their decisions for them. But this is counter-productive, because human nature is such that the only way to learn how not to make mistakes is to make a few. So, *on appropriate occasions*, as a parent, one exercises restraint and bites one's tongue, because you know that this is the only way to achieve the good you desire. But it is risky and demanding. Likewise I, as a Christian teaching in a school which does not have a Christian basis, have to restrain some of my natural and legitimate inclinations to propagate my faith. I do this because I respect my pupils' freedom and the fact that they may hold to a very different meta-narrative from my own. They have a right to grow in faith within that. But as a Christian I do not have a problem with this, because Jesus, too, bit his tongue.

As well as the practice of a degree of restraint, another ingredient in the success of a coalition is that there is a clear code of conduct as to how the members will behave in order to achieve their shared goals. In relation to RE, this will particularly regulate the manner in which a teacher shares or expresses their own faith commitment and deals with faith commitments different from their own. The coalition of RE teaching is already developing some of these. For example, the Westhill Project proposed the widely adopted principle of 'owning and grounding language' (Read *et al.* 1992: 66–7). By this is meant that the language used in an RE classroom is not presumptive in the sense that it does not assume commitment on the part of the pupils to a particular religious position. It gives everyone the freedom to feel it is okay for them not to accept any given teaching or practice, but it allows the introduction of controversial views for study and for debate.

Conclusion

Should we be afraid of commitment in RE teachers? Will it automatically lead to indoctrination? The answer is most certainly no, as long as every RE teacher is prepared to be honest about the commitment they have to their own meta-narrative and to respect the fact that this will not be shared by many other teachers and most of their pupils. Indeed, committed teachers are essential for quality RE. How are pupils to learn the skills of judging truth and of dialogue and debate in the search for truth? How are they to learn how to develop harmonious working relationships with others of very different commitments from their own? How are they to learn the skill of working in coalition and negotiating shared goals with people of faiths different from their own? Only if they are systematically taught these skills by teachers of commitment, who model them on a daily basis.

However if any teacher is unwilling or unable to recognise the controversial nature of their own commitment, or is unable to exercise appropriate restraint in the classroom and thereby impose their own view, then indoctrination is a danger. Certainly there are evangelical Christians and Muslims who behave like this. Most people recognise that particular danger. However, I would suggest that the less visible danger is posed by the more liberal/radical approaches, which assume that their meta-narratives are educationally superior, are not committed in the same sense as their more evangelical brethren and are, therefore, uncontroversial.

Questions

1 What are some of the features of your own meta-narrative? In what ways have these been shaped by your life experiences? Are there any features of your meta-narrative that might influence the way you teach RE?
2 What views do you have on the debate between realist and non-realist approaches to religion?
3 Can you list some of the statements that might be included in a code of conduct for RE teachers? In what ways might these require you to exercise restraint in relation to your own meta-narrative?

Notes

1 For a fuller discussion of story and RE see my chapter in Cooling (1996).
2 This is a controversial assertion concerning John Hicks's position. See Cooling (1994) for a fuller justification.
3 See Groothuis (2000) for an example of a detailed justification of a realist position by an evangelical Christian.
4 This idea is reflected in the following description of the achievements of fifty years of RE: 'That RE teaching could now be seen as a legitimate and fulfilling career (as opposed to a Christian vocation) was part of this achievement' (Copley 1997: 190).
5 This idea is derived from what has come to be known as the phenomenological approach.
6 For a detailed consideration of the notion that Religious Studies and Theology are *religious* activities, see Webb (2000).
7 Lesslie Newbigin is a leading exponent of the dangers of privatisation of faith; see for example Newbigin (1989).
8 A leading exponent of the idea that relativism should be the basis of RE is Clive Erricker; see for example Erricker (1998).
9 For other detailed discussions of similar approaches see Johnson (1996), Hill (1982) and Schwartz (1998). The Qualifications and Curriculum Authority has also produced helpful guidance; see QCA (2000: 19–21).
10 The debate about the controversial nature of truth rests on different epistemologies. For a fuller treatment of the debate see Cooling (1994) and Thompson (1996).
11 For a more detailed exposition of critical realism and religious literacy, the reader is referred to the work of Andrew Wright; for example, Wright (1993). Hobson and Edwards (1999) also give a full treatment of critical realism.
12 This is a very superficial treatment of a complex subject. For a detailed discussion of indoctrination see Thiessen (1993).

5 Issues in the teaching of Religious Education

Assessing achievement in RE from early years to 'A' Level

John Keast

Teaching, learning and assessment

Assessment is an integral part of the cycle of planning effective teaching and learning in any subject. There is a saying: 'A lesson is not taught until it is learned'. Managing the learning as well as preparing the teaching is part of the role of the teacher; indeed, they are two sides of the same coin. Into this process of teaching and learning must come feedback to the pupil. If we take the endeavour of pupils seriously they have a right to know how well they are doing. This requires not only the identification of teaching and learning objectives in the first place, but some assessment against them to establish the progress a pupil has made. Teachers need to know this too, not only to be able to report to others how well a pupil has achieved, but so that they can plan the next stage of the pupil's learning. All this is as true of RE as any subject.

Stressing the integral links between assessment and teaching and learning is not simply to reinforce the link between assessment and the curriculum which is well known but also serves to indicate how, in RE, assessment can get caught up in philosophical issues about the nature and purpose of RE in the school curriculum. These issues are covered in more depth in other parts of this book. The connection is mentioned here simply to indicate that such issues will arise from time to time in this chapter because some particular difficulties in dealing with assessment in RE are due to conceptual questions about what RE is for in schools.

Another point to be drawn from making clear the connection between assessment and teaching and learning is that it demonstrates that teachers of RE have always been assessing the progress and achievement of pupils. It is impossible to imagine that in all the generations of teachers and cohorts of pupils there have been in RE since, say 1944, no assessment has occurred! Much of this assessment may have been individual and subjective, intermittent and unstructured, private and unreported, conscious or unconscious, perhaps not even thought of as assessment, but it has undoubtedly taken place. Teaching and learning could not have happened unless some assessment had taken place also! It may have been accurate or inaccurate, valid or invalid, clear or muddled, but it has served to feedback performance to pupils and report progress to parents. We cannot pretend assessment is not, and has not always been, part of teaching RE.

Impact of GCSE Religious Studies

In the days before the National Curriculum (NC) was introduced in 1989 the only nationally structured and agreed forms of assessment in RE were in 'A' Level, 'O' Level and CSE examinations in Religious Studies. The first two of these had relatively long traditions of assessment based on university marking. Their processes were not generally well known by many teachers, and sometimes were rather opaque. 'O' Level and CSE were combined in 1988 to become GCSE, and aspects of the new assessment process changed assessment thinking and practices in RE very considerably in secondary schools from then on. The training that accompanied the introduction of GCSE in 1988 accustomed secondary teachers of RE to K, U and E. This set of three letters – Knowledge, Understanding and Evaluation (KUE) – identified three assessment objectives that became almost a mantra for teachers in making their assessments. These objectives in turn linked back to teaching and learning objectives for examination groups. Their usage raised the awareness of assessment among teachers and sharpened considerably their thinking about the cycle of planning, teaching and learning. A shared language had been developed not only among teachers but also for use with pupils and parents too. Feedback to pupils became easier, as did reports to parents. It was as if the components of progress had been identified, and made teachers more proficient in tracking it.

One particular aspect of the development of GCSE that promoted this awareness was the requirement for coursework by candidates. Teachers had to set tasks that met the aims of the new examination, one of which was differentiation. Teachers also had to mark the projects that resulted from the tasks. At first there was some abysmal practice. At least one examination board saw a task set by a school that was simply 'Mark's Gospel'! No further indication of what candidates should do was given. Marking of this task consisted of an impression based on neatness and length, with almost full marks being given for material largely copied from commentaries! Despite a minority of bad practice most teachers soon learned to mark using KUE criteria and to set tasks that allowed achievement of these learning objectives to be demonstrated.

Very few teachers objected to the introduction of KUE, though there were (and still are) debates about the distinctiveness of the first two categories, and the nature of the third. It was thought by many to be a regrettable step when, in 1996, the criteria for GCSE Religious Studies combined the first two assessment objectives, then subdivided them by content into *elements* and *effects* of religions. Fortunately, the GCSE (Short course) also introduced in 1996 kept the distinction between them to a large extent, and these were used in 2000 as the basis for the assessment objectives in the combined full and short course GCSE Religious Studies criteria we now have.[1] The distinction between K and U is not to be regarded as helpful in suggesting there is a complete separation of knowledge from understanding but because it helps teachers to focus their planning on learning objectives. These are easier to identify when separated, even though a review of planning objectives will make inevitable and useful connections.

That Muslims believe Muhammad is 'the seal of the prophets' is an item of knowledge, and whether pupils have that knowledge is relatively easy to assess. Recall is both a skill of demonstrating and assessing knowledge. What being 'the seal of the prophets' means is a matter of understanding. Being able to explain the meaning of the term, its origin, its significance in Islam, its links with other religions, etc., is a means of demonstrating and assessing understanding. This would not be possible without the basic item of knowledge. There are, however, more complex forms of knowledge than just more detail and a greater range of material, that stray close towards understanding. Knowing what the 5 Ks of Sikhism are constitutes part of knowledge in RE. Knowing what each represents in terms of Sikh practice or belief – is that knowledge or understanding? Such symbols may be learned by rote, giving a good example of knowledge masquerading as understanding, and understanding learned as knowledge. Such phenomena do not in themselves obliterate the distinction between knowledge and understanding nor diminish its general usefulness. Good assessment processes allow for them.

What we can assess

Assessing even apparently straightforward knowledge can be tricky. Take the examination question, worth one mark, 'When was Jesus born?'[2] On reflection it is easy to see there is no single or simple answer to this. 'Two thousand years ago'; 'In 6BC(E)'; 'In the days of Herod the King'; 'A few months later than John the Baptist'; these are just a few of the right answers! Not only does this indicate that the learning objective needs to be clear when setting the question, or that the mark scheme needs to be comprehensive, but also it points to the different styles of learning that pupils may have. Knowledge is more complex than mere facts!

Even more vexatious is the debate as to what constitutes evaluation. Being able to make a judgement about the value or worth of something is what lies behind this assessment objective. However RE in our common schools and in our external examination system is not about passing judgement on the individual views of pupils. It is the quality of the argument they deploy or the case they can make out which forms the basis of the assessment of their progress and achievement in evaluation. Do pupils have reasonable arguments? Are the arguments logical? What evidence can they adduce to support them? This is relatively uncontentious. However, to prevent such assessment being simply the rehearsal of personal viewpoints, evaluation in RE is also seen as necessarily related to the religious beliefs and practices that give rise to the issues being considered. Thus, pupils must not just convey their own viewpoint but their arguments must be related to the knowledge and understanding of religions they have gained. There is a significant difference between the following questions: 'Is it a good idea to go on a pilgrimage?' and 'Do you think that the Hajj should play such an important part in the practice of Islam?' Some questions try to ensure that the pupil's own view is linked with a critical assessment of religious phenomena, such as 'To worship is a funda-mental need in human beings. What is your view of this statement? Link your answer to the religion(s) you have studied.' Such questions can be rather cumbersome, but are designed to ensure pupils evaluate the significance of what they learn. Higher levels of evaluation may involve pupils critically analysing the views and arguments of others in shaping or reshaping their own.

Why assessment is underdeveloped in RE

This very brief discussion of the issues within evaluation helps to explain several of the reasons why, apart from external examinations before 1989, assessment in RE was very largely undeveloped. First, the identification of KUE was uncommon and certainly not universally practised. Second, the difficulties of distinguishing knowledge and understanding were discouraging. Third, and more important, the uncertainty about evaluation discussed above illustrates a view, almost universally held, that RE was not something that should be assessed. Its purpose in the school curriculum was greater, even nobler, than that which could or should be assessed.

RE was about personal development, certainly moral development, and maybe even religious development. (The use of the term 'spiritual development' was uncommon before 1989.) To assess personal, moral and religious develop-ment was distasteful. Nobody would seriously suggest that the holiness of a priest or a saint could be assessed! Furthermore it was an imposition on the privacy, integrity and personality of individual pupils and their families. Whether assessment in RE was thought possible or not was therefore not gener-ally a question, but if it was, it was soon dismissed. GCSE Religious Studies could get away with being different because it did not pretend to be the same thing as Religious Education. GCSE and 'A' Level (though assessment objec-tives were much later in featuring in its criteria) were regarded as objective, neutral study. The kind of evaluation they required was narrower than the wider purposes of religious education, particularly for younger pupils.

There are at least two submerged contradictions here that did not surface until later in the 1990s. The first is given that some assessment must have been going on consciously or unconsciously, such assessment in RE was likely as not to have been subjective and partial, and in that sense uneducational. Progress in RE would often be more to do with the pleasantness and effort of the pupil than objective standards or achievement. It might even be affected openly or covertly by the religious affiliation or practice of the pupils.[3]

Second, RE was largely regarded as phenomenological in schools and agreed syllabuses. That is, it was an education into the phenomenon of religion and the phenomena of religions. It had ceased to be confessional to a large extent, a change symbolised by the undebated clause in the Education Reform Act 1988 which changed the name of the subject from Religious Instruction to Religious Education. Much of this change was due to the influence of

Lancaster, Ninian Smart in particular, and the Schools' Council.[4] Schools and teachers welcomed the change as it recognised and regularised what had happened in many classrooms since about 1970, when the appearance of followers of religions other than Christianity in Britain became common, and the influence of the new theology of the 1960s caught on. Yet the original concept of phenomenology of religion allowed for pupils to come to a judgement about religious phenomena. Critical evaluation, even empathy to an extent, was a part of the phenomenological methodology. For schools however, this aspect of phenomenology was less prominent and a phenomenological approach became synonymous with neutrality and objectivity. Pupils were to be allowed to make up their own mind about what, if anything, to believe. Schools therefore did not enter this territory. How pupils might do this was not a proper subject of enquiry.

Such an attitude resulted from the much-feared accusation of indoctrination in the 1970s. Teachers of RE were afraid of this for a variety of reasons. Parental complaint was clearly one, and pupil pressure was another. But it was also partly a response to other projects like the Schools' Council material and the Schools' Humanities Project. It was also the times in which they lived, and if now many might regard such a response as a little unthinking – a judgement of hindsight rather than foresight – it was a response shared by many other teachers.

Yet many schools and teachers still clung to the implicit notion that RE was different from RS. They felt there was a dimension to RE that was more personal than RS. They sensed that what might now be more readily identified as 'values' – issues that cannot be denied – were still important in RE. RE can no more be value-neutral than any other subject, and if RE indoctrinated pupils so too did history, science, English, etc., in the assumptions they made about secularism. It is ironic therefore that RE in schools had adopted a methodology with potential for evaluation but on the whole steered clear of it. Its potential was really only begun to be developed when external examinations identified evaluation as an assessment objective. Even then, it was mainly the examination groups that began to enjoy the excitement and exploitation of that potential.

Some teachers were aware that, within the Christian tradition, there was some interesting work going on by Fowler on faith development.[5] This attempted to track stages of progress in faith development that characterised higher levels of faith and practice. Teachers who were aware of this tended generally to think that such tracking was only possible within a faith tradition. It therefore tended to reinforce their views that such a form of assessment had no place in schools or in pupils' development in RE.

National Curriculum developments and their influence on RE

This state of mind persisted in schools mainly because there was no instrument or means of altering it until the National Curriculum came along. Publication of the programmes of study and levels for assessing progress in the attainment targets of each of the National Curriculum (NC) subjects caused a revolution in the school curriculum from 1989. A whole new world of assessment came about, but not in RE. One of Her Majesty's Inspectors (HMIs) illustrated this when he said at a conference in Birmingham in 1989, 'If it moves assess it. If it does not move, assess why!' The core subjects of the NC were massively changed when attainment targets, assessment and reporting in levels became statutory from 1989. There were also debates, for example among teachers of music, art and PE, about whether a scale of levels of attainment was appropriate in their subjects. How could progress in such creative subjects be captured in such scales? At first it was not, and so 'End of Key Stage descriptions' that were more flexible than levels were imposed. Pupils' progress was measured only in terms of working towards, at or beyond the descriptions. It took the best part of ten years before 8 level scales became a statutory part of these subjects alongside the revised 8 level scales for Key Stages 1–3 of the other National Curriculum subjects.

In RE, some university schools of education and RE centres began to look afresh at assessment. Three projects in particular took place that influenced subsequent developments in RE through agreed syllabuses or through national curriculum development in RE. One was a project on assessing RE undertaken by the Association of RE Advisers Inspectors and Consultants (AREIAC) that resulted in advice to RE advisers and thus to LEAs about how pupils' progress in RE might be assessed.[6] The advice looked at the NC approach but did not offer that kind of assessment for use in agreed syllabuses.

A second project was held at Westhill College, Birmingham, where staff of the RE Centre were engaged on an exciting, innovative, pioneering and influential RE curriculum development project. This involved conceptualising RE into interrelated fields of enquiry: traditional belief systems, shared human experience and individual patterns of belief. The project had immense influence on agreed syllabuses in many LEAs for many years to come. Accompanying publications on assessment and attainment[7] were disseminated that greatly influenced teachers' thinking about assessment. There was a real feeling of excitement in breaking new ground as the issues of assessment thrown up by the NC were discussed and proposed as models for RE. Many RE advisers and teachers felt a dilemma then. Were the NC developments themselves so new and relatively untried, and would they prove to be so bureaucratic, that such assessment arrangements would not survive? Or would RE lose even more status and become even more marginal if it did not go along with them? (Remember that the first version of the NC had ten levels in each attainment target, that each level had descriptors to be checked, and that Science alone had about ten attainment targets!) Should RE, not being a NC subject, seriously take to itself, when it was not being asked to, an assessment process that most teachers of RE were untrained to use and that might collapse under its own weight? John Rudge, Director at the Westhill Centre, illustrated the dilemma in one of the more memorable quotations to come from that time when he asked: 'Should RE jump into a pit from which others were already trying to escape?' As it turned out, the original NC arrangements did not survive in their fullness, for it was not long before the assessment burdens were lightened, the NC itself revised, the subject content slimmed and the number of Attainment Targets dramatically reduced in the mid 1990s. Nobody in 1989 knew that was going to happen, RE did not adopt the NC kind of assessment at that time, and some subjects did escape from the pit to a certain extent. The Westhill project did, however, mark a significant milestone in the story of assessing RE.

A third project was the Forms of Assessment in RE (FARE) project at the School of Education, Exeter University, led by Dilys Wadman and Vicki Coddington under the auspices of Terence Copley and Jack Priestley. After two years of action research a thorough report was published, which is still worth reading.[8] It recommended three attainment targets for RE, and drafted an assessment scale for each. This report was to influence the development of agreed syllabuses in the South-west of England and their assessment guidance, whose LEAs had financially supported the project and whose teachers had not only contributed to the research but attended INSET throughout the project.

Impact of central initiatives in RE

The first national advice on the RE curriculum and related matters, largely controlled by LEAs since 1944, came in 1992 when the National Curriculum Council (NCC) published guidance for agreed syllabus conferences[9] on how agreed syllabuses for RE might use the way in which NC subjects were structured. Much of this advice was, however, overshadowed by a related controversy concerning the balance between teaching about Christianity and about the other principal religions represented in Britain. The NCC had analysed agreed syllabuses extant in 1991/2 and published lists that implied some syllabuses were outside the law in this respect. The 1993 Education Act passed soon afterwards required all agreed syllabuses to be reviewed following the 1988 Act if they had not already been, and then every five years subsequently.

To aid this process SCAA published two national *Model Syllabuses for RE*[10] in July 1994 as guidance and resource material for LEA agreed syllabus conferences. These have been significant in many respects. Among the influences they have had has been the widespread adoption of two attainment targets for RE: learning about religions and learning from religion. The draft version of the models published in January of that year for consultation contained an 8 level scale for RE based on these targets, but the July final version omitted them. Instead, the models included 'End of Key Stage descriptions' in line with art, music and PE earlier. These were widely incorporated into agreed syllabuses along with the targets.

However, whilst these projects and central initiatives were going on, schools were struggling with a NC assessment burden now acknowledged as absurdly excessive. As noted above, this was slimmed in 1995 in the Dearing Review under pressure from teacher associations, and was followed by the announcement of a five year moratorium on curriculum change. The principle of a NC subject having attainment targets and levels of attainment did however survive, and was further maintained in the review of the National Curriculum carried out by QCA in 1998–9.

As part of the preparation for that review, research, carried out on behalf of SCAA/QCA in 1996–7, revealed that teachers did not want the NC assessment system changed again when the much-anticipated review of the NC was to take place in 2000. Findings showed that teachers preferred the 8 level scale to anything else, not because it was perfect and free of problems, but because they preferred the devil they knew to the devil they did not know! Teachers, it seemed, took about eighteen months to internalise the meaning of the 8 levels, but once they did, they were confident in its use. They acknowledged that the scale improved their planning of teaching and learning, much as described at the beginning of this chapter. They found they became more accurate in their assessment, and that judgement arrived at by close study of matching the elements of a level descriptor with a pupil's work was little different from a more intuitive and quicker judgement, once the scale had been consistently and properly applied over time. There were issues arising from the use of the scale. These included the varying judgements by primary and secondary teachers of pupils allegedly at the same level; the lack of use of data gained from assessing the level of pupils at primary school by secondary colleagues; and the varying ways in which scales are linked to programmes of study in different subjects. Nevertheless, the targets and scales have survived and the data that their use has yielded has played an enormously important role in target setting, school evaluation, diagnosing weakness of transition, and identifying issues of continuity and progression ever since, especially in the core subjects of the NC.

From the perspective of RE, the continued use of this system has been very important also. First, because in individual schools and in some LEAs the use of the NC assessment process has influenced practice in RE. Many secondary school RE departments were (and are) required by their head teachers to use a similar system, even though there is no national programme of study for RE, no statutory assessment scale or requirement to use one, and none in their agreed syllabus. This has resulted in individual scales for RE being used in many schools. Some LEAs, partly in the light of this, partly because of the assessment projects described earlier and partly because they judged it best for the subject, developed assessment scales of their own in their agreed syllabuses. Kent and Bradford, for example, have had scales since 1995.[11] These syllabuses took a different line from those that followed the national models.

In the period from 1995 onwards therefore practice of assessment in RE, whilst becoming more common, was quite diverse. The diversity encompassed:

- forms of assessment used in external public examinations in Key Stage 4 and beyond;
- use of two attainment targets (or variations of them) with end of Key Stage descriptions in many syllabuses;
- the same targets with 8 level scales (or variations) in a smaller number of syllabuses;
- individual scales in some schools, mainly secondary;
- poor or non-existent practice in the majority of schools, in spite of what agreed syllabuses were beginning to say.

All reflected to some extent the history of hesitancy if not suspicion about the desirability and ability to assess RE. It is not surprising that, in terms of quality and use of assessment, RE has consistently been bottom of OFSTED's league tables! Monitoring of RE by QCA from 1997–9 confirmed this view. Many teachers have disliked being in this position, and wanted to be able to manage RE in ways comparable to subjects of the NC, not just because they wanted similar status for the subject but because they could see the emerging benefits of better assessment for raising standards.

The review of the NC in 1998–9 was greatly influenced by the Labour government elected in 1997. The NC had hitherto been a creation and a creature of the Conservatives. The new government saw an opportunity to steer the NC in the direction of its general social and education policy, with an emphasis on inclusion, key skills, employability and citizenship. When the NC was being revised in these directions in 1999 QCA took a decision that its guidance in RE needed parallel development to reflect some of these momentous changes, even though strictly speaking no review was needed in RE. Alongside the publication of the revised national curriculum in 2000 was *Non-statutory guidance in RE*.[12]

National expectations for RE

Among the developments contained in this publication was the publication of National Expectations for RE. These take the form of an 8 level scale for the two attainment targets for RE, set out in a standard form and a grid, under certain strands, with examples and a table of progression to inform the creation of a customised form of the scale for a particular agreed syllabus. The impetus for this publication also came from the monitoring mentioned above, and a desire to help put assessment of RE on a much firmer and common foundation than was currently the case.

The scale has been widely circulated among LEAs and some schools, and is beginning to produce a more considered and common structure for the assessment of RE. For full effect the scale will have to be incorporated (either directly or modified) into agreed syllabuses, become part of the planning cycle of teaching and learning in RE in schools, and enter the thinking of advisers, teacher trainers and inspectors of RE. Time will tell whether this becomes so, but prospects look promising at present.

The scale attempts to do several things. First, it is based on the end of Key Stage (KS) statements of the model syllabuses and so tries to maintain continuity with those agreed syllabuses that adopted them after 1994. Second, it attempts to mesh the upper levels of the scale with GCSE grade descriptions, so that the assessment model based on attainment targets in Key Stages 1–3 moves more naturally into that used by GCSE. This is increasingly relevant as more and more agreed syllabuses promote GCSE Religious Studies as their required programme of study for KS4, and more and more schools enter pupils for this examination. Third, it tries to do justice to the scope and nature of RE. Again the connection between assessment and curriculum reappears, as do controversial issues about the nature of RE! The scale offers an exposition of what progress in learning about religions might mean, and what learning from religion might mean. The latter is very important, for monitoring and inspection of RE has shown that not only has assessment in RE been generally very weak, the provision of teaching and learning from religion has also been weak. Fourth, the scale tries to allow for a variety of uses. Summative assessment is important for being able to track the progress of pupils, report it to the next teacher or phase of education, and to parents who are now well accustomed to progress reports using levels. More important, perhaps, is the formative use of the scale, where the level descriptions can be used to help pupils move forward in their learning. Most important of all, perhaps is the use of the scale in helping teachers to plan a comprehensive coverage of the RE curriculum and devise appropriate tasks for pupils to aid learning and consolidate it. Task setting in RE especially at KS3 has been shown to be limited and relatively undemanding for pupils.[13]

Learning from religion caused particular difficulties in devising the scale. What the scale does with levels for this target has to be seen in the context of another part of the non-statutory guidance on RE, which expounds what this attainment target is about. Essentially, learning from religion is regarded as the ability to respond to what is learned about religions. It is a developing skill of response, using not only knowledge and understanding of what is learnt about religions but also using pupils' own experiences, ideas and awareness of themselves, their families and their communities. The national expectations then provide a scale for identifying the levels of skill development. This was not easy to do since the range and extent of learning from religion goes beyond what is learnt in the classroom. It slides into what is learnt from life, from home, from the media, and which is processed by the reflecting, thinking and activity of pupils in the whole of their lives.

Learning from religion is closely connected with pupils' spiritual, moral, social and cultural development. Can these be measured? Most teachers believe not, certainly not in the sense that the subjects of the school curriculum are assessed, using a predetermined scale of eight roughly equal steps from age 5–14 and beyond. Pupils' spiritual, moral, social and cultural development is just not like that! However, stages in developing a skill of responding to what is learnt (for example, with thoughtfulness, evidence, reason, argument, anticipating the view of others, engaging with them, etc.)

can be discerned. This leads into the kind of evaluation that GCSE requires. Confidence that such a progressive process could be tracked across the Key Stages has led to the development of levels for the attainment target of learning from religion.

The most obvious drawback to the devising of the national expectations is the lack of a national programme of study on which to base them. This disadvantage is also to be observed in the schemes of work for RE published by QCA and the DfEE also in 2000. With about 150 agreed syllabuses in use in England, no scale can be devised to meet the particular requirements of them all. Much work had been done, however, by AREIAC in 1998–9, which took account of the way many agreed syllabuses had developed since 1995. The QCA scale took advantage of this. QCA worked closely with AREIAC and consulted widely with other RE organisations such as the RE Council, Professional Council for RE (PCfRE), and National Association of SACREs (NASACRE) in its development of the scale.

Trying to meet so many objectives and operating with such constraints has consequences. First, it means that the scale is not of universal application just as it stands. It needs to be contextualised into agreed syllabuses, in a similar way to its use as a progression measure in the exemplar schemes of work for RE. While some diversity in scales is therefore inevitable, one of the most lasting benefits could well be that assessment in RE now takes on a common form across agreed syllabuses and schools. This would be a great advance even if the exact nature of the levels of the scale varies from place to place. Second, it is a compromise, devised from the various starting points and developments that have taken place in the 1990s. Some may think this a weakness. In one sense of course it is, since a single process of development such as the NC subjects experienced is likely to have been more coherent. On the other hand the RE developments that had taken place could not be undone, and the legislation governing RE cannot be ignored. Previous developments can, however, be used, and the national expectations offer a foundation for future work. To take full advantage of future opportunities for curriculum development a national non-statutory framework for RE is a logical step. This would provide the basis and coherence for the various national developments that have taken place, enabling the schemes of work and national expectations to build on national model syllabuses and keep pace with developments in the NC, especially citizenship and the 'on-line' curriculum.

One further national development needs to be documented before turning to some specific issues and concluding this brief resume of assessing RE. Published in 2001 was QCA's *Curriculum Guidelines for Pupils with Learning Difficulties*.[14] They contain generic guidance for teachers working with pupils who will still be working towards or at Level 1 when they are sixteen years old. Accompanying the generic material are subject booklets with specific guidance and 'P' levels. These are levels preceding Level 1, so that the progress of pupils with learning difficulties can be assessed and reported on even though it is within the first level or two of the NC scale.

There is little specific research to base the 'P' levels on. As the first three are generic, detailing basic steps in communication, the task that fell to the developers was to devise steps 4–8 to differentiate learning in RE to fit with the first level on the QCA scale. Although testing was involved, and many people offered comments, until there is some extensive usage of the 'P' levels it will not really be known if the scale is effective or fully accurate.

Early years

Discussion of these early steps in assessing progress in RE leads to reflections on early learning in general. The introduction of the new Foundation stage leading to Key Stage 1 will prove to be an important development in early years education. The legal requirements regarding RE and agreed syllabuses are unaffected by this. However, the fact that both the early learning goals themselves and the associated guidance has reference to and space for religious and moral development means, that over time, a surer foundation will be laid for RE in Key Stage 1. There is no talk of assessing how effective such a foundation might be. Baseline assessment is being made more efficient at the moment of writing but the broad areas of development it measures are not being refined in terms of subject-specific elements. Any harvest of improved RE in the early years will not be reaped until Key Stage 1 assessment of RE takes place, if it does, in schools.

Key Stages 1–3

Primary practice of assessment in RE will be enormously varied, even if the QCA scale has wide currency, in the same way as RE in primary schools varies in quality in spite of the universal requirement to teach according to local syllabuses and faith group guidelines. Lack of specialist teachers to lead assessment practice and develop techniques in schools, combined with unequal access to specialist advisory support and to continued professional development (CPD) will ensure enormous diversity of practice and quality. Nevertheless, the direction has been set, and with time and further effort, practice will improve.

The improvement will find its way through to parallel improvement in secondary schools, where the common structure for assessment across the subjects of the statutory curriculum will remain for some time, even though the core subjects will inevitably be laden with specific targets, external tests and extra requirements about reporting.

General and vocational qualifications, the qualifications framework

At least, that will be the case until the end of Key Stage 3. From 14–19 there is likely to be much more diverse provision for pupils to choose from and individual programmes for them to follow. The Green Paper *Schools: Building on Success*, published in early 2001 (DFES 2001) and the White Paper of September 2001 foreshadow significant change here. Whatever these turn out to be, there should be a place for religious and moral education, perhaps with more philosophical elements than at present. This may be coloured, first by other developments such as 'Education with Character' in that such a term could perhaps host the statutory provision of RE and citizenship. Second, it may equally be coloured by the emphasis (even if more flexible in the future) on appropriate qualifications. The growth of Religious Studies at GCSE will prove significant in identifying the pathways young people follow. This might be more so if vocational qualifications in religion were developed and admitted to the National Qualifications Framework. Then the diversity and choice of 14–19 education and training will create more options for religious and moral education.

In both scenarios assessment will be important. How young people achieve and why, will be fundamental to the first, if only from the point of view of accountability and value for money. In the second, assessment is an intrinsic part of qualifications, and so RE assessment will continue to be important. There are general factors that will affect not just RE but many other subjects in bringing such developments about. What becomes of the current break-point at 16? How will the issue of performance table data be handled? Is anyone brave enough to tackle the anomaly of differing requirements for post-16 students in schools and FE colleges? All these will eventually need resolution.

It is harder to estimate what will happen to Religious Studies at AS Level and 'A' Level. Numbers have grown in 2001 as a result of students taking more AS Levels in Year 12 than they did 'A' Levels in Year 12 in the past. Rises in GCSE may inspire more students to progress beyond the short course to AS study. The depth and specialist nature of 'A' Levels combined with the greater availability of other courses, however, is likely to mean relatively small growth. Nevertheless, issues of comparability, fitness for purpose and distinctive contribution to national provision that are raised by the National Qualifications Framework mean that the validity and purposes of assessment will not diminish in this scenario. We shall need to know the progress made by students and be sure of the standards they achieve in this more diverse world of education and training post-14.

Future trends

The description offered above of how RE may develop in England may seem to be rather idealistic. It is not difficult to conceive of a coherent and meaningful experience of RE from early years to adulthood, where continuity and progression are clearly to be seen, and where the subject plays an important contributory role in pupils' spiritual, moral, social and cultural development, or as some would prefer, the development of the whole person. It is how to put that ideal into practice, how to realise the vision for all our young people in schools and colleges, that is the hard bit!

Here we have to face realities such as lack of training, finite resources, competing priorities, overload from other work, apathy, ignorance, prejudice, inefficiency and other facts of life. These and other counter-pressures, such as stereotypical attitudes and perceptions of religion by the public, tend to sap energy, reduce morale and cloud the vision. When this happens, teachers and others may look to ease pressures, remove what is difficult and stick to the essentials – teaching and learning. A cry may go up: 'Why assess children's progress in RE? Why use a scale as in NC subjects?' These questions take us back to the fundamentals. Religion (and religions) is a powerful dimension in human life and society. Children need to be educated about it. So we are back to the beginning of this chapter. Assessment is an essential part of teaching and learning in RE. The real question is one of quality – how best to do it!

Questions

1 How true is it that assessment is an essential part of teaching and learning? What are the aspects of RE that are properly to be assessed?
2 What are the merits and demerits of assessing RE in ways similar to other subjects?
3 What should the results of assessment be used for? What needs to happen to make assessment in RE more effective?

Notes

1 *Criteria for GSCE Religious Studies*, QCA 2000.
2 This question was actually used in a real GCSE examination paper in the mid 1990s.
3 Examples may be found in the FARE Report, pp. 300ff, mentioned below.
4 Schools Council Working Paper 36, (1971). *Religious Education in Secondary Schools*, Evens Brothers & Methuen Education.
5 Fowler has written several books on faith development. A book that makes his writings accessible is *How Faith Grows*, ISBN 0 7151 4809 5, published by The National Society/Church House.
6 Copies of this document probably do not exist except possibly in the archives of AREIAC.
7 *Attainment in RE* and *A Handbook for Teachers: Assessing, Recording and Reporting RE*, published by Westhill College and later by other publishers.
8 *Forms of Assessment in Religious Education* (FARE) published 1991: ISBN 0 9518 041 0 3.
9 *RE: A local curriculum framework*, NCC (1991): ISBN 1 872676 59 6.
10 *RE Model Syllabuses*, SCAA (1994): ISBN 1 85838 038 3/039 1. Also available on QCA website, *www.qca.org.uk*.
11 Copies may be available from the LEAs or for study in a RE Centre.

12 *Non-Statutory Guidance on RE*, QCA (2000), Ref QCA/00/576. Also available via QCA website, *www.qca.org.uk*.
13 OFSTED inspection evidence produced in 2000.
14 *Planning, teaching and assessing the curriculum for pupils with learning difficulties: RE*, QCA (2001), Ref QCA/01/750. Also available on QCA website, *www.qca.org.uk*.

6   Inspecting Religious Education

Can inspections improve Religious Education?

Jan Thompson

Introduction

> I am clear about one thing: objective, external inspection must remain a vital
> part of both the accountability and improvement mechanisms.
> Mike Tomlinson, HMCI, *Times Education Supplement* 2 February 2001, p. 16

OFSTED stands for the Office for Standards in Education. It came into existence as a result of the Education (Schools) Act 1992 and its purpose was
'improvement through inspections'. It set out to raise standards in education in
maintained schools through independent inspections, public reporting and
informed advice. In the quotation above, Her Majesty's Chief Inspector still
upholds inspection as an 'improvement mechanism', whilst modifying its claims
in the final quotation of this chapter.

It was Section 9 of the School Inspections Act 1992 which dealt with
OFSTED inspections, later changed to Section 10 of the 1996 Act. Section 13
of the original Act dealt with the inspection of denominational aspects of
Voluntary Schools and so their inspections came to be referred to as Section 13
Inspections, becoming Section 23 in the 1996 School Inspections Act.

This chapter asks: 'Can inspections improve Religious Education?' with the
implications of 'How?' and 'To what extent?' Without research into a whole
range of issues on the subject of inspecting RE (both OFSTED and denominational inspections in both Anglican and Roman Catholic schools), I write
largely from the point of view of my own experiences, with the intention of
offering something of practical use to teachers. The chapter raises some of the
issues in relation to whether, how and to what extent inspections can improve
Religious Education in schools, but focuses mainly on helping teachers to:

- understand how OFSTED and Section 23 inspections work;
- make the most of their school's inspection of Religious Education.

I have taken this approach because I believe that it is necessary for teachers to
understand the inspection process if they are to make the most of their own

inspection. And it is necessary for them to make the most of their own inspection if it is to contribute to raising standards in teaching and learning in their subject.

Who would be an OFSTED inspector!

> *Inspection is, by its nature, a stressful event – even for the inspectors.*
> Mike Tomlinson, HMCI, *Times Education Supplement* 2 February 2001, p. 15

When Mike Tomlinson took over from Chris Woodhead as Her Majesty's Chief Inspector of Schools, he set out some of his views on OFSTED inspections in an 'Opinion' article in the *Times Education Supplement* which was given the title, 'We're really not that cruel'. And it is true. Most OFSTED inspectors, like most teachers, are decent people, passionate about their subject, committed to the education of children and young people, hard-working and concerned to do a good job within the constraints of the system. Returns from schools inspected by OFSTED in 2000 indicated that 95 per cent were satisfied with all aspects of their inspection.

Yet few of us would introduce ourselves as OFSTED inspectors: it is even more of a party-stopper than telling fellow students that you are studying theology or telling your neighbours that you are an RE teacher! Why is that? When OFSTED inspections first started, they came as a shock to many schools. Admittedly, there were some Local Education Authorities that already had in place a rigorous inspection system, but not all. Prior to OFSTED, Her Majesty's Inspectors' visits to schools were rare compared to the 4,000 now inspected every year on a four-yearly cycle. Some were simply not ready to have every aspect of school life put under scrutiny, and many schools had a mammoth task ahead of them to put the required paperwork in place. And it was new. No one really knew what to expect. But we are now in the second cycle of inspections; there are fewer surprises; short inspections have been introduced for schools which require only a 'light touch'; less paperwork is required, and schools are less disposed to photocopying everything in sight and writing policies on every-thing that moves.

The changing face of OFSTED

> Inspection should be something done *with* schools, not *to* schools.
> Mike Tomlinson, Chief Inspector, Foreword to *Update 34*, Winter 2000

There have also been improvements from OFSTED since those early days. Inspectors now have to prove that they are qualified and experienced to inspect their subjects in different phases, and there is also a separate endorsement for the inspection of Sixth Form Provision. They are required to have on-going OFSTED experience and training. The OFSTED Handbook for the Inspection of Schools is now in its third new edition (for use from January 2000) and

OFSTED publishes '*Updates*' to its inspectors, which keep them in touch with new emphases and developments. There will always be some inspectors who are better than others, but OFSTED does its best to ensure high quality inspections and consistency of standards.

One of the most important changes has been the subtle shift in inspector mode. There is now much more encouragement for inspectors to engage in a professional dialogue with teachers. It is still not an inspector's place to tell schools how to improve, but there is now much more open discussion about possible ways forward, and many teachers and senior managers make the most of this. With the recent training of schools in self-evaluation using OFSTED techniques, there is every indication that future inspections will not be done *to* schools but *with* schools. It is up to schools how they respond to this. If teachers are nervous and tearful on the one hand, or defensive and aggressive on the other, then it makes it difficult for the inspector to work with them. If however they are reflective practitioners, confident about their strengths, but recognising that they can always improve on their personal best, then they will get a lot from an external inspector who is looking at the situation with new eyes and has much experience to draw on from his or her own background and from seeing other schools.

The OFSTED *Code of Conduct* for inspectors sums up the high standards expected of them and emphasises the concern for teachers who are being inspected:

- Evaluate the work of the school objectively, be impartial and have no previous connection with the school, its staff or governors which could undermine your objectivity.
- Report honestly and fairly, ensuring that judgements accurately and reliably reflect what the school achieves and does.
- Carry out your work with integrity, treating all those you meet with courtesy and sensitivity.
- Do all you can to minimise stress, in particular by ensuring that no teacher is over-inspected and by not asking for paperwork to be specifically prepared for the inspection.
- Act with the best interests and well-being of pupils and staff as priorities.
- Communicate with staff purposefully and productively, and present your judgements of the school's work clearly and frankly.
- Respect the confidentiality of information, particularly about teachers and the judgements made about their individual teaching.

(*Inspecting Schools*, OFSTED Handbook 1999)

Finally, may I have one last word about inspectors. Since RE teachers are supposed to be good at empathy, they should make some attempt to understand the OFSTED inspector's lot. The school to be inspected may be on the other side of the country, requiring a long-distance drive the night before (always through driving rain or thick fog) and B&B in some dodgy hotel. The inspector works excessively long hours, in new surroundings, under extreme pressure to gather as much first-hand evidence as possible in a limited time. In all this, he or she has to keep alert, make clear judgements and behave with the utmost consideration to others. So why do they do it? Many advisers do it to keep in touch with the inspection process so that they are better able to advise their schools. Others do it because they are well-qualified for it and have perhaps taken early retirement from headship or an adviser's post. Taking into account the pay and conditions, it is extremely unlikely that OFSTED inspectors would continue to do the job if they did not believe that they were doing something worthwhile and making a significant contribution to improving the quality of education in schools.

RE inspectors

> By law, RE must be taught according to the locally agreed syllabus in all main-
> tained schools except voluntary-aided schools and schools of a religious character
> where RE is taught according to the trust deed or faith-community guidelines.
>
> *Religious Education Teacher's Guide*, QCA 2000, p. 3.

OFSTED inspectors of RE have additional pressures. Each Local Education Authority has its own agreed syllabus for Religious Education. They are not always the easiest documents to find your way around quickly, but inspectors have to become familiar with the relevant agreed syllabus for each inspection. In other subjects, the National Curriculum orders remain the same anywhere in the country.

Despite the law that RE should be taught to all registered pupils, and is the only compulsory subject in the sixth form, it is ironic that there may be very little RE going on in schools, and it can usually be inspected in secondary schools in two days. This means that RE inspectors may not be there for very much of an inspection, or that RE may be inspected along with other subjects, usually by a Humanities specialist. It is worth mentioning here that the school is given the list of inspectors with their CVs beforehand. If a secondary head of RE wants an RE specialist to inspect the RE department, rather than say a history specialist who is endorsed by OFSTED for inspecting RE, then you should ask for one. But beware. An RE specialist should be much more use to you, but will not necessarily give you an easier ride.

In primary schools, RE may not even be observed. If there is no RE timetabled for the days of the inspection, inspectors have to make judgements on the basis of the school's documentation, pupils' workbooks and talking to pupils and teachers.

Section 23 inspections

> By law, RE must be taught according to the locally agreed syllabus in all main-
> tained schools except voluntary-aided schools and schools of a religious

character where RE is taught according to the trust deed or faith-community guidelines.

Religious Education Teacher's Guide, QCA 2000, p. 3.

Religious Education is one of the denominational aspects of Voluntary Aided Schools. These are mostly Church of England and Roman Catholic schools, but there are others, such as Jewish, Muslim and Sikh schools. Voluntary Controlled schools will usually be expected to follow their local agreed syllabus for RE, unless parents have requested that denominational RE is delivered instead.

In schools where denominational RE is taught, it is the responsibility of the governing body to procure a Section 23 inspection. This usually has to be done in the same academic year as their OFSTED inspection. Many schools like the two inspections to take place together, since this causes less disruption to the school and the inspectors can confer on common aspects such as the opportunities the school gives pupils for spiritual, moral, social and cultural development. However, when the inspections take place at different times, the school is under less pressure at each inspection and in primary schools it is easier to arrange for a good selection of RE lessons to be seen. This makes for a more comprehensive inspection, with more time able to be spent with more teachers. When the inspection is completed, the governing body fills in a DfES grant request form and sends it to the DfES with a copy of the inspection report. The current grant is up to £800 for a secondary school and up to £400 for a primary school.

Section 23 and OFSTED inspections compared

The National Society and almost all the Diocesan Boards of Education recommend that governors of Anglican schools should only use inspectors who are on The National Society Register to inspect their schools under Section 23.

The National Society's Inspection Handbook, 2000 p. 1.

Whereas schools are notified by OFSTED of their inspections and given inspection teams, the governing body of a Voluntary Aided school has the right to choose a Section 23 inspector and to negotiate the date of inspection. Although most will go through their dioceses, there are some who will exercise their right to a free choice. Such inspections may or may not be rigorous and objective. When the governing body of a school acts independently, there is no outside body to maintain the standard or usefulness of the inspection.

Whereas OFSTED inspectors are trained, accredited and endorsed by OFSTED, which keeps an up-to-date register of all its inspectors, there is not the same centralised control for Section 23 inspectors. Each Anglican and Roman Catholic diocese advises its Voluntary Aided schools on Section 23 inspections and will keep a list of their approved inspectors. Most Section 23 inspectors for Anglican schools are trained initially by The National Society, which has published an *Inspection Handbook* as their main point of reference.

The National Board for Religious Inspectors and Advisers (NBRIA) fulfils a similar role for Catholic inspections. These inspectors may be given additional training, and sometimes supervision, by the diocesan RE adviser. Some dioceses have their own standard format for Section 23 inspections, and sometimes charge inspectors for administering the inspection for them. However, unlike OFSTED, there is no one central body with control over diocesan inspections and no standardisation of format or quality of judgements. The comparability of OFSTED inspections means that it can enter its inspection data into a computer and produce national figures and trends; but there is no equivalent for denominational RE. It is up to individual dioceses, if they so wish, to track and report on standards as best they can.

Another big difference between Section 23 and OFSTED inspections is that OFSTED inspectors are part of an inspection team in the school led by a registered inspector. This team gives support, and the registered inspector gives guidance. In contrast, Anglican Section 23 inspectors are usually on their own, with no one to regulate their judgements, although Catholic inspectors often work in small teams.

> Judge not that you be not judged.
>
> (*Matthew 7:1* – written up, presumably by the
> head teacher, and attached to the inspectors' door!)

Although dioceses differ in their expectations, it is likely that, in many cases, the OFSTED inspection process is more rigorous than that for Section 23. For OFSTED, evidence is recorded on a standard evidence form and assessed against a seven-point scale (going down from 1, 'Excellent', to 7, 'Very Poor'). Judgements are entered in the subject inspection notebook, with cross-references to the evidence forms (which are all numbered), so that inspectors have ready access to the evidence and examples to back up their judgements. Copies of everything are kept by the contractors and are available for scrutiny by OFSTED. In addition, OFSTED inspections are scrutinised by Her Majesty's Inspectors who can (and frequently do) descend on an OFSTED inspection without notice. Schools like nothing better than to hear that their own OFSTED inspectors are themselves being inspected by HMI! In contrast, many Section 23 inspectors make their own notes during an inspection that are never seen by anyone else. However, they will be required to back up their judgements with evidence both when feeding back to teachers, heads of departments and head teachers, in their written reports and if they are asked to present the report to the governing body. It is therefore in their own interests to keep their notes thorough and orderly.

Although these quantitative differences would seem to favour OFSTED inspections over Section 23 inspections, there is a qualitative difference with Section 23 inspections which counts in their favour. However positive the attitude of the school towards an OFSTED inspection, there is still usually a resentment of the inspectors and a feeling of 'us and them'. By contrast, a Section 23 inspector is usually seen as 'one of us', is invited to take a chair in the staff room, and the head teacher may off-load onto the Section 23 inspector all his or her worries about how the OFSTED inspection is going. Schools are much more open with their Section 23 inspectors, seeing the process as more a matter of friendly advice than inspection. In my experience, they are willing to listen to advice and to act upon it. Church schools need, however, to be a little bit cautious in being too relaxed about any inspection. It is a great shame, for instance, when this leads to the school having everything up to scratch for the OFSTED inspection but little in place for Section 23. Church schools should also beware of being too open about their weaknesses, and often need to be more confident about their strengths.

Another plus for Section 23 inspections is that the head teacher and governing body of Voluntary Aided Church schools can be expected to take RE seriously. RE is expected to have a secure place in the curriculum and to be valued for its contribution to the spiritual, moral, social and cultural development of pupils. The RE inspector does not have to be on the defensive about the subject, ready to justify its existence with senior management. Instead, they can together celebrate its importance and achievements, and can work with the school to make it even better, for the benefit of the pupils. This is in pleasant contrast to some OFSTED RE inspections in primary schools where little or even no RE teaching may be seen, or short inspections where it is unlikely that RE will get a look in. In aided Church schools, both Anglican and Catholic, RE is always fully inspected since it is an important denominational aspect of the school. There is no equivalent in Section 23 to a short inspection.

The inspection process

The inspection process is similar for OFSTED and Section 23 inspections. Inspectors look for evidence of strengths and weaknesses in the subjects in order to make their judgements, and the sources and processes will be basically the same. All OFSTED inspectors will use the same format for gathering evidence and making their final report. This cannot be said for Section 23 inspectors, even sometimes within the same diocese.

The main difference in the process is that OFSTED inspectors are 'team inspectors' and their judgements may be helped by the insight of other team inspectors or regulated by the registered inspector. For example, the registered inspector may read a lesson observation evidence form and query whether sufficient evidence has been recorded to justify the grades given. There are no such checks on a Section 23 inspector, which is why The National Society does not recommend the use of grades. In an OFSTED inspection, the inspection team is organised by, guided by and answerable to the registered inspector. All evidence is recorded on EFs (Evidence Forms), copies of which are checked by the registered inspector and personal feedback may be given to each inspector. The whole team meets together at the end of each day to contribute to a picture of the school which gradually builds up throughout the week. This helps inspectors to look out for particular issues, for instance: 'Do pupils know how well they are doing in your subject?' 'Are boys being given more attention in class than girls?' 'Is there any evidence of the use of IT in your subject?' 'Do lessons start promptly?' 'Is behaviour worse in the afternoon?' and so on. It is good when a Section 23 inspector picks up similar issues in teaching and learning independently of the OFSTED team, but the shared concerns of the team help an inspector to notice things that might otherwise have been overlooked.

Preparation

The watchword is: 'Be prepared!' You would not go into an interview without preparation, and it would be foolish for the subject leader to go into an inspection with the attitude that 'They can take us as they find us!' If you want a fair assessment of your subject's strengths and weaknesses, then you need to make sure that the inspector sees as much as possible. If, for instance, you *do* use artefacts in your department and you *do* have pupils working together in groups, then make sure that the inspector sees this, even if you would not normally have done it during that particular week. Look at your RE displays and make sure they show a good range of pupils' work including the use of ICT. Try to show pupils' responses (perhaps in speech bubbles) as well as the information about religions that they have accumulated.

Pre-inspection documentation

It is helpful if you give the inspectors the documents they need and ask for, but also give them the information you want them to know. Pre-inspection documentation helps inspectors to form an initial picture of the strengths and weaknesses of the subject. The documentation should include:

- A policy statement (setting out clearly and concisely the principles and practice of RE in your school).
- In a secondary school, the departmental handbook may take the place of the policy statement, and will be much fuller.
- An overview of the scheme of work for each key stage, identifying units of work.
- The agreed syllabus for Religious Education for OFSTED inspections of RE.
- Examination results where applicable.
- The previous inspection report.

This documentation is only useful if it is up-to-date and describes accurately what is really happening in RE (rather than what should be happening or what you wished was happening!). Inspectors will form hypotheses from the documentation, which they will test out during the inspection, and which may shift or even change completely. Questions will be raised by the documentation that may need answering, and these will form the agenda for the interview with the subject leader.

Interview with subject leader

This will usually take place early on in the inspection, and contact will be kept with the subject leader throughout the inspection both to report on how things are going but also to pick up information that may have been missed earlier. There should be an on-going professional dialogue with the subject leader, whereas other teachers will only be given feedback after their lessons. Subject leaders should feel free to come back to the inspector after the interview if they remember something else that they wish they had said, or to show the inspector some relevant evidence for something that had been discussed.

The role of the subject leader has changed in the last few years, and this is reflected in their new title, used by OFSTED, the DfES and the TTA (Teacher Training Agency). Their job is no longer just to *co-ordinate* or *manage* everything to do with the subject, but they must take the lead in ensuring high-quality teaching and learning in their subject. Whether in primary or secondary schools, they must be more than good classroom practitioners themselves; they must take other teachers with them.

To do their job, subject leaders must know what is going on in their subject throughout the school. This is easier for secondary than primary teachers, since secondary schools have RE departments and departmental meetings. But in most primary schools, every teacher teaches every subject, and therefore they will need to feed information to nine other subject leaders (ten in Wales) as well as gathering information on their own subject (or subjects) from all the teachers. There are many ways in which schools can monitor teaching and learning in a subject. They include talking to pupils and teachers, and looking at pupils' work and teachers' plans, as well as lesson observation (which is far more difficult to organise because of the time-tabling implications). However they do it, subject managers need to be in touch with what is actually happening in their subject. The inspector will expect them to know.

An interview with a subject leader will focus on the achievements or progress that pupils make in RE and the standards of attainment at the end of each Key Stage, as well as clearing up any questions that were raised by or not answered by the subject documentation. It is important that the subject leader has a secure knowledge of (and not just a gut feeling about) the standards being achieved in RE. At primary schools, the subject leader should be able to make comparisons with progress and attainment in other subjects. Subject leaders are dependent on their agreed syllabus for setting standards, but where levels and end-of-Key Stage statements are not given, then they could use the QCA (Qualifications and Curriculum Authority) levels and exemplifications of standards, for a better picture of how their school measures up against national standards. Once again, RE is in a different position here to the National Curriculum subjects, and OFSTED RE inspectors must remember that their judgements should record to what extent the school's attainment in RE is in line with the expectations of the local agreed syllabus. Examination RE and RS is different, of course, and accurate comparisons can be made with national statistics.

Since the focus is on progress and attainment, all other factors will be seen as contributory to this. For example, you could be asked about the impact on standards of the following:

- The scheme of work
- Specialist and non-specialist RE teaching
- INSET
- Resources
- Teaching methods.

For example:

- Does a thematic approach to the study of religions lead pupils to get confused between different religions?
- Do pupils do better with specialist than non-specialist RE teachers?
- What follow-up has there been to recent INSET and with what results?
- Are resources challenging enough for higher attaining pupils?
- Are some teachers' methods less stimulating than others and is this having any effect on achievement?

Such questions are useful, because they help to focus the subject leader's energy on outcomes. It is all too easy to be busy for its own sake. This approach will help them to get the most out of what they do.

Subject leaders will also be asked about progress since the last report. It is a good idea to write a report on what has been achieved in your department and your short-term and longer-term targets. It is equally important that, as far as possible, these are in line with whole-school development plans.

Lesson observation

Lesson observation used to take up 80 per cent of the inspection. It still constitutes a major part, but there has been a shift in the distribution of time, with less spent in lessons and more on work scrutiny, to avoid too much of a 'snapshot' inspection. About 60 per cent of inspection time is now spent in lessons. As far as possible, lessons are seen from each Key Stage, especially the last year of the Key Stage. It is preferable for the inspector to remain for a whole lesson, though this is not always possible. However, an OFSTED observation must last at least thirty minutes. All teachers will be seen at least once and, as a rule, no teacher should be seen for more than 50 per cent of their lessons each day. It is unfair, but unavoidable, that in secondary schools with small RE departments, teachers are likely to be observed more frequently than their colleagues in big departments like English. Some teachers do prefer this because they feel that the inspector has a sounder view of their teaching.

It is helpful when teachers prepare some information for the inspector about the lesson, and many schools do this as a matter of course. This should tell the inspector where the lesson fits into the unit of work, what the teacher intends the pupils to learn during the lesson, and information about differentiation and special educational needs.

The OFSTED observation forms used to be divided into 4 sections:

Teaching: the teacher's subject knowledge and understanding, expectations of pupils and challenge, differentiation planning, preparation, questioning skills, sensitivity, methods and grouping, class management, pace, use of resources, use of homework and assessment.

Response: pupils' attitudes to the subject, behaviour, relationships with the teacher and other pupils, ability to work on their own and with others.

Attainment: what the majority know, understand and can do; high attainers; low attainers.

Progress: consolidation of previous learning, new learning and achievements.

Each of these sections would be awarded a grade and it was expected that teaching and progress would be closely aligned. In other words, inspectors are not judging the teacher's performance *per se*, but they are looking to see if, how and to what extent it enables the pupils to learn.

The current forms used for lesson observation are the Evidence Forms used to record any type of evidence. It is essentially a blank form with boxes at the bottom to give grades for: Teaching; Learning; Attainment; and Attitudes/Behaviour. The blank form allows for more of a narrative style, to give a more specific flavour of the lesson seen, but also to make the connection between teaching and learning (formerly called *progress*). For instance, you might say that the teacher maintained a good pace (*teaching*), which helped pupils to complete a lot of work during the lesson (*learning*). Or that the variety of methods used (*teaching*) caught pupils' imagination and contributed to their enjoyment of the lesson (*attitudes*). Or that the discipline maintained during class discussions (*teaching*) encouraged pupils to listen carefully to each other (*learning* and *attitudes/behaviour*).

Teachers can sometimes get so concerned about their performance (and of course good teachers *are* performers) that they may need to be reminded that the most important thing is the outcome in terms of what pupils have learnt. It is also true that teachers are not always aware of everything that is going on in their lesson, and it takes an impartial observer to point out, for instance, that they always ask the boys to answer and not the girls, or that they relate better to the pupils in the front of the class than at the back, or whatever it might be. Lesson observation can, of course, be done in-house, and this is being done with school self-evaluation and performance management. But it is likely that teachers will get a more honest and rigorous evaluation from an external observer than from a colleague.

Teaching is graded – not teachers! Remember that Grade 4 means that you have taught a sound lesson. It is satisfactory, i.e. acceptable. A Grade 4 is given where there are both strengths and weaknesses in the teaching, but the strengths outweigh the weaknesses. In other words, a Grade 4 is a positive assessment.

Work scrutiny

Much more attention is now paid to work scrutiny because this gives evidence of progress over time, rather than the snap-shot view of teaching and learning that one gets from lesson observation. Inspectors are encouraged to look at pupils' work within the lessons as well as the sample that has been put aside for them. It is important that you keep examples of pupils' work for an inspection. There is nothing more frustrating for an inspector who is carrying out an inspection early in the autumn term to find that all pupils have been issued with new books and there is no sign of any previous work.

Many things can be learned from work scrutiny, and subject leaders would be well advised to do this for themselves, rather than wait for an external inspector to point things out to them. For example, taking a selection of books from low, middle and high attaining pupils, you can see:

- pupils' attitudes to their work
- the standards being achieved
- the emphasis given to each attainment target
- how much of the syllabus has been covered
- to what extent the work becomes more challenging over time
- the variety of work set
- how well the work is marked.

The draw-back, of course, is that pupils do not record everything in their RE books, especially since discussion and creative work is an important part of RE; and indeed at Key Stage 1 pupils may well not have RE books. But this is just one source of evidence alongside all the rest, including talking to pupils in the lessons about their work.

Feedback to the subject leader

This covers the same areas as the subject report (see below), but will be fuller because it will draw on more examples. Although the report has not yet been written and this verbal report is to some extent provisional on the inspector taking time to assimilate and review everything, there should not be any surprises in the written report. The subject leader will have a member of senior management for support and to take notes, leaving the subject leader free to listen carefully. Teachers need to listen for the positive messages as well as the criticisms, since teachers are only too willing to do themselves down. Although the reporting is to the subject leader, it is a good opportunity to make sure that senior management hears about RE, particularly if it plays a less than prominent role in the school curriculum. It is an opportunity to praise the RE department, where appropriate, and to draw attention to issues, whether it's the poor quality accommodation for the RE department in a leaky mobile on the other side of the football pitch, or that the RE books look as if they had come out of the Ark. These messages do usually go home, and many RE departments have reason to be thankful to their OFSTED inspections for improvements in accommodation, resources and even curriculum time. It is not always the best policy to try to pretend to OFSTED inspectors that all is well, as they can be a powerful ally when the need arises.

The subject report

The final subject report does not need to be lengthy, nor descriptive. OFSTED subject reports set out clearly and concisely, with some specific examples, the judgements reached about the strengths and weaknesses in the subject under 4 areas:

- Pupils' attainment (related to the attainment targets of the Agreed Syllabus or public examinations, and assessed against their average expectations);
- Achievement, i.e. progress made in relation to prior attainment;
- Pupils' attitudes to learning;
- Any strengths and weaknesses in teaching, and other factors which contribute to the standards achieved in the subject.

Somewhere in the subject paragraph will be a comment on RE's special contribution to pupils' spiritual, moral, social and cultural development (SMSC). This will also contribute to a separate paragraph elsewhere on pupils' personal development which includes the schools' provision for SMSC throughout the school.

Important issues for RE in an OFSTED report may simply remain within the subject paragraph or may contribute to the school's key issues for development if the registered inspector decides that they seriously affect the school's standards.

Section 23 reports do not have to follow the same format, and usually report on RE more fully than an OFSTED report which covers all subjects and all aspects of the school. However, Section 23 inspectors should still focus on clear judgements of strengths and weaknesses, rather than giving a blow-by-blow account of everything that happened in each lesson. They should also highlight just a few issues for the schools to work on. It is embarrassing when a Section 23 report has more key issues than the whole of a school's OFSTED report!

Conclusion

> Inspection does not improve schools. Teachers improve schools.
>
> Mike Tomlinson, lecture entitled 'Education: Building on Success',
> Medway, 5 April 2001

OFSTED set out to improve standards, but it is only one factor in the improvement of schools and, as has been said, its effectiveness depends to a large extent on how far schools and the OFSTED team work together. Subject leaders and senior managers have to be receptive to the outcomes of the inspection and, in practice, they usually are. Subject leaders are expected to improve the weaknesses identified within their subject, with the school's support.

The OFSTED inspection is given more weight by the fact that the report is a public document, a summary of which is given to parents; and the governing body is responsible for drawing up an action plan on the key issues within forty days of the report's publication. Schools with good reports make good use of them in advertising their schools. Schools which are identified as having 'serious weaknesses' are given extra help by their LEA. It is rare but not unheard of for a school to have 'serious weaknesses' identified in RE (this honour is usually reserved for more important subjects!). Schools which are put into 'special measures' (for poor standards of teaching and learning generally or for poor management) are monitored by HMI visits as well as being given special LEA support.

OFSTED's unique role is to gather information about schools on a wide enough scale for it to have national relevance. It can analyse this information and feed it to the policy makers (the DfES and QCA) which, in turn, impacts upon schools. Most years, OFSTED has used its data to produce subject reports, highlighting improvements and common strengths and weaknesses. Many local authority advisers have used these national indicators (or, in larger authorities, have done their own analyses) to give a focus to their own support for schools in the areas of weakness, such as assessment in primary school RE and the Key Stage 3 RE curriculum.

Standing Advisory Councils for Religious Education (SACREs) use the published OFSTED reports as one means of monitoring the standards of RE in their local schools. Many also receive the Section 23 reports from their aided schools. This information helps SACREs to advise the LEA about RE in its schools and to offer appropriate support. In the past, SACREs have not been bashful about complaining to OFSTED about the quality of such reports or the judgements made, but now many are bemoaning the fact that RE does not appear in the short inspection reports! So one can only assume that these OFSTED reports on RE were in the main helpful to SACRE in supporting RE in their schools.

In Section 23 inspections, the good will and advisory nature of these inspections and/or the authority of the diocese, often make the inspectors' judgements and advice more acceptable to the school.

External inspections are currently one of the improvement mechanisms in education today, intended to help teachers improve their schools. It is questionable whether it could be proved one way or another if inspections improve RE in schools. For some inspections, of course, the negative factors may outweigh the positive (how far the stressful nature of inspections affects the performance of both teachers and inspectors; whether a bad report does more harm than good; the competence of individual inspectors; the variable nature of Section 23 inspections). But positive factors remain and can be made use of to improve Religious Education.

Questions

1 What are the strengths of my subject, and what developments have been made since the school's last inspection?
2 What would I identify as the key issues for development in my subject?
3 How can I make the most of my OFSTED/ Section 23 inspection?

---

7 Religious Education in the European context

Peter Schreiner

Introduction

Europe has become a decisive element of daily life, whether we like it or not. In twelve of the fifteen member states of the European Union a new common currency, established some years ago, is now visually in evidence in coins and notes. The European Union has provided plans for enlargement of up to twenty-seven member states in the years ahead, and at the same time initiatives are under way to deepen the existing cooperation. The European economy is no longer focused on national or regional contexts but operates on a global level, looking for good opportunities for production and to develop consumer markets all over the world. Media programmes and advertising for products are now crossing regional and national boundaries. The field of education, also, becomes more and more international not least in the competition for a good education which meets the criteria of a flexible, multi-lingual and well trained working person who can meet the needs of the global economy and its local servants.

With this background, it could be of interest to have an introduction to the situation of Religious Education in other parts of Europe. Which models for RE can be found around Europe? What is the status of RE in the different societies? Are there similar problems, questions about RE, its aims and content, its place in the curriculum? What is the image of RE like in the perception of the pupils? How do RE teachers understand themselves?

Of course this short contribution cannot deal with all the mentioned aspects. The main purpose is to show the value of a comparative approach and the need to deepen mutual exchange in the area of RE.

Overview: The 'biographies' of Religious Education approaches

In most countries of Europe Religious Education is part of the curriculum in public schools (Schreiner 2000), but the regulations are different. Following John Hull (2001), existing models of RE can promote education *into* religion, education *about* religion or education *from* religion. Education *into* religion introduces pupils into one specific faith tradition. It looks to be the case that in many central and eastern European countries this form of RE is given a high priority. It should be mentioned that the implementation of RE is taking place at different speeds and in different contexts. It is hard to say how far the negative image, which was given to religion by the official ideology, still has an impact on the external and internal conditions in (re)establishing Religious Education.

Education *about* religion refers to religious knowledge and religious studies. Pupils learn what a religion means to an adherent of a particular faith tradition: it involves learning about the beliefs, values and practices of a religion, seeking to understand the way in which they may influence behaviour of individuals and how religion shapes communities.

Education *from* religion gives pupils the opportunity to consider different answers to major religious and moral issues, so that they may develop their own views in a reflective way. This approach puts the experience of the pupils at the centre of the teaching.

This rough differentiation is idealistic because good RE should include elements from all these perspectives. In this respect it would be more sensitive not to label too quickly existing models of RE in Europe but to look more carefully at theoretical discourses and the practice of RE (Heimbrock *et al.* 2001).

RE in Europe is grounded in factors like: the religious landscape in the country; the role and value of religion in society; the structure of the education system, history, and politics. Each approach to Religious Education is shaped by a specific composition with different layers. Where there is a Catholic dominated population, as in Italy, Spain, Portugal and Poland, Catholicism is deeply embedded in the culture. Any kind of RE in those countries will be influenced by Catholicism. Even if legal rights guarantee the freedom of religion, which is the case for example in Italy, Spain and Portugal, the dominance of one religion, or denomination, is obvious in culture and society. This is the reason why the small Protestant Churches in Italy do not use the legal opportunity to provide Religious Education for their pupils in schools. The dominance of Catholicism nurtures resistance against any kind of denominational RE in schools.

Where there is a strict separation of State and religion, with France as an extreme example due to the basic principle of *laicité*, religion has no place in public schools. If one takes into account the fact that France has a well developed area of private (Catholic) schools, which 20 per cent of all pupils attend, one can follow the argument that there seems to be no need for a major discussion about RE in public schools. In recent years, however, a serious discussion has started about the need for 'religious knowledge' in school. Teachers recognised that pupils cannot understand history or art or even French without a basic knowledge of religion(s). Additionally Islam now has an increasing influence on French society. Initiatives were taken to provide opportunities for teachers to include religious knowledge in different subjects (Kaempf 2000).

In other countries the relation between public and private schools influences the status of RE. Two thirds of all schools in the Netherlands are still Christian schools and one third has a 'neutral status' regarding religion and worldviews.

When, in the last century, an emotional and serious discussion took place in society about the value and place of Religious Education, a solution was found in the 'pillarization' of the country where nearly every part of the society was structured according to its religious or non-religious worldviews. The State guaranteed the same rights and support for 'private' schools which were then founded mainly through the initiatives of parents. Denominational RE exists in the Christian schools and in general no Religious Education takes place in the 'neutral' public schools. Increasingly parents in public schools ask for opportunities in RE and worldviews which are then provided by the Reformed Church or the Humanistic Union.

In general it is possible to differentiate roughly between two main models of RE in Europe: the *Religious Studies approach* and the *denominational or confessional approach*. One has to be aware that this simplification can nurture prejudices and stereotypes.

The differentiation between 'denominational' and 'religious studies' refers to the fact that the content of RE, the training and facilitating process of teachers, the development of curricula and teaching material are mainly the responsibility of religious communities or of the State. Where RE is denominationally oriented, it must be emphasised that this approach is not necessarily understood as being the consequence of a State Church or of a majority religion; rather it is considered the realisation of State neutrality and the individual freedom of religion. The State does not have to influence the content of the subject, but to be neutral in religion and in worldviews. Where RE is denominationally oriented (such as in the south of Europe, partly in Switzerland, Austria, Belgium, Germany, central and eastern Europe) different kinds of Religious Education are offered. In Austria, Belgium and parts of Germany denominational Religious Education is not limited to Catholic or Protestant teaching but includes also Orthodox, Jewish, Muslim, Buddhist and other forms of Religious Education. In many cases there is an opportunity for pupils to opt out and to choose alternative subjects such as ethics or philosophy.

Most of the countries with a Religious Studies approach (for example, Denmark, Sweden, Norway, England and Wales, Scotland, the last three being the exceptions) do not have a general right to opt out, although in some countries it is granted to members of religious minorities. The general aims are to transmit religious knowledge and understanding, as well as dealing with human experiences. The neutrality of the State and the right of religious freedom are guaranteed with this approach. It occurs in a different way, however, than with denominational Religious Education. The religious studies approach is carried out under the authority of the State. Instruction is not to be neutral in respect to values but should be neutral in respect of worldviews including religion, a demand which corresponds to the religious neutrality of the State. From this perspective, this neutrality guarantees that this kind of Religious Education is equally acceptable to all denominations and religions.

A schematic overview of the place of RE in the school system and the different responsibility can look like the following:

Responsibility: religious communities	In co-operation between religious communities and the State	Responsibility: religious communities
Denominational		Religious Studies
Voluntary subject	Voluntary/compulsory subject	Compulsory subject

Different approaches, different aims?

Different approaches have different aims. The more denominationally oriented RE can focus on the 'identity formation' of the pupils with particular reference to the religious dimension. The more 'religious knowledge' oriented approach is concerned more with the knowledge and understanding of religion.

Looking to the different RE classrooms in Europe, I would argue there is a tendency for practice to converge in spite of the different 'theories'. This can be underlined through an increasing awareness of the relation of religion to the pupils, their own individual religious practice and their 'religious needs'. This view includes a recognition of the active-meaning capacity of the students being in parallel with a dynamic understanding of religion. Comparing aims of religious education from different national contexts (Schreiner 1999) we can find similarities. Many catalogues of aims of RE include:

- to encourage pupils to be sensitive to religion and the religious dimension of life;
- to provide orientation of the variety of existing religious opportunities and in ethical understanding, which are rooted in religious experiences;
- to give knowledge and understanding of religious beliefs and experiences.

Looking for reasons for this convergence one can say that there is a central awareness of Religious Education as a pedagogical enterprise. Another reason is an increasing awareness of the life-world and the day-to-day situation of the pupil.

This change of perspective includes a different understanding of religion and culture. Both are seen as dynamic interwoven areas with every definition having no more than a preliminary status. There is no religion or culture that has not changed in history: more emphasis is given to the concrete 'gestalt' of religion with each individual. A change in the perception of religion from an institutionalised tradition to personal aspects of believers, and the acceptance of the 'Children's right to religion' (Schweitzer 2000) could become a new stimulus for a European-oriented discussion about RE. The orientation of education, the orientation of the life-world and the experiences of the pupils can also provide arguments for discussion about the different existing RE approaches.

Speaking about 'biographies' of religious education in Europe can encourage a careful look at, and the readiness to explore, different understandings of RE. It can sharpen one's own view about RE and provide opportunities for dialogue among RE practitioners and scholars without nurturing the perspective to develop *the* European RE approach, which would ignore the richness of cultures and religions in Europe. It should not hinder any discussion of some common or specific challenges to RE.

Challenges

All approaches are challenged by a radically changed situation of societies. Issues such as secularisation, individualism, pluralism and globalisation are markers of changes which influence the field of religious education. In most of the western European societies modernity came along hand in hand with the secularisation of society. The idea behind the 'secularisation theory' is quite simple: modernisation leads to a decline of religion, both in society and in the minds of individuals. Having an awareness that there are good arguments to underline the view of the 'de-secularisation of the world' (Berger 1999) and that the relation between religion and modernity is rather complicated, we can state that 'Certain religious institutions have lost power and influence in many societies' (Berger 1999: 3). One consequence of this is the trend for religion to become more individualised. 'Religion like so many other things, has entered the world of options, life-styles, and preferences' (Davie 1999: 75). We have to be aware of the situation of plurality which means that European societies are characterised by the presence of different political attitudes, cultural backgrounds, ethnic identifications, religious convictions and worldviews.

These developments have consequences for RE. The existing *denominational approach* can no longer focus exclusively on one specific faith tradition. A much stronger emphasis is needed on ecumenical and inter-religious learning for the sake of mutual understanding and the promotion of respect towards other faith traditions and worldviews.

The *Religious Studies approach* has included from the very beginning a variety of other religions and worldviews; a comparative dimension concerning issues, festivals of rituals, etc., was a decisive element. What appears to be missing is cooperation with faith communities, associations and organisations which give authentic testimony about beliefs and religious views. In a consultation of the World Council of Churches the value of RE in this radically changed situation was underlined:

> In societies where religious indifference, cultural intolerance and rapidly changing norms and values seem to prevail, RE can be the space in which young people learn how to deal with challenges to identity, manage conflict and develop sensitivity in interacting with difference. The task of conceptualising RE, in dialogue with other faith traditions is an essential way forward.
>
> (World Council of Churches 2000: 1)

Any model of RE can be asked how best to contribute to the following tasks:

- to deal with questions and challenges of identity formation;
- to develop ways of handling conflicts;

- to encourage ways of dealing with differences.

This short description makes clear that one cannot separate RE from school development even if the role and place of RE is contested in some education systems. The issues of a religious dimension in general education and of RE in school seem to be unavoidable in the context of the following questions, which in turn raise challenges for the whole education system:

- How can school contribute to a necessary understanding between the existing cultural and religious traditions and views in a society?
- How can religious and ethical education be organised appropriately in order to deal with the existing plurality in society?

In this respect RE can become 'popular' in the general debate about education. RE is confronted with expectations, that it should act as a problem-solver for conflicts in society, to contribute to the peaceful cohabitation of people with different cultural and religious backgrounds.

Parents expect that school will provide a Religious Education which they cannot or will not provide for their children at home. There is also the expectation of religious communities that the way religious traditions are presented in RE will be authentic and in coherence with their self-understanding. But: who represents the religion(s) in the classroom? This can lead to the situation where RE is confused with catechetics and Religious Instruction which should be done by the religious communities themselves for their believers.

Politicians too have expectations of RE especially by reference to the inherent ethical potential of religion. However, education and Religious Education cannot be seen as magic healers for problems and conflicts which are rooted in other areas of society. It is a charming but nevertheless dangerous temptation when politicians claim Religious Education can and should solve existing problems of living together in Europe.

Current developments

In Bosnia-Herzegovina a process has begun to introduce a new subject in all public schools: 'Culture of Religions'. In the canton of Zurich in Switzerland, a new subject was introduced in the upper level of the public school which substitutes the existing confessional-cooperative approach. And in the Bundesland of North-Rhine Westphalia in Germany, a new syllabus was introduced which gives more attention to the pupils and to 'other worldviews'.

Bosnia and Herzegovina: introducing a new subject: 'Culture of Religions

Five years after the end of the war in the former Yugoslavia the political situation and the development of the society is difficult. Bosnia-Herzegovina is a complex State consisting of two nearly independent political entities: the Federation of Bosnia-Herzegovina and the Republic of Sprska. Sarajevo is the common capital. The three main religious communities are the Serbian Orthodox Church (33 per cent of the population) the Islamic community (44 per cent) and the Catholic Church (17 per cent), and religious affiliation goes in line with the ethnic affiliation (Bosnians are mainly Muslims, Serbs belong to the Serbian Orthodox Church and Croats are mainly Catholics). One tragic result of the war is the ethnic cleansing which produced more separated areas of living than before. The Dayton Peace Treaty encouraged the cooperation of the three main ethnic groups in the fragmented society. This does not happen effectively today. It was the power of the High Representative of the international community who forced the institutions of the State to cooperate. In 1999 he dismissed twenty-two local politicians because they resisted the return of refugees from other ethnic groups. The second local elections in April 2000 encouraged nationalistic oriented politicians and parties.

In the Federation of Bosnia-Herzegovina the Department of Education has implemented new curricula in 1994, making RE a voluntary subject under the responsibility of the faith communities (Islamic, Catholic, Orthodox, Jewish, Adventist). The main responsibility is with the administration of the ten Kantons, and so the regulations differ: RE can be found as compulsory, as voluntary or as compulsory with the opportunity for choice. For most of the schools, information is not wholly available but RE is organised by the main religious community.

In the Republic of Srpska the Orthodox Church has the status of a quasi-state church, because 'the Serbian Orthodox church is the church of the Serbian people' as it is written in the constitution. The State supports and cooperates closely with the Orthodox Church. RE is compulsory for all pupils who are members of the Orthodox Church.

Efforts have been made by the Departments of Education of the Federation of Bosnia-Herzegovina and the Republic of Srpska on the initiative of the Office of the High Representative and the Council of Europe in May last year. The decision says that measures shall be implemented to teach about all great religions in the country of Bosnia-Herzegovina for at least one hour per week in all classes of primary and secondary schools. This initiative should help to overcome the separation and fragmentation of society and to encourage tolerance and reconciliation through education.

After a difficult process of preparation, a consultation took place in the spring of 2001 where, for the first time, representatives of the different religious communities (Orthodox, Catholic, Muslim), representatives of the Departments for Education of the different political entities (areas), and of the international organisations who work in Bosnia-Herzegovina, came together to share their opinion about this proposal. The biggest outcome was that the consultation took place and different views about the proposal could be discussed. The task was to work out the shape of the planned new subject, its name, the aims and the pedagogical concept as well as guidelines for teacher training and the cooperation of the churches and other faith communities. The development of guidelines for curricula was also an issue. The difficulty of organising this event can be underlined by the fact that the consultation had to be postponed twice due to internal disagreement among some of the involved groups.

The consultation has enabled an exchange of the different perspectives and brought some agreement that the process should be continued. There was a common understanding that teaching RE should be formative and informative. Teaching should include information about the existing religions in the country, their history and their current status. RE should also encourage mutual understanding of other faith traditions. It was also agreed that the denominational RE of the religious communities should not be substituted by a new subject but that all RE teaching needs to be opened up to promote tolerance and reconciliation with regard to other religions. It was agreed that the dialogue shall continue. This example shows the highly political character of RE and the danger when RE is dominated by political interests. A good solution for RE in Bosnia-Herzegovina needs the contribution of all involved groups in society and it should recognise pedagogical and religious concerns, but it cannot solve deep-rooted problems of a segregated society.

Switzerland: a new subject in Zurich: 'Religion and Culture'

In Switzerland the main responsibility for education is with the regional governments of the twenty-six cantons. Due to differences in the religious landscape, tradition, history and politics, denominational and 'neutral' RE can be found (Eggenberger 2000).

In the canton of Zurich the existing RE in the upper level of the public school (Years 7 to 9) will soon be changed. The denominational-cooperative RE will be substituted by a new subject called 'Religion and Culture'.

The old and the new subjects are both compulsory with the right to opt out. The new subject is taught 2 lessons per week in Year 7 and 1 hour per week in Year 8. The churches can offer a lesson in their own responsibility in Year 8 and they have the opportunity to offer religious oriented projects for four half days during a term.

The decision of the responsible education council said:

> Today we are living in a pluralistic, multicultural and multireligious society, which should be able to organise the living together of different world views. The model of a denominational-cooperative RE is too narrow for the aim of integration. The development of this subject shall enable to introduce all pupils in our religious and cultural roots as well as in values of different religions and world views.
>
> (Bildungsdirektion 2000: 4)

The description of the new subject of 'Religion and Culture' includes:

> The religious dimension is part of a holistic (comprehensive) educa-
> tion…A further development of the subject concerning the contents shall
> deal with Christianity as well as with other religions and worldviews on an
> equal level.

And the attainment targets include:

- to deal with questions of meaning from the perspective of different world
  views and religions;
- to enable pupils to clarify their own values and to give reasons for them;
- to encourage pupils to question their own value-based decisions (cf. 5).

The opportunity of weekly Religious Education by the Churches in Year 8 and
the right to use four half days for teaching projects will be enlarged to other religions. Those who do not participate in these projects have to attend normal
lessons. This fulfils the demand of religious communities: the provision of a
home for their young members. The central task of the new subject and also
one guideline of the material is to combine religion as a source of meaning with
experiences and questions of the young adults.

A new set of teaching and learning material has been developed. It consists
of a teacher handbook with basic articles about the new subject and proposals
on how to use the material. Three student books (for 13–15 year-olds) and
respective manuals for teachers are worked out around the strands, 'People live
with questions', 'People live in traditions' and 'What people see as holy'.

The general teacher handbook gives information about faith development in
adolescence using material and theory based on faith development theory and
developmental psychology. Another chapter includes articles about
Christianity, Judaism, Islam, Buddhism and Hinduism from their own perspectives.

A *thematic approach* is used in articles about prayer in different religions and a
calendar of religious festivals. Information and didactical advice about methodologies, for example working with texts or pictures or Bible dramas and how to
use art in RE are also included.

Some observations:

- The privilege of one main religion, Christianity, no longer exists. Other
  religious communities can use the newly given space for their own projects
  in the school.
- The life-world of the student is a central focus in the teaching material.
- The themes are presented in a way that own views can be developed and
  encourages more than to be introduced to religious knowledge.
- RE is organised in co-operation between the Churches/religious communities and the Department of Education and covers the interests of both sides.

Protestant RE in the upper secondary school in North-Rhine Westphalia

Religious Education in Germany follows a denominational approach. It is based in the constitution that RE is given 'in accordance to the guidelines of the religious communities' (art. 7.3). In each of the 'Bundeslander', agreements exist between the regional government and the Protestant and Catholic Churches about Religious Education. The Jewish religious community and the Orthodox Church also provide RE in some places. In some of the 'Bundeslander', discussions are taking place in order to introduce Islamic RE.

Another aspect is that in many regional constitutions a religious dimension is mentioned as an integrated dimension of education, for example in North-Rhine Westphalia:

1   To arouse reverence for God, respect of the dignity of human beings and readiness to act socially is the primary aim of education.
2   Youth should be educated in the spirit of humanness, of democracy and freedom, to tolerance and acceptance of the other, to responsibility for the maintenance of the natural resources of life, in love to its people and home, to the family of people and to peaceful driven convictions (art. 7).

Looking at the aims of Protestant RE, it is worth noting that they are embedded in the overall aims and attainment targets of this level of school. These are mainly 'to facilitate an academic oriented basic training and to give encouragement for a personal development of social oriented responsibility' (Ministerium 1999: XI). RE is regarded as a subject for dealing with existential issues and questions:

> Christian faith is in the centre of the teaching with its biblical-evangelical form, its effect on history as well as the reality in society and its impact on it. This is done through dialogue and examination with decisive opportunities and demands of other religions, other religious stances and worldviews. Therefore RE contributes to the search for answers to existing existential questions of one's own and to encourage finding new questions.
>
> (Ministerium 1999: 5)

RE is composed in dialogue of three areas:

1   Statements of faith traditions and theology (theological issues).
2   Questions and experiences of the students.
3   Comparative views of other religions and worldviews.

And three other dimensions play a central role in the teaching:

4   Forms and expressions of religious language.

5   Methods of hermeneutics.
6   Perception and production by the students.

These six structural elements form the framework for Religious Education which is then realised through various methods like projects, practical experiences, cooperation with other subjects in cross-curricula work, etc., and through different themes.

Some observations:

- The new approach includes competitive views of other religions and world-views.
- The situation of the students is a decisive element in RE concerning process and content.
- RE is providing space for a common process where teachers and pupils are working and learning together by sharing their stories and experiences.

'Europeanisation' of RE?

The overview shows that Religious Education in Europe is rooted in a specific complex situation in each country, and all existing RE approaches are challenged by recent developments in society and in Europe. Three examples demonstrate how RE is dealing with the expectations of society, state, parents and others. Taking this information for granted, it is worth asking: how can we compare the different REs, and is there a tendency to 'Europeanisation'? Confirming the need and benefit of international exchange and cooperation in RE, we should be aware of existing obstacles and problems which can be experienced at any European conference on Religious Education:

- *The problem of terminology.* What do we understand when we talk about Religious Education? A common starting point could be that we deal with a school subject as part of a general school curriculum. But then we soon recognise that the term RE is embedded in a specific context with different starting points, backgrounds and histories. Are we sensitive to these differences? Are we open for views other than our own? It seems to me that it is better to dance with the differences than to ignore them.
- *The problem of language and culture barriers* that lie between many of the European countries. In most of the cases the linguistic communities correspond to cultural communities shaped by a common history. Language is a mirror and tool of culture and different languages carry different bags of culture. There is no other way than to find ways of dealing with these existing barriers. Crossing boundaries can be a fruitful experience.
- *The differences in the existing education systems.* Religious Education depends not least on the frame and the structure of the education system. In any society the right of the parents to be responsible for the education of their children as well as the right of religious communities for

authentic self-interpretation are decisive criteria for RE. The debate about the role, place and value of RE is an ongoing process for the sake of facilitating religious competence of the pupils and young adults. It is a debate about good education where the religious dimension must not be ignored.

These and other obstacles are areas of concern for exchange in Europe.

A 'Europeanisation' of RE shall not be limited to the demands of economy or politics often expressed concerning education and Religious Education. Another significant area is the exchange and co-operation of religious educators in Europe on these issues. The triennial conferences of the Inter-European Commission on Church and School (ICCS) and the European Forum for Teachers of Religious Education (EFTRE) provide good opportunities for deepening European RE concerns and exchanging information about national developments. A general theme is the relation *between education and religion* which is valued differently in the different approaches. In RE circles 'education' and 'nurture' have been used with the effect of polarising phenomenological and confessional approaches. Increasingly it seems that this distinction is not always helpful, but combining these different roles is a challenge to be faced by the teachers. Another area deals with the *meaning and significance of pedagogy for RE*. Religious Education is first and foremost an educational task. This view is increasingly shared by those who encourage a denominational RE approach. Dealing with RE needs to be aware of the underlying pedagogy, the understanding of teaching and learning, the aims, methodologies and contents:

> Teaching RE is an exacting and complex process which requires approaches to teaching and learning to be informed by pedagogical principles that draw upon psychological theories of learning and human development.
>
> (Grimmitt 2000: 15)

How can religion(s) and education be brought into a relationship with the situation and the needs of the students? How can we deal with the tension between encouraging open-mindedness and seeking to transmit values through RE? The relation between a more content-centred approach which transmits knowledge from a teacher who 'knows' to a student who 'should know' and a pupil-centred approach which takes students as the 'active meaning-makers' seriously and provides a safe space for their own development is a debate for those involved in RE. Paulo Freire has called the 'transmission' approach the 'banking method' where the educator makes 'deposits' in the educatee. He and others argue for a transformation approach where learning and teaching is mutually interwoven, where teachers become teacher-learners and learners become learner-teachers (Wardekker and Miedema 2001). Religious Education is a decisive area where critical contributions can be made to this ongoing debate.

Questions

1 'Instruction is not to be neutral in respect to values but should be neutral in respect of worldviews, including religion'. Is this possible?
2 Is the apparent willingness for the study of different religions in schools across Europe built upon Christian models and understandings of religion? What implications does such dialogue have for European understanding?
3 In the context of such educational, social and religious diversity is it possible to speak of a rationale for RE in Europe?

Part II

Religious Education in the classroom

8 How far do Programmes for RE relate to the Social and Psychological Development of Pupils?

Development through Religious Education

Brian Gates

Development, like music and motherhood, has got to be a good thing. Or at least that is a common assumption when the word is used. But what if development involves deterioration, regression even? What if development takes a form which so transforms the individual that they become a distortion of who they formerly were? Just as musical tastes differ, so do perceptions of what would be desirable, or less desirable, 'development'. It is even conceivable that one person's cacophony could be another's symphony. Motherhood too can be a mixed blessing. In the form of an unwanted pregnancy, it may be perceived as a curse. In the way it is experienced and managed, it can become destructive for both the mother and the child, and others can be destroyed in the process. Development may be highly desirable, but the criteria for making that judgement deserve some prior inspection if it is to be accepted with any professional confidence.

Three different sources of critical awareness regarding use of the term development warrant immediate recognition, the more so when religion is involved. These are ones from the human sciences, from humanists rejecting religion as stunting of human growth potential, and from men and women of religious faith concerned for the enrichment of common humanity. Teachers may be influenced by any or all of these sensitivities.

The first source comes from the *human sciences* as applied to the context of education, as in 'child development', 'human development', 'social and psychological development'. Here, development carries evolutionary overtones which may arouse suspicion of biological determinism. That children's thought forms must go through a set sequence of stages to arrive at maturity might appear to challenge individuality. And yet, with growing boys and girls, just as there is a genetic unfolding of sequenced physical development, so there are certain continuities found throughout the world in respect of developing capacities for dependence and independence, for elaborated reasoning, for short-term and long-term aspiration, and for a sense of boundaries both near and far. The forms such capacities take vary enormously, as their psychogenetic givenness is changed by human interaction and individual reflection, as also by exposure to religion. But that they do emerge as complementary expressions of our outward and inward being, as analysed socially and psychologically, remains constant. Proponents of the human sciences include a wider following than university academics. Intellectually, they all share the view that development is fundamental to human being and that it can be pursued in ways that are liberating of humanity, or quite the opposite.

The second source of critical reservation regarding the use of the word development comes from *humanists* who, on taking stock of the impact of religion in human civilisation, conclude that it is divisive and stunting of human growth potential. They have seen that religious beliefs can be conflictual and contribute to war, seeming on occasion even to legitimate acts of gross barbarism. They have noted an apparent correlation between the secondary status of women and male predominance in the history of religions. They have remarked on the mixture of hypocrisy and guilt often associated with religion where sexual behaviour or personal wealth is concerned. In consequence, they fear that any promotional references to religion in relation to educational development could well be in contradiction of the development which they themselves would want. 'Humanists' in this sense may not formally use the word to describe themselves, but they are people anywhere who have read and pondered human behaviour and concluded that the role of religion is only ambiguously for the good of individuals in society. They want this wariness to be heeded.

The third source of critical concern for how 'development' is best understood for education is that of *men and women of religious faith* who believe that exposure to religious tradition will contribute significantly to the enrichment of common humanity. They certainly believe this in respect of their own faith, if not also of selected others. They may be confident as individual Christians that, once experienced, the quality of life, which flows from association with God in Christ, will transform each person and relationships for the better. Likewise, as individual Muslims, they may know that the knowledge of God disclosed in the Qur'an is creative of a sense of justice and peace for everyone. Or again as individual Buddhists, there will be clear vision that, once we are tuned in, this way enlightens the whole of life and death. Of course, these same individuals know that their respective traditions have been used on occasion to encourage human development in terms which can be characterised as exclusive, inhumane, or even destructive. But by and large they would see those tendencies as going against the grain of the religious development intrinsic to the tradition at its mainstream best. Accordingly, whether as leading theologians or ordinary modest folk, they will find wanting any talk of development through education which is not open to such authentic religious insights.

Because of the process of general cultural osmosis prevalent in a society so extensively exposed to mass communications, it is very likely that RE specialist teachers in primary and secondary schools, no less than specialists in other subjects, will be influenced by one or more of these kinds of critical perspective. Almost inescapably, we breathe each others' air. If not personally, then professionally, or vice versa, we will know that psychology and sociology can be used

to explain religion. That may be to try to explain it away; i'
acknowledge its vitality. Similarly, our general human bear'
how religion can sometimes be contaminated with evil. A
that religious faith has the potential to be transformative †

Given all these different voices, what development sh
RE?

Taking the part of the Other

There is a phenomenon remarked in the activity of young children, known as 'parallel play'. Two children play alongside each other, and appear to be playing together. In fact, there is little or no direct interaction between them. They are each locked into an internally coherent play world whose meaning subsists independently of anything that the other child is intending. Child A may feature in the play of Child B, but entirely on the basis of meaning projected on to him and without reference to any aspect of the play in which he himself is engaged. Whether or not either child is in fact capable of more genuinely inter-active play at that particular age and stage of their development matters less than that each child does come to be able to include both these forms of play in their personal repertoire (Durkin 1996, ch. 4).

There is a phenomenon known as the giving of presents. Again it is initially experienced during childhood years. It may begin with the delight of receiving such gifts, from a parent, relative, sibling or friend, but it commonly extends to pleasure also in giving gifts to others. There is often a clear pattern of reciproca-tion which can be interpreted as in different degrees self-serving. I enjoy receiving presents, and arguably one way of ensuring that the practice continues is to give presents to the very persons who might be expected to be givers. But there is also the experience of pleasure in giving genuinely to please the other person. This still betrays a self-satisfying element, but more in addition to that is involved.

There is a third phenomenon on which hospitals throughout the UK depend: giving blood. This gift relationship is unpaid, and though again there may be an element of self-insurance involved, it depends largely on the good-will of a minority of men and women, who recognise the worth of being ready to share their blood with others.

These three phenomena illustrate a developmental priority which makes good educational sense. The principle involved is that of reciprocity and it is as fundamental to human life and relationships as it is to religion. Without recip-rocal giving, the *sangha* would not survive, the sacrament of holy communion would make no sense, and the life of dedicated professional giving would lose much of its purpose. Accordingly, it matters greatly for Religious Education that pupils are encouraged to understand the process of giving and receiving. If their understanding is deepened in the context of learning about and from some reli-gious story or festival, then that religious insight may prompt their appreciation of a fundamental principle for personal and social life, as well as their own enjoyment of giving. If they already know this in their own experience, they are placed to recognise why acts of generosity are so central to religious ponse and tradition. Either way, they are capable of looking beyond themselves and taking the part of the other.

Such a capacity is at the root of altruistic behaviour. Though the cynic might dismiss all talk of altruism as self-serving, that is not how courageous intervention to save the drowning child or the victim of anti-Semitism feels to the rescuer or rescued. As socio-psychological research has demonstrated, an educational environment which deliberately promotes extensivity of recognition for others in their differentness will challenge any easy assumption that unquestioningly devalues what is different (Oliver 1998, ch. 10).

Arguably, one feature which is absolutely fundamental to good RE is its promotion of empathy. Irrespective of their own individual viewpoints, it invites pupils at every Key Stage to imagine what it is like to be a Muslim, or some other particular faiths. This 'taking the part of the other' then feeds directly into personal and social development more generally.

It also relates to another key aspect of development.

Extending horizons

It is remarked that primary school children, typically during Key Stage 1, may have some difficulty in conceptualising the relationship between the village or town they live in, the country in which this is situated, and how they all relate to other towns, cities and countries. As with the phenomenon of parallel play, this was remarked by Piaget. In the aftermath of the Second World War, with encouragement from UNESCO, he was exercised about the understanding of belonging which local Swiss boys and girls were able to demonstrate in relation to their hometown, nation and wider human community (Piaget 1951).

It is also remarked that youths, like or unlike their parents, can be constrained within certain cultural, ethnic, religious and other social boundaries, with potentially negative consequences for the wider community. Intensive exposure from family beliefs and attitudes, and/or from those of particular peers, can promote reductive stereotypes of other groups, thereby providing licence to think ill of them. Notorious examples of this have come in the past from Northern Ireland. They also come from grandparental stories of inter-religious feuding drawn from experiences on the Indian sub-continent and told to children within the family home. More recently they have come from Bradford. The Report *Community Pride, not Prejudice* (Ouseley 2001), published in the wake of the 2001 riots, suggests that sectional community recruitment to particular schools, combined with after school intensive teaching associated with one particular faith and culture, has had the effect of insulating whole sections of the community from other sections. In consequence, other faiths and cultures in all their wealthy diversity are never met on their own terms.

Religious Education can then be presented as creating the problem rather than contributing to its solution. But that would be a perversion of good RE and the mainstream teachings of world religions.

By definition, world religions are global in their horizons. In this respect, they contrast sharply with what might be termed 'tribal cults', in which loyalties and horizons are in effect confined to an immediate group. It is intrinsic to the Jewish tradition that there is affirmation of being both a Chosen People and simultaneously part of the whole of humanity created by God. The same is no less true for Christians and Muslims, and in all three religions there are radical demands for transformation according to the spirit of justice and generosity which flows from God. Though the Hindu tradition has until relatively recently thrived more on the sacred soil of India, its celebration of the plurality of divine forms gives licence for universal openness. Sikhs drawing parentally on that tradition, as on Islam as well, also assert a strong conviction of human oneness before God. And Buddhists diagnose dis-ease as universal to the human condition and warranting a radical re-ordering. All told, though they may do this in different ways, each of the religions which is prescribed for attention in LEA agreed syllabuses, as also in the National Models, challenges constrictions in thinking to anything less than global belonging.

Classroom RE is rich in incentives and resources from religion to promote horizons which go beyond those of any one group. Transcendent reference points in God, in Divine Reality, or in the transience of all being, give no encouragement to misplaced tribalisms. Sociologists have remarked about the historical role of religion in challenging the 'tyranny of kin'; the same applies now to 'family firstism' and to little Englanders, as it does to the racism of the British National Party or anyone else. Any local church, gurdwara, mosque, synagogue, temple or vihara points beyond itself to a wider humanity and communion of saints; schools can encourage their pupils to look through them as windows to that larger world.

'Faith Schools' are just as much committed to extending horizons as 'Community Schools'. Though their programmes for RE are different from those in Agreed Syllabuses, the 'world faith' with which they are specifically associated has global dimensions intrinsic to it. Moreover, they still operate within the framework of the 1988 Education Reform Act with its requirements that the National Curriculum be followed and that the curriculum 'promotes the spiritual, moral, cultural, mental and physical development of pupils at the school and of society' (ERA 1988, ch. 40.1.2.2). For RE not to extend the horizons of pupils would be a contradiction in terms.

Literal and symbolic sense

It may be said of someone, at any time, that their understanding does not go beyond surface meaning. Again, it may be said of the same person, or another, that they seem only to be interested in the literal meaning of words or pictures. In either instance, that person's human understanding would become more developed were they to learn to read and interpret how meaning is often layered and expressed on several levels.

This is an area of development that is central for RE in two respects. First, religious meanings will be only partly understood without an appreciation of both letter and spirit. Second, the stuff of religion is richly fertile for growing such insights.

According to cognitive developmental psychology, a tendency towards concrete thinking predominates between infancy and adolescence. Whereas the younger child might delight in fantasy and fairy tale, and enjoy games of pretend that may bear little relation to matter of fact reality, it is observed that, for a boy or girl moving into Key Stages 2 and 3, matters of fact come to be of more predominant concern. Thinking becomes more readily concrete and circumstantial; symbols become brittle. And yet, from those earlier years, recollections do persist of the representative pliability of words and things. The newly dominant mode of thinking does not need to freeze out further appeal to symbolic sense, or to delay it into later adolescent years when intellectually more elaborated reasoning tends to flourish. Teachers of children across these different ages would simply recognise that their readiness to operate in terms of picture language and symbols will require appropriate classroom conjuring.

According to the theologian Paul Tillich, the great art of the religious educator is to overcome the problem of literalism (Tillich 1959). Misplaced concreteness can otherwise prevent the substance of religious teaching from having any vitality of its own and reduce its credibility to nil. That risk is perhaps especially evident in respect of scriptural text, but it extends also to all other forms of religious expression.

Take the example of biblical literalism. To be sure it is important to acknowledge that, for some Jews and Christians, biblical text should be taken literally, with its meaning still carefully pondered. But it would be wrong to give the impression that literal interpretation of the Bible has been the norm until the last hundred years, only retreated from in the wake of scientific discoveries. Picture language, powerful metaphor and colourful hyperbole abound in the Hebrew Bible, as they do also in the New Testament parables of Jesus, and in Pauline and Johannine apocalyptic. Their suggestiveness in this regard has been exploited by Christian theologians and artists across the centuries.

The Old Testament story of Jonah is demeaned if it is presented as an historical account of a man eaten by a whale. It is much more engaging as a story of a man who does not want to pass on a message to foreigners, rather than to family and friends, one who gets his come-uppance, and sulks. It takes on fuller force if it is then interpreted allegorically to represent the relation between Israel and the nations of the world, or as a parable about the same relationship affirming that the whole world is in God's hands. Similarly, the main point of the gospel story of Jesus walking on water is lost if it is left at the level of magical performance as found in similar stories from ancient Greece or India. Decoded as might be done for an advert, the message is that this Jesus and the power of God in him is recognised as totally dependable and present in even the most stressful of circumstances.

In approaching scriptural text, it is fundamental to RE that regard is given to the position in which it is held within its faith community. But openness to the meaning of what it says is different from deference to literalism, and scriptures are not possessions belonging exclusively to one group. They are given to humankind. Attention to spirit and letter of text leaves space also for any student to work at it with the best intelligence they can bring to bear (Nielson 1993).

This can also be seen in the other forms of religious language, a further example of which is that of artistic expression (Holm 1996). There is considerable sensitivity in religions regarding visual representations of the Divine and, in a western context, an easy disdain at the very notion that God might be conveyed in, such as, the form of an elephant. But this is where literal mindedness fails a basic tuning test. Behind the friendly and strong sense of security associated with Ganesh, or Gumpati, is a living cultural experience of elephants as immensely strong and capable of removing major obstacles, as capable of great remembering and trumpeting playfulness. During the festival in his name, a carved statue of him may be feted and reverenced, and as a way of sensing Godness and responding appropriately. But what is appropriate may well extend to processing the carved figure to the river and there allowing the elephant form to be swallowed up and carried away in the great flow of water, shortly to become one with the greater ocean which surrounds our being in the world.

Unfortunately, literalised understanding can on occasion become a very dangerous force. Caricatured versions of what is intended in a statue of the Buddha, or a Catholic image of the Virgin, have fuelled the violent antipathy of the Taliban's recent destruction by dynamite of ancient rock carvings in Afghanistan, or centuries ago the Protestant marauding of Christian visual expression in the Churches of the British Isles. Good RE has the potential to make a real political difference!

The classroom then can be the arena for developing both literal and symbolic sense, if pupils are encouraged to bring to religious texts the quality of personal experience with which they interpret much of what goes on around them outside of school, and if in turn teachers know the material well enough to prompt the links and connections that will ring true.

Critical thinking and wondering why

Just as constraints of cognitive development can be used as a disincentive against the promotion of symbolic understanding before a certain age and stage, the same can also be invoked to discourage any priority being given to critical thinking.

It may be that, as boys and girls move into Key Stage 2 (KS2), questions such as 'Did it really happen?', 'Is it true?', 'How do you know?' are more frequently asked. Similarly, comments such as 'It's just made up', 'It's not true really', and 'You can't prove it' may be more abundant. For some, perhaps later in Key Stage 3 and into Key Stage 4, this predominant emphasis may give way to different kinds of comments and questions, which may ask what is meant or intended in the first place by the statement made or belief being asserted.

However, such an age-related and linear developmental progression again strikes some as too simplistic. Children do ask these kinds of questions and may well with sensitive prompting be capable of pursuing them at a younger age than is often supposed, even in KS1 (CAM 1993). At the same time, questions of historical verification, scientific scrutiny, and empirical check-out do get more systematically asked and pursued as children get older, by both them and their teachers. Indeed, this interrogation will be encouraged as a curriculum priority. What may be overlooked in the course of this happening, is that it is no less important that the rigorous questioning should take place in RE than, for instance, in Science and History and Geography. Arguably, it may be even more important because RE has a special concern for 'why' questions in general, and ultimate 'whys' in particular: why is there a universe when there might be nothing? Why is there cosmos and not only chaos? Why does it matter that right thoughts and actions should prevail over wrong ones? (Isaacs 1930 Appendix A)

Theological and philosophical discourse has a strong place in each of the religious traditions which feature in the syllabuses. They include tracts of credal material which is didactically assertive in its form and content, but they are even richer in material which seeks to interpret, explain and justify what is being believed and taught as central to each faith. Thus, there are discussions about such questions as the following and many more besides: the injustice of innocent suffering, where life comes from, whether there is anything beyond death and what form it might take, if evil can be defeated, how to tell the difference between true and false prophecy, what God looks like, whether the individual self has any continuing identity. These all go beyond surface meanings. They connect with questions that any person might want to ask at any time in their life. Exposure to such material in RE can promote thinking skills at any age and at the same time give companionship to boys and girls in facing any tussles, which they find themselves in, regarding overall purpose and meaning in life and death.

As part of this process of scrutiny, it is important for the integrity of religion that its engagement with critical scholarship is presented, so that this is recognised as an indicator of health and vitality in the tradition and not simply defensiveness. For instance, the insights from secondary disciplines – such as archaeology, ethnography, geography, history, psychology and textual analysis – are important and variously informing of the teacher's confidence. And insights from primary sources, as generated from within each religious tradition and interrogated by scholars in its own particular terms, are even more fundamental for the teacher's repertoire. Their forms will be greatly diverse: literary and liturgical, in music, dance and drama, socially ordering and spiritually deepening, visually stimulating and morally demanding. Throughout, the questions provoked and affirmations claimed present a high order of philosophical challenge.

RE does indeed have an interest in promoting cognitive development. It has vehicles and resources that lend themselves to stretching of thought and imagination. It is not at all shy of wanting to engage pupils in wondering why this, and that, and the other. A curriculum that invites them to wonder cannot help but be all about development.

Being, knowing and sensing finitude

The contributions from RE to the social and psychological development of pupils are significant: in building empathy and a sense of neighbourliness, in stretching horizons and loyalties beyond those nearest to hand, in creating an appreciation of the depth and power of language, and in promoting critical thinking and pursuing the question 'why?' In the midst of all this lies another contribution which focuses in the person at the centre of all these thoughts and feelings.

This focus has been left till last for three reasons, two negative and one positive. The first of these is that there is much in contemporary western culture which takes as unquestionable norm that the goal of education is human autonomy. Enabling each pupil to think for themselves becomes the over-arching goal of every curriculum subject. This is a healthy challenge to rote learning and any cultural tendency to want to predetermine the thinking and behaviour of its youth. However, the cultivation of the individual can have very isolating outcomes, which are at the expense of other relatedness and relational belonging. The 'I' is supreme, but entirely solitary.

Second, there is a wariness in religious traditions not only with self-centredness, but with the very notion of self having any reality. Jews, Christians and Muslims press the case that neighbour be loved as much as, or even more than, self. Buddhists challenge the very notion of an individual self: it is illusory. If therefore Religious Education were to guise itself as primarily an exercise in self-exploration, it would easily invite dismissal from across religions that it was merely navel-gazing.

Yet, third, religious responses to life in the world do invariably involve a sense of contingency, of transience and of human limitation, and each of these is fundamental to personhood. Death stalks the heart of religion, as of all humanity, powerfully. Much of the sentiment expressed in petitionary prayer is admitting relative helplessness and dependence. Much of the contemplative reflection found in acts of meditation seeks to go beyond the ordinary givenness of physical sensation. Religion and RE, almost by definition, raise questions in the pupil of any age as to 'who' is the 'I' who is learning, and to what lasting end. Without sooner or later coming to recognise the relative precariousness of being, human capacity for self-deception translates more readily into delusions of grandeur.

Without engaging with the prospect of individual mortality, the opportunity to reflect on short- and long-term purpose in individual and collective life may well be delayed or dulled. Similarly, motivation, and the will to act, is less quickened than it might have been.

Children in their play already demonstrate their awareness of the transitory and of death. It is in the substance of rhymes and gestures from an early age. RE is able to work with this primal sense and to connect it with the stories and rituals that abound in religious tradition as making sense of the finitude that is involved. As the Nupe story from Africa has it: 'only the stones didn't have children and so they never die' (Beier 1960, pp. 58–9).

Such basic 'knowing in the bones' that is often communicated through story is also connected with a developing awareness of 'ought' at the centre of individual being. Though it may be too grand to tag this straightaway as 'conscience', the synoptic sense of being that accompanies more immediate knowledge and general awareness is fertile ground for growing both moral and religious insights, and with them an enriched humanity.

In the context of RE, boys and girls can be encouraged to explore their finitude in ways that heighten their sense of the specialness of human being. The awareness that emerges moves on ground which many would regard as both moral and religious. Therein too lie criteria for checking that any associated development is indeed enriching of humanity.

And so?

In conclusion, effective provision of Religious Education has much to contribute to the development of pupils. Its absence, or poor quality of provision, is by contrast likely to be genuinely debilitating. Opportunities to enhance both social and psychological maturity are significantly missed; instead the risks of individual hollowness and communal splintering are magnified. In a very real sense, personally, socially and politically, the world suffers underdevelopment from lack of genuine RE.

Questions

1 What trends can be identified as typical of children's social and psychological development?
2 Why are some people nervous about invoking references to religion in connection with educational development? How can they be professionally reassured?
3 What activities which are central to the religious traditions studied in the RE programmes of a particular school exemplify the significance of identifying with the needs and interests of others?
4 How might a teacher enable pupils in a particular age group to understand the respective claims and loyalties which arise from belonging to several different groups – the family, friends, the country, the European Community, and a world Religion?
5 What can be learned from the teaching of English and art regarding developing the pupil's sense of metaphor and the power of pictorial expression? Taking examples of some key words and images in any two religious traditions, show how they can be opened up in both literal and symbolic terms.
6 Examine with pupils several creation stories from different religious traditions. What 'why' question(s) are they asking? What are they wondering about? What are they wondering at?
7 By what criteria can good educational development be distinguished from its opposite?

9 Ethnography and Religious Education

Eleanor Nesbitt

RE teachers stand to benefit from insights arising from ethnographic studies of faith communities. That is the contention of this chapter which first outlines ethnography and then addresses two questions: how does current ethnographic research influence our understanding of what constitutes a religion? And, what are the repercussions of this for resourcing Religious Education and, more fundamentally, for religious educationists' methodology? In answering this second question we will note the implications of ethnography both for conceptualising religion and for pedagogy. As religious educationists we need to realise that there is a big difference between the lived experience of many who identify as Buddhists, Hindus, Muslims and Sikhs and the 'Buddhism', 'Hinduism', 'Islam' and 'Sikhism' as packaged and presented in RE.

This realisation is unsettling, and can add to a teacher's insecurity. Instead, it must be allowed to empower us, so that we are less likely to feel threatened by discovering from our Buddhist, etc., pupils that what is central to curriculum Buddhism is unfamiliar to them, and that much of their own experience is missing from these materials.

The chapter suggests the value for RE teachers of (a) reading published studies of communities, of (b) becoming alert to the key issues of representing and interpreting others' worldviews, and of (c) ourselves conducting studies, however small in scale. Field studies suggest that RE can influence some pupils' identification with a particular 'religion' as well as their understanding of it. Besides providing data for producing, or at least critiquing, curriculum materials, ethnographic research suggests principles for enhancing pedagogy, in both primary and secondary phases, through adopting an interpretive (or interpretative) approach.

Ethnographic research

Ethnography – literally nation (or people) writing – has several overlapping meanings. The term is used for a qualitative style of social research which relies mainly upon field studies consisting of in-depth interviewing and (above all) participant observation (Hammersley and Atkinson 1995). Although ethnography ideally – and some would say necessarily (Stringer 1999: 43) – entails prolonged immersion in the community concerned, I am using ethnography here to include smaller scale qualitative studies too – such as the field studies that MA students, most of whom are full-time teachers, conduct for an assignment. One can speak also of 'an ethnography' i.e. a report of a field study, usually in print, but also through other media such as film.

Increasingly scholars are questioning the distance between qualitative and quantitative methodology (the latter using, for example, large-scale questionnaire surveys which produce data in a form susceptible to statistical analysis) and suggesting the value of a complementary approach (Brannen 1992). For example, an ethnographic study may suggest hypotheses for testing by means of a larger scale piece of quantitative research, or the statistical findings of a quantitative study may provide a framework and perspective for a micro-study employing ethnographic methods.

For the purposes of this chapter, ethnographic research means field studies conducted not to test hypotheses or to produce generalisable results, but to provide 'thick descriptions' (Geertz 1973) of cultural activity. 'Thick description' refers to a way of reporting which involves layers of interpretation. It will include verbatim quotations from 'subjects', plus interpretative commentary upon these and discussion of themes emergent from analysis of the data as a whole. Ethnographers listen out for the 'grammar' of the culture in question, noting the relationship between constitutive elements: for example how a festival, or one detail of its observance, connects with both the total calendar and with celebration in this community generally. As another example, a boy's avoidance of eye contact with a female teacher would be misunderstood unless situated in the wider (e.g. South Asian) understanding of respect in the context of both gender and seniority.

So, ethnographers examine what individuals say and do with attention to the contexts for this behaviour; and in doing so they look at relevant publications both by spokespeople (e.g. from the same congregation or denomination or ethnic group) and by scholarly observers. Ethnographers must be on the alert for both similarities and differences between ways in which members of the community use terms, and for the conceptual distance or overlap between their own assumptions and those of the community that they are studying. As we shall be seeing, all this has implications for Religious Education practitioners.

Today's ethnographers are successors to nineteenth-century European folklorists and to those colonial administrators and their wives who kept enthusiastic records of their observations in, for example, rural India. They inherit a tradition of fieldwork skills deployed overseas before being honed by sociologists and social anthropologists who wanted to understand social patterns nearer home, in urban Britain. A late twentieth-century embarrassment at ethnography's colonial beginnings has stimulated theoretical debate concerned with the power imbalance between those who are subjects of research, on the one hand, and the researcher, on the other hand, who exercises power not only by carrying out the fieldwork but also by reporting and so representing the subjects in the public domain. Feminist critiques have also contributed to debate about the processes involved in ethnography and awareness of its interactive nature. For more reflection on how the researcher and 'subjects' impact upon each other, and are changed by the experience, see for example Nesbitt (1998a: 110) and Nesbitt (1999a).

None of this should obscure the fact that all of us are already amateur ethnographers every day in our homes, classrooms, staff rooms, congregations or other membership groups. This is because we are mixing with people and so talking, listening, participating in activity and observing it, noticing patterns of behaviour and anomalies, forming and revising judgements and reporting to others, in ways they can relate to, what we have experienced. All these activities – if carried out methodically, purposefully and rigorously – are the basics of an ethnographer's tool-kit.

The impetus for the present chapter comes primarily from the experience of nearly twenty years of ethnographic research in what is currently the Warwick Religions and Education Research Unit (WRERU) in the Institute of Education at the University of Warwick. The year 1984 marked the start of a series of eight ethnographic studies directed by Professor Robert Jackson (summarised in Nesbitt 2001). To give one example, in 1995–6 I interviewed twenty-two young Hindus in depth. In age they ranged from 16 to 23, and all had family roots in the Indian states of Gujarat and Punjab. These young people had (when aged 8 to 13) been the focus of two earlier studies (Jackson and Nesbitt 1993 and Nesbitt 1991, respectively). The 1995–6 study explored their perceptions of, and relationship with, the Hindu tradition. I examined the twin themes of religio-cultural continuity and change with particular reference to (among other aspects) their dietary attitudes and practices (Nesbitt 1999b) and their sense of identity as British, Asian and Hindu (Nesbitt 1998b). This included their feelings about caste membership (Nesbitt 1997). Their 'beliefs' – or at least their evolving ideas and hunches – and the impact of a visiting religious celebrity, Morari Bapu, provided related strands in this enquiry (Nesbitt 1999c and 2001).

In addition to this series of studies our graduate students at Warwick have contributed to WRERU's experience of ethnographic research. Field studies conducted by our MA in Religious Education and Ph.D. students have included several with a Muslim focus. Angelika Baxter's concern was Muslim secondary school pupils' attitudes to involvement in collective acts of worship in a Roman Catholic school. Julia Ipgrave's was primary school pupils' understanding of their faith (Ipgrave 1998, 1999), while Sissel Østberg's Oslo-based doctoral study of Pakistani Norwegians discerns processes at work in young Muslims' developing identity (2002).

WRERU's primary concern has been religious nurture, that is the processes of transmission and adaptation that constitute religious socialisation. A few ethnographers elsewhere have shared this focus, among them Nora Stene Preston, who has studied the religious nurture of Coptic Orthodox Christians in Cairo and London (1997, 1998). Her work has drawn attention to Coptic Christian perception of children as particularly like angels, and has also highlighted the changing relationship of Arabic, Coptic and English as languages for cultural transmission.

Of course ethnographic studies of religious socialisation are a sub-set of ethnographic studies (published and unpublished) of cultural continuity and change in Britain and elsewhere. From the ever-growing wealth of published studies of diasporic communities in the UK the collections edited by Burghart (1987) and by Ballard (1994) certainly need to be recorded, as significant pointers to the religious and cultural diversity within and between South Asian communities in the UK. Key factors are people's region of origin, their caste, migration history and spiritual allegiance.

Problematising 'religions'

It will come as no surprise, then, that these published studies offer religious educationists a mass of detailed information to fill out – and challenge – their existing knowledge of the faith communities concerned. As Ron Geaves has reminded us, the model of studying religions that has been adopted from traditional Christian scholarship is theology, textual criticism and history (1998: 23) and so, importantly, 'field studies attempt to restore the balance and provide a methodology that can move away from [this] model'.

At the same time, more challengingly for the RE teacher, even if the particular studies do not foreground religion, or the issues implicit in it, the reader is likely to start questioning the very framework within which Religious Education is conceived. This is because Religious Education syllabuses in the UK are based on six 'world religions' and these world religions are presented as discrete belief systems to which people adhere or at least as faith communities to which people belong. Religion is separated out from culture. What a reading of ethnography does is to make one wonder about how 'religion' relates to the other ways in which particular groups behave and identify themselves. One starts puzzling over the relationship between ethnicity and religion and the meaning of both. And how do culture and community overlap or intersect with ethnicity and religion? In Baumann's terms one is dealing with numerous cross-cutting cleavages (1999). Portraying these intersections at a micro level, as it does, ethnographic research precipitates theoretical debate about the very framework within which Religious Education is conceptualised. What is more, as we shall see, the separateness of one 'religion' from another comes to appear more and more suspect.

Robert Jackson has devoted a chapter of *Religious Education: An Interpretive Approach* (1997: 49–71) to the representation of religions. He traces the history of the concept of both religion and religions in European discourse and looks critically at the evolution of the term 'world religions'. He emphasises Edward Said's exposé of Orientalism – that is of the Western nations' exercise of power in not only labelling but also defining weaker groups (1978) – and he situates the naming of 'Hinduism' and 'Buddhism' at the beginning of the nineteenth century. Jackson also suggests that Wilfrid Cantwell Smith's preference for 'faith' and 'tradition' rather than 'religion' points a helpful way forward (Smith 1978), although he himself uses the term 'tradition' differently from Smith, and leaves 'faith' aside as a theologically loaded concept. Jackson goes on to suggest that in approaching the Christian tradition, the Jewish tradition and so on it is useful to employ a 'three-tier model'. This he envisages as a 'matrix', consisting of individual faith, membership group (such as denominational or ethnic categories) and tradition (1997).

So, to return to Gujarati Hindus, an individual in Bradford could be a devotee of Krishna, a Gujarati in terms of ethnicity, a *mochi* (shoemaker; see Knott's contribution to Ballard 1994) not by occupation but by *jati* (caste), a follower of ISKCON (the International Society for Krishna Consciousness) by *sampradaya* (a term denoting the followers of a line of gurus). To describe this person as simply Hindu is to overlook the reality that one is not a Hindu in a vacuum, but by virtue of membership of one or more of these groups. In this imaginary case the individual belongs to two of the groups (Gujaratis and *mochis*) by birth and may be an ISKCON follower not by birth but by decision as an adult. Her particular devotion to Krishna would probably be in line with her family's devotion over many generations or it might be more individual. Each of these constituencies may influence her day to day practice, such as her domestic *puja* (worship) and her family's life cycle rites, as well as her philosophical or theological understanding, her attitudes to other Hindu groups and so forth.

However, as Jackson would be the first to emphasise, ethnography challenges any over-simple application of this three-tier model. This is because real-life individuals often do not fit neatly like the smallest of a set of *madrioshka* dolls inside successively larger dolls (the membership groups and tradition or 'faith community'). One reason for this is that both groups and traditions intersect and overlap. For example, returning to the 'membership groups' of our imagined Gujarati, there are *mochis* (even if called by other regional language names) who are not Gujarati but hail from Uttar Pradesh or Tamil Nadu, and for that matter who identify themselves not as Hindu but as Christian or Muslim. Moreover ISKCON has followers from many parts of India, as well as from European and African families.

Also – at the 'tradition' tier of the model – even Hindu and Muslim are not always such distinct categories as we might assume. Ron Geaves has pointed out (1998: 22), quoting Oberoi (1994: 11), that in the 1911 census '200,000 Gujaratis declared themselves as Mohammedan Hindus'. Leaving identity aside, cultural norms that individuals often regard as religiously defined in practice sweep across any lines of religious demarcation. To quote Mary Searle-Chatterjee (in fact critiquing Jackson and Nesbitt 1993):

> Much of what is described in *Hindu Children in Britain*…would be equally true of Muslims and Sikhs of similar class backgrounds originating from the north and west of the subcontinent. Examples of this are the account of family roles and gender distinctions…
>
> (Searle-Chatterjee 2000: 503)

On the basis of fieldwork among Punjabis in the UK and north India, Geaves (1998) shows how problematic the boundaries that religious educationists often assume run uncontroversially between 'Hinduism', 'Sikhism' and 'Islam' are. Ballard's account of 'Punjabi religion' provides an insightful contextualisation in Punjabi society, which leaves the 'world religions' looking uncomfortably dislocated from the real world of healers and holy places (1999). My own study of religious socialisation among Coventrian Punjabis from two *jati*-specific congregations, the Valmikis and the Ravidasis, provides a local illustration of the arbitrariness of any Hindu/Sikh boundary when applied to the experience of members of the two most stigmatised communities in Punjab, who have suffered discrimination at the hands of both Hindus and Sikhs, but whose religious terminology and ritual practice consist of elements (such as worship in a gurdwara or worshipping Mata, the divine mother) that are associated by religious educationists with either one 'faith' or the other (Nesbitt 1991).

In addition to exposing the complex relations between individual, membership group and tradition, our WRERU studies disclose something of the dynamics at work which manifest in appearances of religio-cultural continuity and change. Examples of this concern food and fasting, individuals' principles, preferences and practices (Nesbitt 1999b) and their assumptions about gender roles and spouse selection. The endlessly diverse patterns of innovation, compromise and conservativeness, within a single lifespan as well as from generation to generation within a family, make statements that 'Hindus believe this' or 'Muslims do this', let alone 'all Sikhs believe or do…' palpably untrue.

Let us shift our attention away from the apparent syncretism of Punjabis, and of South Asians more generally. In so doing let us remind ourselves that the (usually derogatory) term 'syncretism' itself springs from a viewpoint that assumes that religions either are or should be discrete. Turning to our increasingly globalised, post-modern society, first-hand observation and recurrent journalism (leave alone ethnographic study) highlight increasingly plural spiritualities insofar as individuals – consciously and unwittingly – combine elements which our textbooks relegate to particular 'faiths'. Increasing belief in reincarnation by people who identify themselves as Christians (Nesbitt 1993) and the growing influence of Buddhist insights, way beyond Buddhists, are two examples.

Ethnographers portray young people from migrant families, whose parental religion/culture differs from the majority's religion/culture in their present environment, as drawing skilfully upon a range of cultural resources. Identity itself is plural, and some ethnographers have stressed its situational character. In different situations our Gujarati cited above would identify more strongly than in others as Asian, British, middle-aged, professional, a Yorkshirewoman, as low-caste, Hindu, Vaishnava (that is a devotee of Vishnu, since Krishna is his avatar) either in solidarity with or in distinction from those around him. In preference to images of culture-clash or the language of 'biculturalism', Østberg argues for 'integrated plural identities' (2002), and it is helpful for religious educationists to think in these terms.

As I have illustrated (Nesbitt 1998b), the individual's identity is constructed through encounters and exchanges, and the narration of these to oneself and others. For example my young Hindu and Sikh interviewees related feelings of cultural Britishness when faced with their Indian-domiciled relatives in India or of Britishness as a civic identity when called racist names in the UK. The ethnographic interview – in-depth and unhurried – itself both discloses and facilitates identity formation.

Ethnographic evidence of the school's relation to nurture

Significantly for us as educationists, among my interviewees' narrations of identity formation were their accounts of conversations in school. It is salutary to realise that as teachers we ourselves contribute to pupils' construction of identity. The following quotations are not typical of large numbers of children, but I quote them because the fact that these instances arise at all should give teachers food for thought. In the first example the speaker is a Punjabi girl, whose family and caste community do not fit into a model that firmly distinguishes Sikhs from Hindus:

> First I used to say [my religion] was Indian, but then my teacher told me that it's not really Indian, it's Sikh. So I start sort of saying, 'It's Sikh'.
>
> (Nesbitt 1991: 31)

A second Punjabi girl told me:

> I just found that I'm Hindu; well my mum told me because this teacher said, 'Are you a Hindu?' and I said, 'I don't know', so she said, 'Go and ask your mum and tell me.' And when I told her the other day she said, 'OK' and she wanted to know about Divali.
>
> (Jackson and Nesbitt 1993: 162–3)

Research interviews indicate that in addition to suggesting – as well as reinforcing – religious labelling, teachers provided content for the relevant religious packages. Karma, caste and reincarnation were Hindu 'beliefs' that young people, who identified themselves as Hindu, mentioned having heard about in RE lessons on Hinduism (Nesbitt 1998a).

At the same time, teachers' reinforcement of a particular orthodoxy, for example, an influential Sikh view that to be Sikh means to be Khalsa Sikh (i.e. observing a discipline that includes keeping five signs of commitment), may marginalise the many Sikh pupils for whom being Sikh does not involve the maintenance of the five Ks, or even an aspiration to do so. It was from her concern at a teacher telling her own son that he was not a Sikh that RE co-ordinator Surinder Lall devoted a Farmington Fellowship term to setting out the diversity within Sikh society (Lall 1999).

What pupils learn and the way in which they learn at school are sometimes dissonant with their experience of their traditions at home or in their worshipping community. On the basis of her Masters field study in Leicester, Ipgrave discusses a teacher's explanation of *wudu* (required ablution before praying) as 'symbolic of inner purification' in relation to the Muslim pupils' understanding of it as a practical necessity, and the teacher's explanation of the open-handed prayer posture as representing 'openness to God' in contrast to the Muslim pupil's knowledge that it was to support an angel on each hand (1999: 151–2).

Implications of ethnography for RE

Clearly, what we do in RE can have formative effects on individual pupils. We need to acknowledge our responsibility, without letting this frighten us. The implications of ethnography for RE include the ways in which reading field studies may change our approach as well as the impact on our teaching of conducting our own field study, and even the effect of simply adopting an ethnographic stance. By this I mean, in true anthropological style, making the mental effort to make the familiar strange (as well as to make the strange familiar). You may have come across my colleague Robert Jackson's exercise for pupils: as a visiting alien to planet earth they report back to base what British earthlings would recognise as a Christmas tree in a living room, with children putting presents around its tub (Jackson 1989: 4–5). This exercise makes us more aware of the levels of understanding that we take for granted in familiar contexts and the need for us and our pupils to take steps to understand what is equally familiar to someone else.

Resources

Ethnographic studies can produce data on which curriculum materials (such as the Warwick RE Project; see Jackson 1997: 104–20) are then based. Judith Everington has reflected upon the issues involved in this process, requiring as it does sensitive negotiation between community members (and their 'leaders'), publishers and teachers (1996a). Among the contributing ethnographer-writers on the Project team were a Warwickshire primary schoolteacher, Margaret Barratt (1994a, 1994b, 1994c, 1994d and 1994e for Key Stage 1), an RE Adviser, Jo Price (see Barratt and Price 1996a, 1996b for Key Stage 2) and a Leicester secondary teacher, Elizabeth Wayne (see Wayne *et al.* 1996 for Key Stage 3). Some teacher fellows (funded by the Farmington Institute for Christian Studies) have spent their term in the Institute producing materials on the basis of interviewing and participant observation. For example Ruth Lambert, a primary schoolteacher from Leicester, prepared materials for presenting Sikh tradition as part of the national literacy strategy (Lambert 2000).

We are not all in the position to produce published materials. But at the most basic level ethnographic studies (our own and other people's) provide data against which curriculum material can be checked for balance and omission. They provide a corrective to writers' tendency to generalise; for example Watton's generalisation to other Hindu temples of what is distinctive of one particular Swaminarayan temple (1996).

Critical awareness

As teachers we will be more and more wary of resources using the terms Judaism, Buddhism and so on rather than speaking of Jews, and Buddhists (or, rather, 'some Jews' or 'many Buddhists') or of the Jewish and Buddhist traditions.

RE materials frequently present principles as the norm, or do not make it sufficiently clear that there is a distinction. My studies among gurdwara-going Sikh families found no child with the five Ks, and few with even the two most frequently maintained Ks (*kara*, steel bangle, and *kesh*, uncut hair), yet few books or schools television programmes make this clear. In the Sikh case, as I have elaborated elsewhere (e.g. Nesbitt 2000), ethnographic immersion alerts one to the mismatch between some curriculum books' presentation of 'Sikhism' and lived reality. This mismatch arises from, for example, suggesting that caste was a Hindu system that was actually overthrown by the Gurus. In fact the Gurus' insistence that one's social status was irrelevant to the likelihood of attaining liberation from the cycle of rebirths, and their establishment of all-caste institutions, namely the Khalsa and the *langar*, did not result in many marriages occurring across caste divides or in the weakening of caste-based stereotyping. Similarly curriculum books portray the five Ks as general to Sikhs – children included – rather than as part of a code to which only initiates into the Khalsa are fully committed. In other words, principles (or particular understandings of them) are presented too often as norms, so leaving teachers and pupils with a distorted impression of how things actually are.

Ethnography cautions us to be on the lookout for the positioning of the author. In what ways is he or she an insider or an outsider? What is his/her agenda as an educationist, as a writer, as a person with a particular cultural and religious background and stance? Articulating the concern of fellow academics, Mukta's condemnation (1997) of Prinja (1996) was salutary in alerting some religious educationists to the dangers of naiveté in accepting a spokesperson's representation and to political complexities and passions of which they had been unaware. In this instance a mainstream Religious Education publisher had published a book conveying the perspective of a particular Hindu organisation, when most readers would lack the background knowledge of Indian politics to be able to contextualise the author's stance.

Of course spokespeople – 'leaders', representatives on SACREs, authors of books – will make statements which have particular political and theological backgrounds. We can feel daunted by the near-impossibility of becoming informed about the history and social dynamics of so many communities. Here the message from the practice of conducting field studies is: carry on hopefully with an open mind, noting down clues to processes at work, for example, from news of the Hindu right-wing parties in India or of competition between Islamic states. Recognise that our own understanding will change, expand, be challenged, and that in recognising that we ourselves are learning we can support this approach in pupils.

Just as the ethnographer is alert to the idiom and vocabulary of individuals and groups, so as teachers we can become more aware of the issues at play. What is the linguistic history and conceptual content of 'God' in statements (made by many Sikhs) that 'we have ten gods' (Nesbitt 2000)? I suggest that on most occasions they use 'God' interchangeably with 'Baba'. This is a term of respectful affection which Sikhs use for the ten Gurus and for living spiritual masters. When some Sikhs refer to *amritchhakana* as 'being baptised', or refer to the *granthi* as a priest, we educationists need to be clear as to why might we decide to echo this usage or to challenge it?

Ethnography suggests, for all practitioners the value of triangulation, of checking – and of encouraging children to check – one book with another, and what books say with what individuals say, without necessarily privileging one source over another. This is not to say that if an individual speaks, say, of the Guru Granth Sahib containing the compositions of all ten Gurus, and a book (rightly) states that the Guru Granth Sahib contains the words of only six of the ten, we pronounce these sources as equally accurate, since statements about the authorship of the Guru Granth Sahib can be checked. If we approach texts critically ourselves, we are better equipped to foster our pupils' skills of investigation and analysis in RE.

Syllabus requirements result in RE teachers – especially at Key Stage 4 – equipping pupils to answer questions on the response of the world faiths to ethical dilemmas. Since the agenda, featuring as it does abortion, euthanasia, etc., has been set in western terms, and arises from twentieth-century anxieties, unsurprisingly there are few clearcut directives in any of the world's scriptures. Simply adopting an ethnographic stance in the community that the teacher knows best (English middle class, Irish Catholic or whatever) reveals the pressures such as 'keeping up with the Joneses' which actually dictate behaviour more often than e.g. Biblical directives. Yet, in presenting the 'faiths' of communities other than one's own it is easy to slip into relying on what (as mediated by, for example, a curriculum book writer) the Guru Granth Sahib or the Bhagavad Gita says. Ethnographic research (e.g. Shaw 2000) reminds us of the imperative of *izzat* (reputation, family honour) which is at least as reliable a clue to South Asian Muslim behaviour in a given situation as Qur'anic verses.

Pedagogy

More importantly than providing data for producing resources, or enabling us to check existing resources, ethnographic experience – even at second hand – has implications for how our pupils learn. The Warwick RE Project's fundamental pedagogical tool – encouraging pupils to 'build bridges' between their own experience and that of others – is the interpretative or interpretive approach of ethnographic research. To engage with this approach you are strongly recommended to read Jackson (1997). An example would be enabling pupils to bridge between preparing for an important event in their

6 Should RE teachers be defining boundaries or defying them? (For example should they be (a) reinforcing the separateness of our RE syllabuses' 'Hinduism', 'Buddhism' and 'Sikhism', or (b) challenging these boundaries, e.g. by helping pupils to understand that from a widespread Hindu point of view Buddhists and Sikhs are part of the Hindu tradition? Should we be encouraging pupils to draw ideas from different traditions for their own 'faith'?)

7 How best can we enable pupils to understand factors in the power of the observer in representing traditions in particular ways? (Factors would include the particularity of an individual's experience and the selectivity of any published account.)

own lives and one Roman Catholic boy, Paul's, preparations
tion (Everington 1996b: 32). Coupled with the bridging
helping pupils to relate parts of a tradition to the bigger wh
to connect Nathan's congregation's experience of the Hol
narrative of Pentecost in the Acts of the Apostles (Everingt‹
with the Christian tradition.

Of course this is not the only approach to use in RE – but i!
tion to the teacher's pedagogical kit. Individual practition‹
further. For instance our MA student, Dave Bennett, a second‹
member of an evangelical congregation in Leicester, explored
pupils to use his own Christian experience as a resource. Julia
about the different 'starting points' that make sense in a M
from, say, a class of pupils with no religious affiliation (1999)
has explored in detail the ways in which primary school RE
that pupils' knowledge is constructed through processes of
been facilitated by the teacher. The opportunities which
carefully prepared interfaith dialogue by e-mail, in her case
pupils in a Muslim majority school and a Roman Catholic sci

Conclusion

JC

I have argued that Religious Education stands to gain
ethnographers, and that there is benefit for the subject if
dip their toes into ethnographic study of religion-relatec
level field studies have challenged the whole framewor
another, both by reading reported research and by condu
study, ethnography enables us to appraise resources m
reveals that as teachers we affect what it is that
Importantly, an interpretative approach can inform our ‹
articulate principles that have long been embedded in goc

Questions

1 What community or issue in my experience would I s
   field study if I had the time? What would be my prac
   related reasons for this selection?
2 What are the problems with 'world religions' as
   syllabuses?
3 As an RE teacher (using my school's RE resources)
   apply any insights from the ethnographic approach?
4 In what ways can an ethnographic approach bene
   mented by other approaches?
5 How do you present a faith when you have pur
   concerned in the class?

10 Not 'either-or', more a case of 'both-and'

Towards an inclusive gender strategy for Religious Education

Dinah Hanlon

Educational inequality

Equality of opportunity and gender equality are issues of social, economic and moral importance, they concern society as a whole and have particular significance for those of us involved in education and in teacher training. In considering the implications of gender equity issues it is helpful to consider the ways that the feminist critique of education gave rise to, and fuelled, equality reforms. The causes of inequalities have historically been conceptualised separately within education. This has led to a failure to take account of the myriad ways that ethnicity, class and gender intersect. In turn, this 'fragmented' approach contributed to the development of different phases, with differing emphases and concerns, within policy formation and reforms.

Equality of opportunity is a vital issue of social, economic and moral importance. In seeking to emphasise the links between educational inequalities and their impact on society, Gilborn and Mirza note that: 'If any individual is denied that opportunity to fulfil their potential because of their racial, ethnic, class or gendered status it is now widely understood that society as a whole bears a social and economic cost by being deprived of the fruits of their enterprise, energy and imagination' (Gilborn and Mirza 2000: 6).

One goal of an 'egalitarian educational agenda' is the creation of democratic, participatory forms of schooling at every level, which raises standards and academic performance. The achievement of this goal demands that all teachers recognise how inequalities, based on 'social class', 'race', 'gender', 'sexuality' and 'disability', are perpetuated through the educational structures, systems and individuals within schools. As Hill and Cole argue: 'we think it is important for students, teachers and others with an interest in the educational community to understand and be able to critique not only what is happening in schooling and the National Curriculum but also why it is happening, and arguments for changing it' (Hill and Cole 1997: 8). Such an awareness is dependent upon the development of a critically reflective stance, the questioning of political priorities and the values that underpin them.

Structural inequalities exploit and oppress individuals in many ways. Myers makes an important point by, in the following extract, emphasising that individuals have 'multiple identities' and do not experience inequalities and oppression uniformly:

> it is crucial to remember that women and girls, men and boys come in variety of guises. Women and girls are present in all ethnic and language groups and in all socio-economic classes. They are able-bodied or disabled. They exist throughout the ability range. They are heterosexual, lesbian, bisexual or celibate. They can be discriminated against for all these reasons as well as for being female. Men and boys are likewise not a homogeneous group and should therefore not be treated as such. Issues of equal opportunities inevitably interrelate...it is important not to look at them in isolation...and it is important to compare like with like.
>
> (Myers 1992: 2)

While inequalities, based on class, ethnicity, gender, sexuality and disability, can be separate and discreet, they are often experienced in a multiple sense by individuals.

Defining terms

Before moving on to consider the focus and changing emphases in gender reforms, it is necessary to define the terms feminism, patriarchy, sexism, sex and gender.

A broad definition of feminism suggests it as a form of opposition to any form of social, personal or economic discrimination which women experience because of their sex. However, two points are worth noting: first, it cannot be assumed or presumed that all women are feminists; and second, men are not necessarily excluded, by virtue of their sex, from being sympathetic to feminist causes. Feminist perspectives are polarised and can be positioned along a continuum from radical or revolutionary at one end, to liberal at the other, with a range of perspectives between the two.

Patriarchy, regarded by many feminists as the principal form of oppression, is the institutional system of male power and dominance over women. Sexism, which includes the belief that men are superior to women, is the ideology used by patriarchy to justify male dominance.

The distinction between the terms sex and gender is worth noting. Sex refers to the biologically given differences between females and males. The term gender on the other hand, refers to the cultural and social constructions of what it means to be a man or a woman. Understandings of sexual differences, interpreted through images, dress, behaviour and language, differ from one culture to another and change historically. In principle, while gender analyses can focus on both the experiences of boys and girls, historically feminist scholarship has focused mainly on concerns about the gendered experiences, and their consequences, for girls.

The passing of the 1988 ERA saw the introduction of a National Curriculum and established the notion of pupil entitlement to the 'broad and balanced curriculum relevant to his or her particular needs'. Whilst the notion of access can encompass equity, the interplay of issues of gender, class and ethnicity is not always recognised. Thus, equality reforms in education developed as separate responses to individual inequalities and emerged in a piecemeal fashion at different times. This resulted in quite distinctive anti-sexist, multicultural and anti-racist policies.

Concerns and emphases in gender reforms

Inequalities based on gender are reproduced through the family, peer pressure, the media and the education system, all of which perpetuate men and women's different experience and position in society. Feminist thinking, which arose out of successive women's movements, has been an influential catalyst in promoting gender reforms in society, the workplace and education. It contributed to the passing of anti-discrimination legislation, such as the Sex Discrimination and Equal Pay Acts and the establishment of the Equal Opportunities Commission. It has thus become possible to challenge discriminatory behaviour in the courts.

The feminist critique of education has been a key factor in fuelling concern about girls' differentiated experiences of schooling and the resulting educational, social and economic disadvantage. For example, gender differences in educational performance, pupil–teacher interaction, the hidden and overt curriculum have each generated considerable debate over the past thirty years. The research of Deem (1978 and 1980), Delamont (1980), Clarricoates (1981), Stanworth (1983), Weiner (1985) and Whyte (1986) highlighted that girls were disadvantaged at all levels of schooling and this has perpetuated the gendered division of labour in society. At LEA level, this research influenced educational policy development which again focused, almost exclusively, on girls, giving the impression that only the gender identity and experiences of women and girls was important (Adams 1986a, 1986b).

Initiatives, on subject choice and classroom interaction, advocating 'girl friendly schooling' developed. The *Genderwatch* Project (Myers 1992) advocated a whole school approach to strategies within both the formal and hidden curricula focusing on teachers' expectations, classroom management, pupil grouping, teacher time and subject choice. Intervention strategies, developed by Whyte (1986) and Walden and Walkerdine (1985), focused on subject competency. Interestingly, in assuming that equalising opportunities for girls in schools would result in greater equality for women, some of these strategies were potentially problematic. Many reforms failed to acknowledge that educational gender differentiation does not operate in a social or political vacuum.

The perceived effectiveness of gender reforms on girls' gains in examination performance has led to expressions such as 'girl power', 'girls on top' and television programmes such as *The Future is Female*. This suggests that concern about educational winners and losers has swung to the other extreme contributing to the development of gender reforms with an almost exclusive focus on boys' underachievement. Three concerns dominate the current educational agenda: first, boys are lagging behind girls in the development of early literacy skills (and later on in English); second, boys are performing less well than girls in GCSE examinations; and third, girls are still not opting for mathematics and sciences in the later stages of their educational careers. It is suggested however, that such perceptions oversimplify 'girl gains' as some analyses of performance between girls and boys does not take account of differences which show that improvements have not occurred uniformly, nor for all girls.

Towards an inclusive strategy

It would be a retrograde step if the present focus on boys' underachievement leads to a marginalisation of the needs of girls. Martin notes that 'women are still under-represented in the majority of jobs with any claim to status and responsibility...there are continuing inequalities of income' (Martin 1999: 114). In seeking to raise standards for all, it is argued that there is a continued need to translate commitment (so often expressed at a national level) into policy, proposals and practice at the local/school level.

From their overview of the current research into educational inequality, Gilborn and Mirza (2000) note that only a few schools have found ways of being equally effective for both sexes. They identify the following factors as being significant in realisation of inclusive education:

- strong leadership on equal opportunities and social justice
- seeking and using pupils' and parents' perspectives
- designing and enacting clear procedures for recording
- acting on racist incidents
- an ethos that is open and vigilant
- developing and communicating high expectations
- reviewing curricular and pastoral approaches
- using ethnic monitoring as a routine and rigorous part of the school's self-evaluation and management.

To summarise, inclusive education encompassing gender equality is an important issue with implications for schools and teachers. The importance of taking account of individuals' multiple experience of inequalities has been noted. Whilst early responses in gender reforms focused almost exclusively on girls, the perceived success of feminist reforms has given rise to an equality agenda with an exclusive male focus. However, three issues emerge as important: first, that there is still a need to maintain a commitment to gender and performance issues; second, this should be done in the context of inclusive strategies; and finally, inclusive approaches must remain sensitive to the findings of feminists.

Feminist critique of religions

In much the same way that feminist thinking acted as a catalyst to promote the development of gender reforms in education, the substantial body of feminist thought on religions has promoted thinking about gender issues within the context of RE.

In the following section, three main points arise out of a discussion of feminists' critique of religion: first, the critique is diverse in nature; second, the differing perspectives reflect differing concerns; and third, they can be conceptualised along a continuum ranging from reform-inclusive to radical-separatist. These points will be discussed before moving on, in the final section, to consider their implications within the context of RE.

Feminism and religion are issues with significance for contemporary life. As Morgan notes, 'Feminism, like religion, addresses the meaning of human identity and wholeness at the very deepest levels, drawing upon a wide range of interdisciplinary insights' (Morgan 1999: 42). The feminist critique of religions reflects a wide, and often opposing, range of political and personal ideological perspectives. The influential writing of Mary Daly perhaps best exemplifies the radical-separatist stance with its call for solutions outside patriarchal structures. In contrast, Rosemary Radford-Reuther adopts a reform-inclusive stance, regarding patriarchy as a misguided state, which can be reformed from within. The differing emphases within these perspectives (referred to as: reforming, rejecting, replicating and transforming) are briefly discussed below.

Reforming

Terms such as 'evangelical' and 'Biblical' define a perspective which suggests that the scriptural base (of, for example, Jewish and Christian religions) contains the message that women and men are created equal in the sight of God. This perspective proposes that the egalitarian message was suppressed and, whilst recognising that the religious systems, structures and written traditions are unjust, it accepts scriptural authority as 'feminist in intent'. This perspective regards it as necessary to work from inside to reform traditions, rediscover women's 'lost' history and liberate the original, 'authentic' message.

Rejecting

Liberationist, radical and socialist perspectives do not accept the notion of a lost egalitarian message. They concede that the Biblical texts are overtly patriarchal and male-centred, and argue that women have been intentionally 'written out' of scriptures. St Thomas Aquinas's well-known view of woman as a 'misbegotten male' is often quoted as an example of men's rejection of women as equals. Thus, the authority of scripture is rejected wholesale, as is the idea of reclaiming an egalitarian message. Instead, the emphasis is on the need to critique the male interpretation of religious experience, reclaim women's lost history from behind the text and affirm women's voices as separate and authoritative in themselves.

Replicating

Separatist or radical feminists aim to redress women's invisibility, marginalisation and subordination, by developing alternatives outside of patriarchal traditions. Some have drawn heavily upon female-centred religions, which existed in pre-patriarchal times but were later suppressed. These attempts to re-validate female experience of the divine have led to the replacement of male traditions with exclusive and distinctive female ones. The replication of a paradigm that replaces one form of oppression with another is however criticised by those wishing to create a comprehensive and inclusive faith for men as well as women.

Transforming

To some extent, the radical separatist position, with its tendency to reject, has alienated men and fuelled calls for transforming religious traditions along more inclusive lines. This view is evident in King's notion of a 'dialogical approach' (King 1988: 4) amongst religions and between men and women which, she argues, must extend beyond criticisms of patriarchy. However, it is equally important that inclusive approaches do not ignore the oppressive dimension of women's experiences because they too may become problematic. Morgan reflects that 'the extreme poles, from reform to radical...need to work towards an integrative paradigm of justice that does not lose sight of the specificity of women's situation' (Morgan 1999: 65).

Inclusive approaches must emphasise and value the different experiences of religions that men and women have. They have led to demands for inclusive language and women's right to participate in public religious roles. Generically male terms to denote all human beings and define experiences are rejected in favour of gender neutral language and the use of female imagery. Concerns for a reclamation of women's participation in, and their right of access to, public religious roles are recognised in calls for the ordination of women as ministers and rabbis. Such calls have not been without criticism or resistance, taken together however, such views have contributed to the large-scale re-examination of assumed knowledge of religions.

To sum up, these four perspectives do not represent a hierarchy, nor a progression of views. Religious symbolism, language, literature, history and doctrine have all come under scrutiny within the feminist study of religions. Though polarised, each perspective contributes something valuable towards a re-shaping of religions and to the content and teaching of RE. Taken as a whole, they demand that RE in primary and secondary schools celebrates women's lives, gives value to women's distinctive voices and makes more visible women's distinctive experiences of religion.

The implications of gender reforms for RE content and teaching

The implications of educational reforms and the feminist critique of religions are explored in this final section in relation to the content and teaching of RE. It is suggested that all those involved in education have an ethical, as well as a professional, role in seeking to understand and challenge the inequalities that are perpetuated in the process of schooling. In particular, teachers must consider their role as agents of change in the implementation of 'education for all'. This section concludes by emphasising that gender issues, as part of the broader picture of structural inequalities, are best conceptualised within an inclusive approach of equalising opportunities for all. Within the context of RE then, it is no longer a case of either-or, inclusive approaches must embrace both-and.[1]

Feminist critique, gender and RE

The differing emphases and orientations within the feminist critique have much to offer RE practitioners. For example, feminists drew attention to gender, as a category for analysing religions, revealing how patriarchal systems render women inferior and invisible. Their critique gave anchorage to the need for the development of a new pedagogy in RE teaching, i.e. the use of critical questioning to explore the causes of women's invisibility in religions. It challenges RE practitioners to eliminate gender differences and requires that teachers support pupils to explore women's contributions to religions in the light of their own experiences.

By calling for such a transformation in the classroom, RE teachers have been asked to confront dilemmas and deal with controversy, whilst remaining 'true' to the religious traditions themselves. This is not an easy task. The process is dependent upon good levels of knowledge and the confidence to use methods that facilitate critical explorations. For some RE teachers, dealing with critical reflection and controversy in classrooms may be regarded as an essentially 'anti-religious' process. Katalushi makes a useful point when he emphasises that agitation for gender equality cannot be separated from tension or opposing viewpoints. He maintains, however, that 'controversy is not necessarily anti-RE' and that 'there can be something creative about tension' (Katalushi 1998: 108). RE has an important role in presenting accurate and authentic understanding of the world's religions, requiring that teachers begin to question the nature of religious knowledge itself.

Aims and assumptions of RE

In common with all those working in education, RE practitioners have a professional responsibility to contribute to the realisation of a broad and balanced education for all, which simultaneously addresses issues of social justice and equality. The aims and concerns of RE, outlined in the SCAA

Model Syllabuses (1994) and reinforced in the QCA/DfEE schemes of work (2000), position it to contribute to this realisation. RE has an important role to prepare young people to live and function in a religiously pluralistic society, enabling them to learn about, and from, the different faith communities within it. Multifaith RE should promote intercultural understanding and sustain tolerance, a view reflected in official documentation (ERA 1988; DES 1988, Circular 3/89). As Skinner suggests, 'it is not unreasonable to hope that accurate teaching about the beliefs and practices of British religious minority communities might at least help to undermine the myths on which prejudice is built' (Skinner 1993: 63).

The notion of accuracy that underpins the realisation of gender equity implies that account is to be taken of the views and experiences of women. Slee (2000) and King (1995) have each suggested that the process of active engagement with plurality requires not simply tolerance, but the seeking of understanding whilst recognising and respecting genuine differences. From the outset of schooling, teachers ought to introduce and help young people to value the rich legacy, experiences and contribution that women have made to religious traditions and systems. As Skinner notes, RE should help students 'appreciate that the truth claims about the nature of God, the meaning of life and the hope of "salvation", which lie at the heart of religions, may not always be reconcilable' (Skinner 1993: 63). Contentious issues, including tensions within religions (for example, over orthodoxy and reform), as well as tensions between religions (for example, contested 'truth claims') need to be addressed by RE practitioners. RE teachers must go beyond the descriptive, beyond learning about religions (Attainment Target 1), and give space and time to learning from religions (Attainment Target 2). It is evident, however, that RE practitioners face additional problems and paradoxes.

Some RE problems and paradoxes

RE has a unique position in the curriculum of English and Welsh schools by virtue of its long history and compulsory nature. Its local implementation is arguably implicitly democratic with parents, teachers, faith communities, local councillors and LEA officers, through the Standing Advisory Council for RE (SACRE), all having an input. RE is a legitimate area of study. In the main it is taught by professionally trained teachers and its purpose is not to proselytise, convert, or deepen pupils' faith in any particular religion. By virtue of its content, RE is well placed to make a valuable contribution to the realisation of inclusive education. Paradoxically, a barrier to this realisation is the erosion of pupils' entitlement to a broad and balanced curriculum, as a consequence of the continued existence of the withdrawal clause. While justified in its historical context, the right of parents to withdraw their children, and teachers not to teach it on grounds of conscience, are problematic. The withdrawal clause 'is amongst factors which undermine the status of RE and leads to much confusion in the minds of experienced and trainee teachers' (Hanlon 2001: 26).

Other barriers identified in the 1998–9 Annual OFSTED Report (OFSTED 2000a) include insufficient time given for coverage of the Agreed Syllabus; low expectations; poor use of resources and poor planning. The legacy of impoverished experiences of RE at Key Stages 3 and 4 are amongst significant factors contributing to poor subject knowledge of many trainee teachers. The multiplicity of locally Agreed Syllabuses, with varying expectations of pupils' achievements, are further contributory factors that continue to 'dog' RE practitioners' lives in their pursuit of equality in the classroom.

The emergence of central support in the form of: exemplar schemes of work (QCA/DfEE 2000); non-statutory guidance for RE; and the production of an eight level scale of assessment, are beginning to have an impact in schools. OFSTED (2000a) has noted some improvement in RE teaching in primary schools, though it suggests secondary teachers have been slow to build on this, as too many assume pupils lack any knowledge of religions. Consequently, work of a low standard is prepared and much work previously undertaken in primary schools is replicated. This may be one of the factors which account for low pupil motivation at Key Stage 3. The lack of commitment on the part of senior managers continues to have a devastating effect on the marginalisation of RE.

Choice, performance and the gendered nature of RE

Having identified a number of barriers that perpetuate the marginalisation of RE it comes as no surprise that the overall numbers of pupils currently entered for examinations is significantly lower than most other humanities subjects. The DfEE/QCA (2001) acknowledges that gender-related subject choice remains fairly robust. So, for example, science, mathematics, technology, IT and PE continue to be rated as 'masculine' by pupils and preferred by boys, whereas English, humanities, music, PSE and RE tend to be rated as 'feminine' and preferred by girls. Whilst there is some evidence that pupils' subject preferences and choices are becoming less gender-stereotyped, girls still dominate the arts and humanities and boys still dominate the sciences, suggesting that patterns of entry have persisted.

Additional factors serve to perpetuate the low status of RE within the curriculum, including the devalued currency of religion in an increasingly secular society, and result in the perception that RE is a 'soft' vocational option. The fact that girls perform significantly better than boys possibly contributes to further reducing its attraction to boys. However, the issues of subject preference and performance are not exclusively 'RE' problems.

In Table 1 the patterns of entry for RE examinations during 1999–2000 are presented. This shows, as already discussed, that the differential between boys and girls opting for RE widens as the level of examination passes from GCSE (short) through to the 'A' level.

Table 1 Figures for RE 2000 in all maintained schools – reproduced from OFSTED *National Summary Data Report for Secondary Maintained Schools* (OFSTED 2000b)

Year 2000	Total All	Girls	Boys	% Girls	% Boys
GCSE (short)	127,674	65,484	62,188	51.3%	48.7%
GCSE (full)	86,253	51,092	35,161	59.2%	40.8%
AS level	1,111	692	419	62.3%	37.7%
'A' level	4,516	3,563	953	78.9%	21.1%

However, there may be some positive news when considering the entries for the GSCE short course, as shown in Table 2 below. First, when contrasted with other subjects, it is particularly encouraging to note the extremely high overall number (127,674) of pupils being entered for the RE GCSE short course. Second, and perhaps of greater significance to the current discussion, is that, at this level of examination course, the gender gap has been held between boys (49 per cent) and girls (51 per cent). If so, this is an encouraging inclusive trend, with a cause for some cautious optimism.

Gender issues within the context of RE

The feminist critique of education and religions revealed the need for practitioners to give serious consideration to choices concerning content and the development of a pedagogy consistent to the realisation of a gender-inclusive RE. A number of issues emerge as significant for RE practitioners and each will be briefly explored by way of concluding this chapter. First, it is suggested that RE teachers have an ethical, as well as a professional, responsibility to reveal

Table 2 Figures for all subjects entering students for GCSE short courses in all maintained schools – reproduced from OFSTED *National Summary Data Report for Secondary Maintained Schools* (OFSTED 2000b)

Subject	Number of 15 year-old pupils entered
Art & Design	2,859
Business Studies	147
Design & Technology	32,297
French	10,690
Geography	4,590
German	3,015
History	4,784
Information Technology	52,461
Music	643
Physical Education / Sports Studies	6,419
Religious Studies / Education	127,674
Spanish	1,509

the patriarchal bases in the world's religions which continue to constrain women's visibility. Second, the achievement of inclusivity requires a pedagogical stance that involves active engagement with difference. Third, RE teachers should strategically exploit the enormous flexibility within local agreed, and examination, syllabuses to consciously write women back into the RE curriculum by using story to teach about women's public and private roles. Finally, it is worth repeating that engaging in gender-inclusive RE, which challenges the status quo, is an activity open to the criticism of being anti-religious. RE teachers thus engaged will inevitably be taken outside of comfort zones into dynamic, but 'messier', RE territory where they will need to wrestle with, rather than find neat answers to, a whole range of paradoxes and dilemmas.

While RE teachers have a professional responsibility to be objective and maintain neutrality, they ought also to acknowledge the patriarchal bases in the world's religions. They thus have an ethical responsibility to challenge 'religious sexism by omission' and minimise their own complicity of unintentionally reproducing patriarchy through content choice and teaching. Telling the other part of the story and teaching about private, as well as public, aspects of men and women's experiences, ought to lead to a more accurate picture of the world's religions.

Second, setting the record straight requires that teachers adopt a pedagogical stance that encourages pupils' critical reflection of diversity. For some teachers this will need a fundamental shift away from straightforward or simplistic approaches towards the inclusion of a range of voices and views. Such a process ought to lead teachers to affirm women's diverse experiences, for example as religious teachers, founders, leaders, mystics, missionaries, prophets, judges, saints, martyrs or wise women. It should also result in validating women's ordinary day to day experiences as faith adherents, for example, acknowledging the important role of preparing the shrine in a Hindu home, or the pivotal role of the mother welcoming in Shabbat on a Friday evening in an Orthodox Jewish home. However, equally important is that such experiences should not be taken as somehow representative of all women's experience of these faiths. Respecting difference means that teachers will need to talk about the differences between men and women as well as between women and women.

Third, a key strategy for exploring women's diverse religious experiences as leaders, preachers and writers of texts is through the use of story and religious narratives. Story has long been used as a vehicle to provide insights into complex beliefs and truth claims and lies at the heart of world religions. The best stories operate on many levels simultaneously and can be retold to disclose something new and different each time. Trevett asserts that, by including women in the taught curriculum, RE teachers can automatically redress three serious omissions: that religion is influential in the lives of women; that women are active practitioners in religious celebrations and rituals; and that there are many faith heroines. She suggests that 'children need heroines of faiths and the knowledge that women, as well as men, have been writers, mystics and faithful observers of the day to day requirements of their religions' (Trevett 1983: 83). Story can be used to reveal contemporary public roles of women rabbis, priests and Buddhist nuns, as well as to retrieve some of the great women in religious history, such as Rabyiah, the Sufi founder, Deborah the Israelite Judge, or Mother Anne Lee, founder of the Shaker movement. The central role of story within RE cannot be overstated.

Recovering the rich traditions that contain many stories of women remains a key task for RE practitioners. Many teachers already help pupils to reflect upon the 'truths' within 'creation narratives', about how and why the world was created and the role of human beings in relation to the created order. The creation story in Genesis 1:1–12 which tells that Eve is created from Adam's rib has historically been used by the Jewish and Christian religious communities to justify, as God-ordained, women's inferior (or equal, but different) status in both traditions. A simple trans- mission of this creation story, without discussion, may unintentionally perpetuate patriarchy by suggesting it is the only, and therefore the true, account. It is not suggested teachers avoid exploration of this narrative, rather they should open up the discussion by exploring other versions (for example, Genesis 2) which convey different 'truths' about men and women. Teachers could also create relational and conversational settings in the classroom by focusing on women's experience as a primary subject within the narratives, i.e. help pupils to explore or re-tell accounts from Eve's or Lilith's points of view, or both. These are small, yet significant, shifts of emphases for RE teachers wishing to avoid collusion with patriarchy.

The act of writing women back into the content will not help to 'disprivilege patriarchy', if it is a tokenistic gesture. As Mantin notes, RE teachers must accept the dual challenge of presenting 'positive images of women whilst at the same time showing pupils ways in which stories have operated against women in the past by rendering them invisible' (Mantin 1997: 18). Stories have long been used by marginalised groups to promote visions of hope when claiming their right to equality. This can be seen, for example, historically in the amazing life of Sojourner Truth, former black American slave and Christian, or in more contemporary experiences of orthodox Jewish *agunot* (chained wives). King notes that, 'a story is like a seed sown, whose shoot if nurtured can provide grafting ground for the deeper understanding of those questions which lie at the heart of our existence' (King 1995: 163).

Finally, minimising complicity with patriarchy will take some RE teachers out of comfort zones into territories where paradoxes and dilemmas abound. Helping pupils towards an understanding of the dynamic, and changing, nature of religions, to appreciate the diversity in women's religious lives and then engage with current debates within religions, is no easy task. Whenever teachers begin to validate women's domestic religious roles, such as Sikh women's contribution to *langar* (the communal meal in the gurdwara), there will inevitably be tensions about women's invisibility from public religious roles. For example, Guru Nanak advocated equality between the sexes and religious liberation irrespective of gender, so why are Sikh women not seen reading the Guru Granth Sahib as 'Granthis'? At the classroom level, teachers may not easily be able to reconcile such tensions by simply asserting that women have an 'equally important' but 'different' religious role to men.

Engaging with difference will also raise tensions, not least because the act of respectful listening, and the validation of many voices, may itself be perceived as fundamentally anti-religious by mainstream or religious conservatives. Teachers will find that dealing with tensions and opposing viewpoints is a sometimes perplexing business as the following questions illustrate. Fourteen centuries ago women's rights and dignities were restored in Islam, so why is it that many Muslim women today deem themselves to be oppressed? Why is it that the very qualities for which Mary is honoured among Roman Catholic, Anglo-Catholic and Orthodox Christians, i.e. as 'virgin' and 'mother' of Jesus, are also those used to problematise female sexuality and non-virgin motherhood? Why are women's roles in Orthodox and Liberal Judaism fundamentally so different? Why is the ordination of women as priests supported in some parts of the Christian church and not in others? An exploration of such questions is perhaps better facilitated when the voices of faith adherents, who are themselves engaging in the debate and reassessing the role of women, are heard. Pupils' encounter with such questions should lead to a wider appreciation of the dynamic nature of religions and help them to develop their own informed stance on gender issues within the wider context of the society in which they live.

Calls for inclusive and conciliatory approaches amongst religions, and between men and women, powerfully support the central theme suggested in the title to this chapter. To realise this, RE teachers must move beyond criticism of patriarchy and adopt a dialogical approach, 'where listening, according equal recognition and respect to others are important features' (King 1988: 4). Inclusive and dialogical perspectives require RE practitioners to take account of the feminist critique of religions and comprehend different dimensions of inequalities that shape the experiences, not only of women, but also of men. They require teachers to consider the quality of relationships in their classrooms, the hidden curriculum of expectations and to question assumptions that perpetuate gender-specific choices. RE content and pedagogy without such breadth or balance will impoverish the experiences and life chances of boys as well as girls.

Questions

1 Is the future really female or has the gender challenge been reversed in education and RE?
2 Are girls equal beneficiaries and participants in the education system?
3 Have teachers done all possible to eliminate factors that hinder the access, progression and accomplishment of girls and boys?
4 Why have feminist calls to integrate women's experiences into RE impacted only slightly on RE content and pedagogy?
5 Will 'writing women back in' help to achieve a more inclusive RE?

Note

1 This sentiment was taken from an article by Heyward (1979).

11 Religious Education and pupils with special educational needs

A dialogue

Lynne Broadbent and
Alan Brown

Introduction

'Three middle aged men came into the church one Sunday morning. They sat down together and as the service got underway one of them began to genuflect and cross himself – not in the correct places – with an intensity borne of familiarity. As the time approached to go forward to the altar rail to receive the bread and wine, I asked the church warden if the three men were also being encouraged to go forward. "I don't think so", he said. I ignored him and told the three of them to approach the altar rail. As I waited my turn, the man who had been crossing himself so fervently stood up to return to his seat. He caught my eye, gave me a thumbs-up sign and in a loud voice said "Great".'

The story above reflects some of the issues that arise when religion, or at least the practice of it, meets people who may have a variety of special educational needs. Indeed, the average congregation in church, mosque, gurdwara or any religious group setting will normally include the wide spectrum of humanity. In this chapter we want to explore where some of those crossing points between religion, Religious Education and the needs of pupils who have special educational needs can provide an insight into providing better quality RE for all in schools. The chapter will also refer to the concept of progress in Religious Education and how this concept can be applied to pupils with special educational needs whether they be in special schools or in mainstream schools; and while the chapter cannot identify strategies for differentiating each and every scheme of work in LEA agreed syllabuses, case studies of activities that have provided access for special needs pupils in various Key Stages and schools have been identified. There will need to be some broad generalisations made about religion for, like education, it is a huge, amorphous and sprawling area of study, as diverse as the variety of special educational needs.

Religions all have, in the main, some academic, philosophical or theological rationale. Behind the daily or weekly practice, there is a thoughtout ideology regarding the universe, the world and how each person and each social group functions within that context. Religions, generally, help their followers to identify and live within a sense of place and time, both historical and spatial. The great thinkers, Aquinas, al-Ghazali, Sankara, Gautama and others, provide an interpretation of events and teaching that create frameworks within which there can be a variety of religious belief and practice, even within one religion or philosophy. Most devout, regular worshippers will not be familiar with the philosophies and theologies that underpin their actions or their faith. They normally follow a pattern of ritual, behaviour and belief that is learned, and having been learned becomes familiar, comfortable and comforting; the pattern also becomes an authentic response to religious need. Religions are multi-sensory, conveying profound beliefs through a range of rich symbolism relating to sound, sight, smell, taste and touch. They are not designed solely for the 'brightest and best' but for all, regardless of intellectual aptitude or physical ability. An individual devotee or follower may not feel able to change the world but through rites and rituals, familiar prayers and mantras, as well as feeling 'at home' within their surroundings, they believe they have a place in the great scheme of things, whatever they may understand that to be.

In speaking about pupils with special educational needs we are addressing a wide range of pupils and needs. One of the great challenges for teachers is how they can meet the diverse and distinctive needs of such pupils. The Government's policy of greater inclusion has meant that in any classroom there will be a demanding range of pupils with special educational needs all requiring support and stimulation. There will be pupils with learning difficulties but there will also be pupils with a physical disability: there will be pupils who exhibit challenging behaviour when confronted with under-challenging tasks; and, of course, there will be gifted and talented pupils too.

Edwin Cox (1983: 39–41) suggested that certain basic awarenesses or sensitivities were a prerequisite to understanding a religious response to experience and that without possession of some or all of these awarenesses, the study of religion would be meaningless or incomprehensible. Cox identified these awarenesses or sensitivities as follows:

1   A sense of mystery in life.
2   A sense of continual change.
3   A sense of relationship to, and dependence on, the natural order.
4   A sense of order in what we experience.
5   A realisation that there are other persons in the universe.
6   A sense of right and wrong.

These sensitivities are essentially common human experiences. Cox's thesis that they need to be experienced before one can make sense of religion may be disputed but the sensitivities themselves raise some interesting issues.

First, these sensitivities are clearly reflected in religion itself and point towards the key concepts that underpin the teaching of Religious Education in schools. For example, a sense of mystery and sense of continual change can be experienced both in a personal sense with those changes marked in religion as rites of passage and experienced in the natural world with festivals such as the harvest festivals. A realisation that there are other persons in the universe relates to an experience of interpersonal relationships and community, an essential feature of religion, while a sense of right and wrong raises questions about values and belongs to a developing sense of oneself in relation to others and the wider world and has obvious links with authority in religion.

Second, these sensitivities are reflected in the aspects of the 'spiritual' identified by SCAA (1994). A sense of awe and wonder, of relationship with the natural world and of relationship or community with others are three of the eight aspects cited.

Third, some of these sensitivities are reflected in a recent QCA document (QCA 2001: 4) which suggest that RE can offer pupils with learning difficulties opportunities to 'understand the world they live in as individuals and as members of groups', 'reflect on and consider their own values' and 'deal with issues that form the basis for personal choice and behaviour'.

So are there basic sensitivities which are prerequisites for the understanding of religion, and can these be introduced to and comprehended by pupils with special educational needs? Religions themselves differ internally and some may lend themselves more easily to Cox's sensitivities than others. Some may lend themselves to some at different times in their history while others may have an endemic leaning to one or more of his 'awarenesses'. Cox's analysis does reflect a western view of religion and is applied less comfortably to religions that arose in the East.

The Education Acts 1993 and 1996 require staff in special schools to provide RE for all their pupils wherever practical. 'Every pupil attending a special school will, so far as is practical, attend collective worship and receive religious education unless the child's parents have expressed a wish to the contrary. It is for schools to decide what is practicable but, in general terms, the Secretary of State would expect the question of practicability to relate to the special educational needs of the pupils and not to problems of staffing or premises', is the guidance given in the accompanying circular.

Staff are free to construct a programme of Religious Education based upon a rich diet of experiences linked to common human experiences and grounded within religion itself. The experiences might be broadly grouped around the concepts of community, change and celebration, and right and wrong.

Religion and communities

The European Enlightenment and the Reformation in northern Europe (unlike the earlier Islamic Enlightenment) encouraged the remorseless rise of individualism. The corporate nature of society was challenged, theologically and philosophically, with much greater emphasis placed on the individual holding the keys to salvation (however that was understood). This contrasted with the strong authoritarian, hierarchical and patriarchal community base of some Christian groups such as the Roman Catholic Church and the Orthodox Churches. Islam has a very strong sense of community (endorsed and encouraged in its own Enlightenment of the eleventh and twelfth Christian centuries), as does Judaism, although there is a wide variety of Jewish practice. Sikhism and Buddhism too have strong communal roots in the Khalsa and the Sangha, while the vast range of religious and cultural activity and belief that is called Hinduism has a firm base in community activity.

One example of such activity in the Christian religion is the L'Arche community founded by Jean Vanier in 1964. It seeks to be guided by God and by the weakest members. Its aim is to create communities which welcome people with a mental handicap, seeking to reveal their particular gifts. The communities of L'Arche want to be in solidarity with the poor of the world, and with all those who take part in the struggle for justice. Frances Young, writing in *Encounter with Mystery*, says: 'what really makes us human is our capacity to ask for help, and that challenges modern claims to autonomy. Community means you never suffer alone' (Young 1997: 169–70). She also provides some food for thought for those who regard religion as the means to the solving of problems when she writes: 'Christianity is not problem-solving but mystery-encountering' (1997: 166), a deep reflection that may well be true for all religions as well as having a message for those who teach Religious Education to pupils of all abilities.

One aspect, then, of educating pupils about religion should be to help them understand and experience the power and importance of community. It is essential for the religious education of pupils of all abilities to identify the key elements of community if effective teaching is to take place. So, starting from the school itself, can the school provide a model community into which all pupils are welcomed for what they can offer to the community? Schools, like religions, are made up of people with a variety of special educational needs; if the school community is not inclusive, accepting difference and diversity, the model for teaching about religion will be difficult to explore. Communities are understood by living in them, by feelings and emotions, not simply through cerebral activity.

Religions, at one level, have a role for everyone; there are those who lead, those who participate through song or mime, those who are given a role and those who simply are there. All are part of the community through their presence, for whatever abilities one has, all are engaged in being part of the whole community: and the very presence of each person contributes to the wholeness of the complete community. The welcoming of the new member of the Church at baptism; hearing the shofar blown at Rosh Hashanah; raising one's hands over the flame on the *puja* tray to receive a blessing all contribute to the activity of the community. Where some pupils can find a difficulty is when stories are read in class, or in the religious community, which tell of a healing miracle, in the case of Christianity. This will raise questions as to why they or members of their family are not healed, and if they are not healed does this make them outsiders, unaccepted and unacceptable within the community?

The concept of community is central to religion. Good RE teaching has to introduce pupils to the importance of community, recognising that there are different models of community within religions but the basic community within which the pupil functions (outside the family/care unit) is the school. How does the school/RE department plan for special educational needs (SEN) pupils? Are the requirements of pupils with SEN at the heart of curriculum planning, school design, disposal of funds and so on, or are they fitted in around the periphery of planning – a necessary but unfortunate add-on?

Religion has wrestled with these problems with varying degrees of 'unsatis-factoriness', from the argument that says 'God made you like that' through the 'God is punishing you/your parents for present/past evil', on to, 'This is the penalty for imperfect living in a previous life'. Religions have a tendency to attribute difficult issues to being part of 'God's, or some Ultimate Being's plan'. A more positive approach is to help all pupils identify religion as being 'mystery-encountering'. Religions will always have dogmatic individuals who praise and condemn with the absolute certainty of egocentricity, yet at the heart of all religion is mystery. Religious Education should help with SEN pupils:

- to engage with the mystery of beliefs and practices;
- to explore the blurred edges of people's lives in relation to religion;
- to be aware that feelings are as important as dogmas in everyday religious practice.

Of course some religions, mainly in the western tradition, can promote dogmatic certainty but human beings grapple with the vagaries and mysteries of life on a daily basis. Good RE recognises this and should be presenting the rich-ness and reality of human experience to pupils to engage them in the mystery – the myth of what it is to be a human being.

Change and celebration

In a recent article published just before his death, Ninian Smart encouraged religious educators and thinkers to take up the challenge of science, to set aside anxieties and 're-feel the universe'. The affective aspect of religion, so impor-tant in the teaching and learning of many pupils with SEN, continues to be the poor relation in RE teaching, though in recent years some RE syllabuses have made a real effort to cater for such pupils. The two attainment targets model, produced by SCAA and promoted by QCA remain flawed, even though accepted by many LEA RE syllabuses, because the AT2 – 'learning from' – cannot focus directly on religion nor can it be assessed effectively in spite of some helpful support from QCA. The AT2 model follows the promotion of the Model Syllabuses (in 1994) that are so content-laden as to ignore any affective aspect of religion. These have now been given official sanction to form an essential part of initial teacher education, even though they were never intended to be actual syllabuses nor are they structured as Agreed Syllabuses in RE; they take no account of the affective, and their content-laden approach makes it much more difficult to apply them to the needs of SEN pupils. Religious faith is largely about feelings and emotions; it is multi-sensory and engages the follower at all levels. The effective learning process cannot be assessed in traditional ways, if at all except through joy, love of learning, wonder, excitement and so on. 'To help pupils understand religion' should be the one attainment target. This would allow teachers to explore the affective, sensory aspect of religion without squeezing it into assessment profiles and meeting content-laden syllabuses.

Smart was very influential in the development of Religious Education in the 1970s and 1980s because he tried to encompass the way in which religion touched the seminal events of so many peoples lives. His phrase 're-feel the universe' complements Cox's 'awarenesses' through recognising that religion is about change and tradition; it is in this paradox that pupils can acquire some insight into how religion has a place and a function in society.

Change is marked in traditional ways: through acknowledging the seasons, through birthdays, through religious and national days. It is ironic that the act of remembering, of bringing the past to life, is written into the fabric of society, yet it is given life through the changing needs of society itself.

Learning about the rites of life and sharing in them are a marker for change. It may be that a young person attends a wedding or a funeral or is baptised and enters into a 'new' community but on each occasion the old is tempered with the new. In each event the key element is the experience of the people involved. At the heart of such experiences lie the feelings of the person. At one bar-mitzvah the sense of belonging was so powerful it was as if all the people in the synagogue were Jewish and welcoming this young man into their community. Most of the congregation were Jewish, of course, but there were non-Jewish pupils and teachers present too. The power of the occasion was tangible, and to share in it was to transcend information; the detail and knowledge of the event was lost in the awesome awareness of what it meant to become a full member of the synagogue; it was a life-transforming occasion.

This is what Smart means by 're-feeling the universe' and Cox explores in his 'awarenesses'. It is the willingness to set aside traditional knowledge and detailed information in order to engage in the experience of what it is to be a whole person. It is a challenge, for one has to allow feelings and emotions to play a part in understanding, and that causes problems to some who measure success and understanding in limited cognitive terms. For pupils with special educational needs, however, it is the unlocking of the gate to learning; for learning is no longer identified simply as intellectual activity and the literary and verbal skills necessary to express that activity. The bar-mitzvah example shows how all pupils can *learn about* a seminal moment of change through engaging in the activity of *learning from* a celebration. They feel it, participate in it, become one with it, without having to leap through the hoops of formal assessment.

One school for pupils with moderate learning difficulties had used music to explore the religious traditions. Some lent themselves to this more easily than others but the aim was to show how the affective aspect of each faith made a significant contribution to the way in which followers responded to the demands of their faith. The school also planted a 'religious garden' where different parts of the garden reflected the different religions studied. Pupils had found the appropriate plants, prepared the ground, planted and cared for the plants as they grew.

This is one of the often-unrecognised aspects of religion, that it exists in a state of fluidity while clinging to the eternal verities as if they were diamonds. Where it helps pupils with learning difficulties enormously is in its ritualistic nature. All pupils understand ritual if only because of the ritual of going to school. Rituals allow for an emotional discharge which can be experienced by all regardless of intellectual capability. A common example is the growing frequency with which roadside tragedies are marked with flowers or messages. This is not a new custom in wider Europe but is relatively new to Britain; there is a corporate sharing of emotion that transcends the worth or value of the dead person in moral terms enabling all to share in the experience. Such events are a means of suspending (or bracketing out) the challenge of the instructional truth claims in order to engage at a spiritual and emotional level. Celebrating, whether it is a bar-mitzvah or giving thanks for a life, is a group activity.

A class of 15 year-olds in a special school in an outer London borough had been studying Islam. They had handled *tasbir* or prayer beads, listened to recordings of the call to prayer and had looked at the patterns on prayer mats. ID cards with iridescent Islamic designs had been placed around the wall surrounded by the brightly painted designs of the pupils. A visit was planned to the Central London Mosque and the staff there had been alerted to the fact that one pupil, Farah, came from a Muslim family and was a wheelchair user. Farah's profound disability had resulted in a sense of low self-esteem, seemingly little interest in her surroundings, and a reluctance to develop a sense of personal hygiene. As the minibus arrived at the mosque, the call to prayer was heard from the minaret. The pupils were taken around the complex of buildings and shown the facilities for *wudu*. Some of the pupils, including Farah, were given the opportunity to experience washing their hands in the same way as a Muslim would in preparation for prayer. When most of the people had finished praying, heads were covered and the pupils were taken to experience the almost empty mosque with its huge chandelier sparkling overhead. The enormity of the building silenced the pupils. Staff reported a distinct change in Farah. Her body seemed to relax in surroundings which held a degree of familiarity for her, and her eyes rose to acknowledge the people and the place. These changes were apparent on her return to school and during the days when the experience of the visit was recounted and recorded.

Right from wrong

There are those who regard Religious Education as the major vehicle for ensuring that pupils know the difference between right and wrong. Indeed, this view has often been supported by RE teachers and lecturers as a means of justifying the place of RE in the curriculum. There is a truth in the opinion because virtually every religion has a moral code, an expectation of behaviour which is held up to its followers. Historically, much of the teaching of RE in the last thirty years has related closely to ethical issues, particularly at Key Stages 3 and 4 and at post-16.

There is the dictum in many religions that one carries out the will of God first and, while that may bring its own problems, the will of God may be neither right nor wrong in human terms. Religion, it can be argued, creates an environment in which individuals can find a place to be, a stone to stand as the flood of life washes over them. Of course there are moral requirements: 'love your neighbour', 'take care of the sick', 'do harm to no living thing' and so on, but they exist within a context: the context of failure, that the high moral level required cannot be wholly achieved. The gods themselves are identified as being above mere human morality, so Krishna can play with the *gopis* and the Jewish and Christian god can, apparently, destroy thousands of people for no obvious reason other than the promotion of the Elect, Israel. There is, surprisingly, no clear constant of right and wrong in religion which is binding upon gods and humans. Buddhism, in some of its forms, may be an exception because of its distinctive philosophy.

Such ambiguity is a delight for pupils with special educational needs who are often led to believe that religion is the moral straitjacket of the young and adolescent. What the study of religion can and does contribute is an awareness that the great religious leaders all challenged the conventions of their time, religious and moral. A cursory glance at the writings of religion would support such a view. Many religious leaders attacked the traditional values of their contemporary culture. If religion teaches anything about right and wrong, it teaches that there are shades of grey, something that most pupils of all abilities recognise instinctively.

This should not be taken as implying that religion has nothing to offer the teaching of values and morality, quite the reverse; its major contribution should be to help pupils acquire discernment and discrimination in order to help them make personal judgements when the time comes. Those teaching RE should reflect on whether they believe religion gives rules to live by, or offers a means of coping with the vagaries of life. If it is the latter then there is an immediate link with those who have special educational needs because they are constantly addressing the vagaries of life. Pupils of all abilities push against the boundaries of life as they grow and will overstep the mark from time to time.

Pupils will learn codes of behaviour through visits. These should be occasions when all pupils begin to recognise that different communities will have different expectations of them. They will be expected to show respect in the place of worship visited. Sometimes they will have to cover their heads, sometimes they will uncover their heads; sometimes they will be expected to remove their shoes; and other times just sit in silence.

Stories are, perhaps, the most powerful medium through which pupils with SEN can share in the vitality of a religion. The stories are evocative enough to speak for themselves, and pupils should be encouraged to seek an angle for themselves rather than be 'teacher-led'. One 9 year-old, after hearing the story of the Good Samaritan, responded to the question, 'who is the most important person in the story?' with, 'the innkeeper'. Why? 'Well how would you like someone like him brought to your house, all bleeding and everything, and would the bloke come back to pay you the money he owed you?' The practicalities were not lost on the pupil, who was not to be led astray by the expected answer of 'the Good Samaritan'. Similarly, the Prodigal Son raises issues of 'Wow, he spent all his father's money and his father still had him back', or, 'The older brother still hated his brother didn't he? He wasn't pleased to see him back.'

There are so many stories where pupils can identify themselves with a character or with a situation. All religions use stories to teach but they are enduring stories because they touch on an aspect of the human condition. They can capture a moment but one often wishes one could know what happened next or what had immediately preceded the moment. Issues of right and wrong are addressed in the dynamism of the story, in questions of fairness and injustice. Perhaps one lesson from such stories is that life is just not fair.

One SLD special school had celebrated Divali. The teachers had told the story of Rama and Sita, both in the classrooms and in the hall. They had experienced sitting, for just a moment, in darkness and then gradually lighting the *divas* until the light flooded the hall. Teachers had decided to aim for greater involvement of pupils and to strengthen the focus of the story on the concept of 'good and evil', contrasting the characters of Rama and the demon, Ravana. As before, enormous models of the characters were constructed and used as the basis for storytelling. However, this year teachers encouraged the pupils' involvement in the story by getting the pupils to 'cheer' or clap every time they saw the character of Rama, and to 'boo' at each appearance of the demon, Ravana. Cheering and booing or hissing is common practice during the retelling of the story of Queen Ester and the wicked Haman at the Jewish festival of Purim. Here it added a greater dimension of greater involvement and for some, though not all, served to reinforce a concept of 'right and wrong'.

QCA guidelines

In *Religious Education: Planning, Teaching and Assessing the Curriculum for Pupils with Learning Difficulties*, the QCA (DfEE/QCA 2001a) has sought, with some success, to address this concern for the affective. Under the heading 'Improving access to the Religious Education curriculum', there is advice and guidance to teachers to use sensory materials and resources through sight, touch, sound, taste or smell; to give pupils first-hand experiences; to adapt tasks or environments and provide alternative activities; and more. What one might add is that these excellent ideas and approaches should be true for all pupils following the RE curriculum. The lesson appears to be that one should *start* with the curricular needs of pupils with learning difficulties and move on from there and not tack these on as an afterthought.

If the teacher has not, within each programme of study, shared with pupils sights, sounds, tastes, smells and given them the opportunity for reflection, then there is no affective (or effective) RE. Some SEN pupils will not be able to share in every sensory activity; but neither might other pupils. The needs of pupils with SEN should be placed at the heart of RE planning and teaching strategies and styles because it encourages good teaching across the ability range. It also ensures that religion is presented more accurately.

QCA again, page 6:

> Teaching RE can help pupils develop their broader communication and literacy skills through encouraging interaction with other pupils as well as staff…These skills also develop as pupils use ICT and other technological aids. Other pupils' skills will develop as they use alternative and augmentative communication, for example, body movements, eye gaze, facial expressions and gestures including pointing and signing.

Surely an approach that should be available to all because religion itself is about those very skills.

QCA identifies (QCA 2001: 4) four ways in which pupils can make progress in RE, namely:

- by moving from a personal to a wider perspective;
- by increasing their knowledge of religious beliefs, practices and experiences;
- through developing understanding of the meaning of stories, symbols, events and pictures;
- through developing and communicating their individual responses to a range of views.

These are in fact ways which should be open to *all* pupils. The path to progress should be the same for every pupil. To suggest otherwise would be both patronising and un-educational, lacking in humanity even, for it would imply that pupils with SEN lacked human integrity. The strategies, however, that are employed to give access to pupils would need to be matched to the specific needs of each pupil: that is the challenge for the teacher, not the pupil.

One challenge to teachers of pupils with Severe Learning Difficulties (SLD) is whether it is easier to adopt a confessional approach to each religion. Given the variety of needs and the diversity of pupils, should RE teaching not require pupils to learn 'about religion' at all but engulf them in a series of stories, activities and experiences that set to one side cognitive learning and understanding? This sounds like heresy in the world of RE, yet so much teaching of RE continues to have a confessional bias. This may be because teachers themselves are unaware of their own endemic understanding of religion or because it is less controversial to teach the religion as the followers want it taught and understood. The onus would be on the teacher to represent each religious tradition taught in class as if it were 'true' and engage pupils with truth claims. Many would baulk at that. In fact it is not dissimilar from play-acting. The actor plays *Hamlet* as if it were 'true', being fully engrossed and engaged in the activity. A problem is that it is clear many people do not distinguish play acting from real life.

Opportunities and activities

The QCA guidance at Key Stage 1 and Key Stage 2 is very helpful and is reproduced here. At Key Stage 1:

> *All* pupils with learning difficulties should have opportunities to build on their own experiences and knowledge of activities from the foundation stage. They experience some of the characteristics and people associated with a variety of religions and begin to appreciate the world and the diversity of the people in it. They are enabled to express their feelings.
>
> *Most* pupils with learning difficulties should begin to explore what it means to belong to a variety of groups and communities.
>
> A *few* pupils with learning difficulties will begin to identify similarities and differences in others and answer questions about such differences.

And at Key Stage 2:

> *All* pupils with learning difficulties are encouraged to learn more about some of the characteristics of, and people associated with, religions. They have opportunities to develop further ways of expressing themselves.
>
> *Most* pupils with learning difficulties realise that they are not the same as others; they do not always think, experience or believe the same things as others. They develop a fundamental sense of right and wrong.
>
> A *few* pupils with learning difficulties who ask questions about, compare and contrast aspects of religion and are able to personally reflect during times of stillness and quietness.

Surely these experiences and forms of reflection should be part of the basic curriculum for all pupils regardless of ability because they are so fundamental to the very nature of religion itself?

RE syllabuses

RE syllabuses must change if attitudes to teaching pupils with SEN are to change. Syllabuses continue to be weighted down with information partly because the religious are most concerned that pupils 'know' everything about their faith and partly because of the obsessive belief that everything has to be assessed. RE educators would perform a great service to pupils with SEN and to all pupils if they could accept that knowledge of the minutiae of any religion is of limited interest and what is more important is the ambiguity of an approach that enters imaginatively into, for example, what it means to be a Sikh rather than just being able to list the 5 Ks. Currently, some pupils are asked to learn details about religions that many followers of that religion are unaware of or find irrelevant! An imaginative approach does not only assist pupils with SEN, it is good effective teaching.

Religion, not as propounded by some of its prophets and teachers, is by nature inclusive because it has to find a place for all regardless of ability, mobility, insight or understanding. How then to teach it in such a way that pupils can be engaged in that inclusiveness? One way could be to use a model based very loosely on a hierarchy of need and adapt it to the classroom:

1   Do pupils understand? Are they aware of the subject matter and can/do they engage with it?
2   Are the pupils able to apply that engagement? Does it make sense? Do they enjoy it? Are there opportunities for them to participate, to show what they know and understand?
3   Are there opportunities to demonstrate awareness and understanding of what has been taught and learned? Does the teaching/learning allow feelings and reasoning to be explored?
4   Are pupils able to demonstrate different skills, concepts and attitudes? Can they begin to display evidence of empathy with others?
5   In what ways can they evaluate their own learning? Are there opportunities for them to evaluate the learning process? Are they able to demonstrate why religious beliefs are important to those who hold them?
6   Are they in a position to share their learning with others and teach them? Does the learning/teaching situation allow/encourage them to practice/learn/teach by doing?

The performance descriptions in religious education in the QCA document above (pages 20–21) are useful as they describe pupils' performance in such a way that indicates the emergence of skills, knowledge and understanding in RE. One has to add that the list should be true for all RE and not just pupils with learning difficulties: why should they get all the best teaching and insights into religion?

Level Descriptors…may be used as a guide to both the current performance of an individual pupil and as an indicator of how future progress may be made. They also indicate individual pupil reactions to the learning encounters provided through:

- experiencing an activity;
- being aware of an activity;
- responding to an activity;
- participating in an activity;
- being involved in an activity;
- demonstrating a learning outcome.

For children with complex learning needs who may be at the extreme margins of the continuum of SEN, teachers will need to provide experiences which invite individual pupils to respond for example through:

- expressing emotion;
- developing self-awareness;
- responding to different environments.

(Brown 2001: 179–81)

If pupils with SEN are to reach their full potential in RE there will need to be general agreement not about what religion is but what it includes. Such pupils have rights: they have the right to experience good teaching; they have the right to know that their presence in the classroom can improve the quality of education for all; they have the right not to be patronised and be listened to with care and integrity.

> My belief is that the metaphor 'barrier to learning' which is now used to explain special needs, does not work for RE. My pupils are drawn into the subject because of the links with their own personal stories of loss, difficulty and struggle. RE is no barrier, but more like a mirror that reflects their life experience, or steps which take them to a higher level of understanding.
>
> (Krisman 2000/01: 83)

The inclusiveness of religion is not always emphasised nor, to be honest, is it always apparent, but unless it is acknowledged, there will be no inclusiveness for pupils with SEN in RE (and perhaps not in the school). Religion has its own ambiguities and its own pitfalls: 'God heals/cures everyone who prays/believes', and so on, and these negative aspects have to be challenged in the classroom in the same way as do the positive aspects: 'God loves everyone', 'God is merciful', 'God cares for creation' (when earthquakes occur killing thousands). Ambiguity is, however, part of life and the challenge of ambiguity in religion can have a very positive educational context when applied to life itself.

Any dialogue between religion and pupils with SEN has to find the first firm stepping stone across the river of mutual understanding and recognition. To move forward RE teachers and RE syllabuses will have to change, there will need to be a recognition of the huge contribution pupils with SEN can and do make across the spectrum of learning. One feature of many religions is humility, and it may be that in any future dialogue the religious educators will need to be more humble if they are to recognise the insights and attainments of pupils with SEN. Then indeed we can all receive a 'thumbs-up' and the experience will be 'Great'.

Questions

1 In what ways do pupils with special educational needs make a significant contribution to RE teaching?
2 How effectively do religions meet the needs of people with special educational needs?
3 Classroom management is the key to ensuring pupils with special educational needs receive their full entitlement. Would you agree?
4 Is religion a cerebral or an intellectual, practical activity?

12 The birth of a new Religious Studies at post-16

Arthur Giles

(The opinions and views in this article are those of the author and do not represent any awarding body. At the time of writing in September 2001 there are a number of developments and changes likely to affect post-16 RS. Up to date information can be found on www.qca.org.uk).

The waters were choppy and the ferry was teeming with commuters. The skyscrapers with their advertising logos were even more impressive than the photographs I had seen. In England it was just after midnight and I was on my way to an INSET conference on post-16 Religious Studies. This, however, was early morning in vibrant Hong Kong. The English Schools Foundation has a number of schools in Hong Kong which enter candidates for 'A' level Religious Studies. These schools produce students of considerable ability who enter universities in numerous countries. So, RS at 'A' level is not just a British phenomenon but is flourishing in this context under Chinese rule.

A second example concerns the sensitivity and professionalism of the teaching and assessing of RS at 'A' level in Northern Ireland. Both Catholics and Protestants work to the highest professional standards in their awarding authority (CCEA) with their united focus on the academic study of religion. Both of these examples from Hong Kong and Northern Ireland indicate the value and possibilities of the study of religion in the post-16 sector in significantly different political and religious environments.

Legal context

Maintained schools have a legal responsibility to provide for the spiritual, moral and cultural development of pupils, and are required to provide Religious Education for all, including those in the sixth form together with the parental right to withdraw their children from RS. Further education, sixth-form colleges and training providers have no legal requirement to promote spiritual and moral development. In this context, the Dearing Report (1996: 3.1) argues that 'such aspects of education are no less relevant to their students. Education about the world we live in cannot avoid moral and spiritual issues and discussion of personal qualities such as honesty, integrity and consideration for others'. The

Summary Report (Dearing 1996) elaborates this by saying (in 7.8) that spiritual and moral development has a double focus, intellectual and personal. The former is concerned with issues and experiences which raise questions of a spiritual or moral nature which need resolving. The latter focuses on the view that spiritual and moral growth is integral to personal growth. Arising from this there are two recommendations (nos. 181 and 182) in the Dearing Report:

- Regulatory and awarding bodies should recognise the potential relevance of spiritual and moral issues to individual subjects, particularly when designing and approving syllabuses.

- All providers of education and training should take spiritual and moral issues into account in the design and delivery of the curriculum and programmes for young people.

Questions

1 Are there questionable assumptions about the relevance of spiritual and moral issues across all approved syllabuses?
2 Are there different types of explicit links to spiritual and moral issues across a range of subjects?

Brief literature review

A trawl of literature indicates that little work has been done recently on RS in the post-16 sector, apart from materials directed at 'A' level studies which tend to focus on the academic content rather than an analysis of RS at this level. (See the bibliography for details about the awarding authorities.) A useful recent article by Vanessa Ogden elaborates some implications of the Dearing Report. Her article contains a helpful, brief annotated bibliography. She provides a clear context to RE in post-compulsory education including the legal and statutory requirements. One of the most useful parts is her analysis of the options available in offering a general entitlement to RE at post-16. She argues that there is much potential for dynamic development in post-16 RE. For example, offering modules of a subject-based or vocational character permitting students to examine RE in a variety of contexts at a number of levels. Some modules could concentrate on religious issues that affect the workplace or national and global public life, such as human resourcing or international team working. Other modules could explore the religious dimensions of community life and citizenship. There is a discussion of the structural and planning issues concerned with establishing a programme introducing inclusive accreditation through GNVQ, Key Skills and National Record of Achievement Certification. She includes specimen strategies and models with practical implications. There is some attention to the transition from GCSE to 'A' level incorporating a few ideas about the demands of certain study skills at 'A' level such as essay writing. The detail about 'A' level is now out of date given the publication of specifications from the awarding bodies. My chapter will not duplicate the constructive details in Ogden's work.

In the 1990s the Church of England Board of Education and the Methodist Division of Education and Youth produced a series of reports on moral and spiritual values in the FE curriculum. The third of these, for example, outlines a number of policy statements from various FE colleges. The bulk of the material consists of examples of curriculum projects and is based around three themes:

- examples in which values are explicit within the received syllabus such as a theological component to the GNVQ in Health and Social Care, level 2 course, or business ethics in BTEC HND.
- second, examples from the college perception of student development and outreach to the wider community such as forging links with various religious communities to reinforce their culture and to develop communication and social skills.
- third, programmes which have been adapted to suit the basic needs of the individual including programmes developed in education departments in prisons and Access Courses.

In the light of these sources it is interesting to note the QCA Annual Report 1999–2000 in which there is reference to a Graduation Certificate. QCA undertook a large-scale consultation using interviews, focus groups and a survey. There was support for a Graduation Certificate which recognises the wider achievements of 18–19 age range incorporating interpersonal skills and personal attributes. This is a matter of on-going debate and clearly RS has a number of interesting proposals to offer in this context.

Subject criteria

Over the years prior to the Dearing Report in 1996, there had been an unregulated approach to qualification development at post-16. This 'qualification jungle' led to an array of qualifications developed at different moments for different needs with some duplication of syllabuses and a lack of opportunities for awarding smaller steps of achievement. Post-Dearing developments have meant that qualifications have to meet stringent criteria to ensure public confidence and also to meet the needs of wide groups of learners. The first set of exams in the Advanced Subsidiary (AS) level are in 2001 and for A2 in 2002 onwards. The generic title for this development is *Curriculum 2000*. (As noted in the preface and in section below there are ongoing reviews of this development, some of which may be far-reaching.)

Specifications in RS are based on the subject criteria for RS published by QCA and are mandatory for all awarding bodies. (QCA stands for Qualifications and Curriculum Authority, the regulatory body for the awarding bodies.) These criteria help ensure consistent and comparable standards across awarding bodies. The intention of the subject criteria is to ensure the rigour of

'A' level is maintained and also to make explicit to a range of bodies and organisations what has been studied and assessed.

Aims

The aims of RS in the criteria are to:

- develop an interest in and enthusiasm for a rigorous study of religion;
- treat the subject as an academic discipline by developing knowledge and understanding appropriate to a specialist study of religion;
- use an enquiring, critical and empathetic approach to the study of religion.

There is an emphasis on the academic study of religion as seen in the use of the terms: rigour, academic discipline, specialist study and so on. This approach is at odds with the view that religion for various reasons is not worth sustained academic study. For example, it could be argued that religion is fundamentally erroneous and not a suitable area for academic study. An argument against RS can be seen by way of analogy. Should a serious study of sport focus on ways of cheating? Should a programme in study skills devote a sustained enquiry into plagiarism and how to get away with it? Similarly, should an 'academic discipline' focus on a fundamentally mistaken belief system with dubious moral consequences (i.e. religion)? The thrust of this criticism is that it is not worth allocating resources and time to a sustained study of something of dubious value. So why study religion which is unproven and has a history of immoral practices?

By way of response it can be noted that these aims do not imply any notion of 'becoming religious'. So one can study religion without making value judgements about its truthfulness or worth. Fair enough, the phenomenon may be erroneous but its impact over many centuries and across many cultures is itself significant and an important area for academic study for an understanding of human nature, societies and cultures. Clearly the analogy with cheating and plagiarism is weak, for example, in terms of the range and scope of the impact of religion compared to the specific features of cheating.

A further criticism raised against these aims concerns the assumption that one can study religion and develop an enthusiasm for such a study alongside an empathetic approach. Some of the problems with this assumption can be seen, for example, in the ideas of Wittgenstein. If one takes his views about 'language games', there is the view that an understanding of a 'game' requires a stance from within that game. In a cliché form this can be expressed as 'belief precedes understanding'. The aims of the subject criteria imply that students can embark upon this type of study with empathy even though they may themselves not be believers in the particular tradition being studied. Clearly this is an issue across RS in general. However, at 'A' level it becomes pronounced in terms of the breadth and depth of areas studied, for example a Muslim studying Buddhism for a unit at 'A' level. From another perspective there are also implications for agnostics trying to study with empathy selected arguments for the existence of God.

In reply there may be reasons for questioning the strength of this Wittgensteinian model with its view of cultural relativism. This could be criticised on various grounds such as the view of the importance of 'extra-linguistic reality' and its impact on our linguistic claims, including the distinctions we make between 'fact' and 'fiction'. A specific example of such a critique can be seen in Hick's essay entitled 'Theology and Verification' (Mitchell 1986: ch. 3). In this Hick argues for 'religious facts' which in this context concern beliefs about life after death. So a Wittgensteinian type of criticism of the aims may have some force but such views are not knockdown arguments against these aims. The issues about empathy are complex but not perhaps decisive arguments against the feasibility of such a study. On the contrary, the opportunity to engage in empathetic skills could be a selling point for the merits of RS. The subject criteria does not state that this award is open to candidates of any religious persuasion or none. It may be thought to be redundant in the sense that such a comment would not normally be made about other academic subjects and RS is on a par with any other discipline. However, it may be prudent to at least be explicit about this in advertising this subject to prospective candidates, let alone prospective RS teachers!

Questions

1 Are there additional criticisms which could be raised against these aims?
2 Do these aims promote the development of independent learners at this level of maturation?

Subject core

QCA's Subject Criteria lays the foundation for what constitutes Religious Studies at 'AS' and 'A' level. The specifications should require candidates to study one or more religions across one or more of the following eight areas:

- textual studies,
- theological studies,
- history of religious traditions,
- religious ethics,
- religious practice,
- philosophy of religion,
- psychology of religion,
- sociology of religion.

Specifications may focus on a single area of study, a combination of two areas or an interdisciplinary approach. As far as the subject criteria is concerned there are no value judgements being made about breadth *vis-à-vis* depth or vice versa.

There is no separate bullet point entitled 'world religions'. This is because these areas are intended to be applicable across a range of religious traditions, including texts and philosophy across various world religions. Another obvious point is the sheer range of this subject area which is multi-disciplinary. This is not unique to the study of religion but it is a significant feature of the complexities of this subject area. This has implications for the synoptic assessment in the A2 (see the section below). Positively, we can note that the multi-disciplinary skills available to RS students can be beneficial to them across a range of academic disciplines and to future areas of study and in transferable skills.

The sheer range of these disciplines reflects the multi-dimensional phenomena of religion. A difficult issue is expressing a judgement about the respective importance of any of these disciplines compared to others. Clearly, the subject core makes no explicit judgement on this matter, although the order of topics may indicate some unstated rationale. As far as schools are concerned some of these areas are much better resourced and more popular than others. For example, philosophy of religion is one of the more buoyant areas with much excellent material readily available, whereas sociology is not well resourced in terms of diversity at this level. (One of the implications here is the rationale behind the Advanced Extension Exam; see below.)

Questions:

1 What are your reasons for selecting two areas for 'A' level study and your reasons for rejecting others?
2 Are there any areas which could be eliminated or any areas which could be included in the subject core?

Awarding bodies and their specifications

Survey

The three awarding bodies in England which form the focus of this article are:

- AQA (Assessment and Qualifications Alliance)
- the Edexcel Foundation
- OCR (Oxford, Cambridge and RSA Examinations)

In addition RS at 'A' level is available in the Curriculum and Assessment Authority for Wales (ACAC) and the Council for the Curriculum, Examinations and Assessment (CCEA) in Northern Ireland.

A survey of the units offered by the three awarding bodies indicates that all eight areas in the subject core are assessed in various units. Two, however, are less well represented. Psychology and sociology of religion figure as options within coursework at Edexcel but are not explicitly studied within the other two specifications. All bodies assess the following religions: Buddhism, Christianity, Hinduism, Islam and Judaism. AQA includes Sikhism as an examination option, and this tradition is available as a coursework option with Edexcel.

Objectives and assessment

These awards are assessed by three units at Advanced Subsidiary (AS) level and then at a more demanding level by three units at Advanced (A2) level. Although these are equally weighted, the demand of AS is that expected of candidates halfway through their 'A' level course. The 50 per cent weighting for AS is valued as such by UCAS and in performance tables. AS provides a certified exit point for students and is designed to promote breadth in the post-16 curriculum. There are clear advantages for RS in terms of the legal requirement regarding the provision of RS in maintained schools which is coupled with the award of AS. It is a way of enabling students to increase their breadth of study over one year and also to defer decisions about specialisms.

Two of the awarding bodies (AQA and OCR) have two assessment points in the year, January and June, whereas Edexcel has June only. The AQA system has written examinations in all its assessment points. OCR has extended essays and no examinations in January at A2 level only. The assessment units may be taken at stages throughout the course or at the end of each year or at the end of the total course. This is clearly an important management decision affecting a whole school policy. (This issue of assessment points is a matter of on-going debate at the time of writing and the QCA review of *Curriculum 2000* has important contributions to make about the manageability of the scheme of assessment; see below.)

The assessment objectives include knowledge and understanding (AO1) and the ability to sustain a critical line of argument and to justify a point of view (AO2). A significant difference between AS and A2 is that there is an increased weighting given to AO2 from between 25–35 per cent for AS to 35–45 per cent at A2. This illustrates the requirement for more developed analytical skills in the second year of study leading to the A2 award. A crucial point to understand is that successful study in RS at this level is not only about mastery of subject content but also the development of evaluative skills. Indeed, this range of 35–45 per cent for AO2 is a significant feature in the differentiation of standard of work across a range of students with implications for the grading of candidates. One implication is the time and focus required in the development of these evaluative skills in an AS/A course in RS. My article 'Evaluation: Why and How!', in *Dialogue* (10 April 1998) focuses on the skills of evaluation. We need to note, however, that some of the details in this article such as assessment objectives are now out of date because of the subsequent publication of the specifications. The article draws attention to the increased weighting given to evaluative skills compared to previous syllabuses and hence the importance of developing these skills across the whole spectrum of study from preparation, reading skills, revision, essay planning and examination techniques.

Given the status of these assessment objectives in the subject criteria it is incumbent on awarding bodies to ensure that centres and candidates know the relationship between various trigger words and particular assessment objectives. If, for example, a part of a question spans the two objectives it must be transparent that there are the relevant trigger words to show this spread of assessment demands.

All specifications may have a maximum internal assessment weighting of 30 per cent which may be split between AS and A2. In practice, Edexcel has a compulsory coursework unit at AS as one of the three units and OCR has optional extended essays at A2 for its January assessment point and AQA has no coursework. Both Edexcel and OCR mark this work externally. The compulsory coursework at Edexcel, for example, is intended to enlarge the range of study such as the inclusion of contemporary religious communities in the UK or the opportunity to investigate psychology or sociology of religion. The bulk of assessment is, however, by means of written examinations with all the implications about preparation of effective study skills for exam work. Both Edexcel and OCR have all their exams lasting one and a half hours and AQA has an hour and a quarter for AS and an hour and a half for A2.

AQA and Edexcel do not have a prerequisite system between A2 units requiring the relevant underpinning from particular AS units, although they state that it is the responsibility of the centre and candidate to ensure the students who have not studied the relevant AS module have the necessary knowledge, understanding and skills to start an effective study at standards required at A2. OCR has recommended routes and states that Advanced GCE should continue to A2 along the route chosen for AS.

Synoptic assessment

The subject criteria state that all specifications should include a minimum of 15 per cent synoptic assessment which relate to both assessment objectives. This aims to assess the candidates' knowledge, understanding and skills learnt regarding the connections between elements of the area(s) of study selected. It should also contribute to the assessment of relating such connections to their broader context and to specified aspects of human experience. It is not permissible to assess this by means of coursework and can only be done via written examinations. This ensures parity across all the awarding bodies. Although this is not permitted, it can be noted that individual students on a multi-disciplinary course could enrich their understanding of connections across discrete and complex areas by means of an individually created portfolio/coursework which is externally assessed. Provided the rigour of scrupulous assessment is in place, there would appear to be some reasons for promoting this type of development in the future especially for a unit which aims for students to create a synthesis within a multi-disciplinary subject.

All three awarding bodies allocate 20 per cent to the synoptic unit as the contribution to the full A2 award which is a greater proportion than any other unit. Within the context of the A2 units the synoptic is worth 40 per cent of that one-year course of study. The implication is that such a proportion has an impact on the amount of learning time devoted to this module. Forty per cent of the learning time in this year's study for A2 is clearly of major significance in the effective use of managing the teaching and especially the learning leading to this award.

All the synoptic papers are one and a half hours. OCR's rubric requires two questions whereas both AQA and Edexcel stipulate one question. Both Edexcel and OCR have global essays whereas AQA has structured questions in the synoptic paper. Those papers which require one question in one and a half hours have important implications about the development of appropriate study skills for this type of examination technique which may be a new demand for these candidates. Hence, they will need to address time management issues and effective means of preparation for new types of demands in this context, including coherent, focused essay planning with a considerable amount of material over this time-scale. My article 'Synoptic Assessment' in *Dialogue* (14 April 2000) considers a number of issues related to synoptic assessment including implications for study skills development. For example, there are brief suggestions about reading and note-making skills focused on synoptic assessment together with related revision and examination techniques. A possible way forward is for students to create their own personal record/port-folio akin to coursework preparation as a means of preparing for the synoptic paper. As far as two of the boards are concerned, a new technique requiring attention is time management, answering one question in one and a half hours, because this may be a new demand for some students. The article encourages students to think critically throughout their synoptic preparation, for example using effective ways of monitoring the standard of trial essays they may do as part of their synoptic revision.

There is a complex issue of the place of 'connections' in a multi-disciplinary subject like RS. Candidates in this type of 'A' level may study a mixture of textual, theological, historical, ethical, philosophical, psychological and socio-logical disciplines. In addition, some may study a diverse range of religious traditions such as ancient Jewish thought and practices alongside more contem-porary Buddhist ideas and customs or there may be Hindu philosophical schools alongside Christian exegesis. Wherein lie connections in this Pandora's box of diversity? One cannot pretend this is a minor problem which simply has to be swept aside because of mandatory requirements. Clearly all the awarding bodies are required to assess the synoptic focus on 'connections'. However, the demands on candidates to examine, at a fairly sophisticated level, notions of connections in a multi-disciplinary subject are substantial. No doubt this is a ripe area for research in terms of the respective demands of synoptic assessment across different types of subjects and how parity of demand can be justifiably achieved.

One implication in the synoptic assessment is the need to clarify the shades of meaning associated with 'connections' across different units of study.

- It may be there is substantial overlap as in, for example, philosophy of religion and ethics.
- One unit may embrace and include another such as New Testament studies and Christian thought.
- Another model is that parts of units are in effect identical to each other such as Old Testament/Jewish Bible and parts of Judaism.
- However, it may be that a candidate studies Christian theology with another unit on Buddhism. The previous three models of connections may not fit as easily with this particular pathway. Indeed, it may distort the characteristic features of these religious traditions to assume a fairly simple 'connection' between them. Hence, a reasonable model of connections may be that given a rigorous study of these traditions the differences are significant and substantial. In that case, a model for 'connections' may highlight the differences and separation between the two. To pretend otherwise is to run the danger of distorting data and evidence which is the last thing anyone wants in an academic study.

On further analysis of such connections it may become apparent that the similarities and differences are complex and subtle and students may need to create a model which addresses such evolving variations and different shades of relationships. So let no one underestimate the conceptual demands of synoptic assessment! However, the development of these skills of synthesis is worthwhile and should be a useful preparation for university work and the demands of creative thinking in various careers.

Key skills

All the specifications provide opportunities for developing and generating evidence for assessing the following key skills:

- communication,
- information technology,
- improving own learning and performance,
- working with others,
- problem solving.

The units in RS provide various opportunities for the development of these five skills. Coursework provision, for example, promotes IT skills and opportunities to target and monitor the improvement of study skills over a period of time with the provision for reflection and improvement. An analysis of the opportunities of building up a student's key skills portfolio across the RS units reveals the range of teaching and learning methods which could be employed, such as:

- group discussions,
- presentation of seminar papers,

- use of a range of media,
- different types of documents,
- variety of IT skills.

It is important to note that the RS specifications will develop a student's skill in investigation, interpretation and critical thinking. These skills are valued within higher education and are also applicable across a wide range of career routes. The QCA review of *Curriculum 2000* is in the process of making a number of recommendations about Key Skills, in particular allowing for a more flexible provision. Up to date information can be found at *www.qca.org.uk*.

Advanced Extension Award

The Dearing *Review* (1996) made certain recommendations concerning young people of exceptional ability. This had been done previously by means of the special papers ('S' levels). In recent years there has been a marked decline in 'S' papers, from 17,400 in 1989 to 9,500 in 1994. Dearing recommends that special papers should be retained but with each awarding body agreeing to take responsibility for a number of subjects in order to ensure cost-effective provision. In addition consideration should be given to developing approaches to these based on the subject cores which will bring them within the range of the teaching resources of more institutions.

The new paper for this group of students is known as the Advanced Extension Award (AEA). It is targeted at the top 10 per cent of students in RS irrespective of the particular specification they have followed. At the time of writing this chapter, Edexcel has been given this particular responsibility. An important feature is that the AEA should ensure that the most able students are tested against the standards comparable with the most demanding to be found in other countries. The examination is based on the subject criteria for RS and independent of individual specifications. The AEA requires greater depth of understanding rather than greater breadth of knowledge and requires application of understanding of critical analysis, evaluation and synthesis. AEAs have an external assessment weighting of 100 per cent and for RS this will be a three-hour examination comprising two elements equally weighted. The first is an understanding of (unfamiliar) textual material which facilitates comparisons and connections on broad themes related to the nature of religion. Second, there is a question reflecting the eight areas of the subject criteria. The assessment will award a distinction, merit or ungraded. The level descriptors for candidates who achieve distinction epitomise the scholarly demands of the rigour and good practice at this level of work. It is worth quoting them in full so as to clarify the nature of the demands and expectations at this level. Candidates who achieve these qualities and standards are on a par with the intellectual demands of any other subject not only in this country but worldwide. In that sense RS can be rightly confident about its academic status and the challenges it poses to the brightest of students.

In order to achieve distinction candidates should:

- deploy effectively a range of carefully selected, detailed, relevant and almost totally accurate knowledge of aspects of the nature of religion;
- demonstrate in depth a clear understanding of the connections between the areas they have studied and their contribution to and links with aspects of human experience;
- show a facility in clearly explaining the relevance of recent ideas, methods and approaches in the study of religion;
- evaluate competently and articulate insights and independent thought, using technical language and terminology naturally and accurately throughout their work;
- sustain an effective and perceptive analytical approach to issues concerning the nature of religion and synthesise ideas in coming to well-reasoned conclusions;
- show a very mature approach to the study of religion, with sophisticated, concise and elegant expression, construction and quality of language, which enables them to communicate with clarity and precision.

The future

One of the concerns in the past has been the problem of small 'A' level groups which may have made some of them unviable. However, with the advances of electronic communications there are various possibilities such as the pooling of lessons and resources across different colleges and centres, for example by means of e-mail groups. Similarly there are enormous possibilities of e-mail groups for large numbers of RS staff on particular topics and/or exam papers.

One aspect of 'the future' concerns the progression of these candidates into higher education. Some will find an explicit link in terms of degrees in RS. However, it is worth pointing out the contributions that RS at 'A' level can make to undergraduate studies. As far as content is concerned there are clearly religious dimensions to a large number of academic subjects including English, history, drama, film studies and so on. In addition, religion figures in interdisciplinary areas such as American studies and also subjects which may not in the past have been associated with RS such as the growing popularity of ethics in business studies. A number of students, of course, use entry into university to embark upon new subjects for themselves, including anthropology, which again would be of interest to RS students. So, one can sell RS in the sixth form in terms of the considerable diversity of courses which include religious dimensions.

Furthermore, this subject has significant implications for a range of study skills and transferable skills which could benefit the quality of undergraduate study and a range of career routes. For example, if we reconsider the aims and objectives (see above) these promote, for example, critical and empathetic skills and an ability to sustain a critical line of enquiry and to justify a point of view; these are complex and demanding skills to develop especially when considering contentious yet sensitive areas for investigation. Such abilities are highly valued in the cut and thrust of undergraduate studies dealing with diverse interpretations and also business enterprises which may include judicious understanding of the significance of belief systems in various communities.

This chapter was written in September 2001. At the time of writing there are various developments taking place and up to date information can be found at *www.qca.org.uk*. Phase one of the *Curriculum 2000* review was published in June 2001 and the second phase in December 2001. The first points out overwhelming support for the principles of *Curriculum 2000*, including the greater breadth of taking four AS subjects together with increased choice and flexibility and better retention rates. However, action is needed to support schools and colleges to make the reforms work more effectively in practice including the overall manageability of assessment schemes and examination arrangements. For example, this may include a linear option for AS of a single combined paper which might reduce two or three units of assessment.

We started off this chapter with RS in Hong Kong and Northern Ireland, indicating that RS can be a lively and worthwhile enterprise across a diversity of cultures and ideologies. The quest for academic integrity and a scrupulous investigation of religious beliefs and practices will continue to tax the most able teachers and candidates. The benefits, apart from any intrinsic value, promote an informed analysis and critical appraisal of this fundamental and perennial feature of the human condition.

Questions

1 What are the reasons and factors for entering candidates for the following assessment points:
   (i) all AS units in year 12 followed by A2 in year 13;
   (ii) some AS in year 12 with the remaining AS plus A2 in year 13;
   (iii) taking all units at the end of year 13?
2 Evaluate the educational justification for the proportion of exams in this asssessment system.
3 In what ways may awarding bodies be unfair to candidates in their restricted range of modes of asssessment?
4 What are the principles which underpin the selection of content in the specifications?
5 If exam questions appear to be unfair, what action can you take?

Part III

Religious Education and the wider curriculum

13 The contribution of Religious Education to whole school initiatives

Lynne Broadbent

Introduction

There is a very real danger that in identifying the contribution which Religious Education can make to whole school initiatives that Religious Education loses its focus as a discrete subject in the school curriculum. This was certainly true in the 1970s when Religious Education, like general studies and social studies, became 'issues based', engulfed in the morality of sex, marriage, violence and war arguments, frequently without the inclusion of a religious perspective. There are those who suggest that Religious Education is a natural vehicle for delivering personal, social and health education and, more recently, citizenship education. Literacy issues became the focus of the *National Literacy Project* (DfEE 1996) and the *National Literacy Strategy* (DfEE 1997) for primary schools and, more recently, the focus of the *Key Stage 3: National Strategy: Language at Work in Lessons* (DfEE/ QCA 2001b). The government's focus upon improving literacy and numeracy has required teachers to address the contribution made by their subject to pupils' literacy, and, in turn, the contribution made by literacy to pupils' learning within the subject area. Government initiatives for including citizenship education within the curriculum have imposed a need for schools to consider where the requirements might be incorporated within the subject areas and where they should be addressed separately. Running parallel to these developments there has been an increasing demand that ICT should play a significant role in the curriculum, while schools have long been aware of the need to make provision for pupils' spiritual, moral, social and cultural development. There are undoubtedly strong links between Religious Education and each of the above aspects, but its contribution to whole school initiatives must be based on an integral relationship rather than any *ad hoc* or tenuous linkage and, equally important, in time firm boundaries between each of the disciplines must be imposed.

Religious Education, language and literacy

A QCA booklet, *Religious Education and the Use of Language* (QCA 1998), states that the development of language skills 'is an entitlement for all pupils', and identifies the need for pupils to have opportunities to:

σ   Speak clearly and effectively to convey information and ideas to a variety of audiences;

σ   Listen attentively to others to take in meanings, intentions and feelings;

σ   Read confidently to gain ideas, information and stimulus from written texts;

σ   Write accurately and appropriately to express understanding and present information and imaginative idea.

(QCA 1998)

Religious Education is abundant in opportunities for developing language and literacy. Learning in Religious Education relates not only to the acquisition of knowledge and the development of skills, but to the development of pupils' conceptual understanding. This involves the understanding of concepts which are essential to the understanding of religion but which may not be exclusively religious concepts. For example, 'forgiveness', 'sacrifice', 'repentance' or saying sorry, and 'authority' are terms in common use with understood secular meanings, however, when used in a religious context, they take on meanings particular to one or more of the religious traditions, and pupils' ability to understand and use these 'secular' and religious terms or concepts in the appropriate context can be a mark of progression in Religious Education.

Equally, the development of pupils' language can be crucial to the development of their understanding of specific religious concepts such as god, prayer, faithfulness and forgiveness. Through paired and small group discussion pupils can explore these concepts and subsequently develop their level of understanding. Two examples might serve to illustrate the point:

> A class of Year 7 pupils were exploring the concept of the divine through a scheme of work on Hinduism. Pictures of Hindu deities were distributed to pairs and small groups and pupils were asked to identify the key features of the image and to discuss possible meanings of the symbols. The pupils noted the fact that the deities were often blue and had many arms, and that some images, such as Ganesh, were in the form of animals. Subsequent discussions allowed pupils to explore ideas related to the power of god and how Hindus, like believers in other faiths, appeal to god to enable them to remove obstacles.

> A class of Year 3 pupils were exploring the concept of prayer. The teacher introduced a range of aids to prayer: including Muslim prayer mats, tasbir, the rosary, kneelers and prayer cards. The pupils were then divided into small groups, armed with clip-boards and a selection of 'post it' notes and asked to look at the pictures on the marked pages of textbooks. The task was to identify features which were 'clues' that the people illustrated might be praying, for example, the position of the hands or facial expression. Key words were noted and reported in the feedback. Subsequent discussion raised some sophisticated discussion about motivation, veracity, forms and efficacy of prayer.

The development of learning in Religious Education also draws upon a wide range of skills and there are strong links between these skills and pupils' language development; for example, developing the skill of investigation involves pupils in asking relevant questions, while developing interpretation requires pupils to interpret religious language and suggest meanings for religious texts. The skill of analysis is marked by the ability to distinguish between opinion, belief and fact while that of expression is marked by the ability to explain concepts, rituals and practices and to articulate matters of deep conviction and concern. The ability to listen to the views of others without prejudging one's response is a feature of the skill of fairness. These skills are challenging yet frequently under used in Religious Education and OFSTED inspections suggest that this lack of focus on the development of skills results in low expectations for the subject, particularly at Key Stage 3 (see PCfRE 2000).

There is a richness in the language of religion. In Religious Education pupils encounter a wide range of sacred and secular texts through which to develop their understanding of a range of genres of writing: the 'adventure' stories of Moses and Joseph, the 'revelation' of God's promise to Abraham, the 'punchy' Proverbs or even the 'raunchy' stories of the Song of Solomon, the poetry of the Psalms and descriptions of the Divine in the Upanishads. Pupils can use these texts as models for their own writing, for example, of creation myths, psalms or koans, or the dramatisation of the story of Elijah and the Prophets of Baal, or the writing of newspaper reports of the crucifixion.

Scripture might be written on parchment scrolls, the paper pages of a book or palm leaves. It may be housed within an Ark, placed on a wooden stand or on a lectern in the form of an eagle with outstretched wings. It may be recited from memory, preached, chanted, read or sung, by individuals or communities in a range of languages. These features symbolise the authority with which the scripture is regarded by the faith community and distinguishes sacred writings from secular texts for the believer. But in today's society, all kinds of secular texts may be imbibed with a sense of 'authority', and this very term itself warrants exploration and evaluation.

Religious Education has the potential for making a significant contribution to the development of pupils' literacy, and in turn, Religious Education is dependent on literacy skills for developing an understanding of religious concepts. This is a relationship between two subject areas which should be fostered both for the sake of the pupils and for the continued development of Religious Education as a challenging subject with high expectations of pupil achievement.

Religious Education and numeracy

With Jesus's twelve disciples, the Four Noble Truths of Buddhism, the Five Pillars of Islam and the Ten Commandments of the Judeo-Christian tradition, Religious Education might appear to have ready links with numeracy. It is however, questionable whether RE can contribute to pupils' knowledge of number bonds, multiplication tables or computation skills, and many of those working in the area of Religious Education are anxious to refute the need for links with numeracy. Nevertheless, there are concepts related to time, pattern and number which are central to an understanding of religion and some of the activities undertaken in Religious Education might serve to support pupils' mathematical development and therefore support the holistic rather than fragmented development of knowledge.

The Christian calendar, based on an early accepted date for the birth of Jesus, provides a common form of dating. Although later evidence suggested that Jesus had been born approximately six years earlier, this date remains accepted as 'the Common Era' and used internationally, it is sometimes difficult for pupils to recognise that this was originally a religious form of dating and that the birth of Jesus was, and is, not the focal point in history for many religious and secular traditions. For Jews, the years are marked from the Creation of the World and in 2002 CE, the year in the Jewish calendar is 5762. For Muslims, the focal point in history was the Hijra or migration of the Prophet Muhammad from Makkah to Medina, where the first Muslim community was established. It is from this date that the years are numbered and 2002 CE is the Muslim year of 1423 AH. Each of these religions has its own time frame usually measured by a lunar calendar, each year with a different number of months, variously named. There are new years which mark the beginning of the religious community such as those of Islam and Sikhism, while others are financial new years (Divali) or even new year celebrations for trees such as Tu B' Shevat in Judaism. Faith communities mark new years differently, planting trees, starting new account books, holding initiation ceremonies into the faith communities, telling stories about good conquering evil or engaging in an extended period of self-examination and repentance before moving forward, casting off old ways, resolved to obey God's law. Even the cycle of day and night is determined not by the hands of an Accurist watch but by scriptural reference. In Judaism, festival days begin as the sun goes down in the evening of the day before the festival, for in the Genesis story of creation, 'the evening and the morning were the first day', while in Islam the Ramadan fast begins when there is enough light to distinguish between a black and a white thread and ends when darkness prevents the possibility of distinguishing between the two.

This religious time frame is also applied to the cycle of birth and death, with celebrations to mark the births and deaths of the divine and the great figures of the faith: for example, the births of Krishna, Lord Mahavira, Guru Nanak, the Buddha and Jesus, the death and resurrection of Jesus and the martyrdoms of Gurus Tegh Bahadur and Arjan and of the Bab. Each adherent enters into the cycle of birth, initiation, marriage and death marked by the religious community with ritual and symbol. For each religion, its key events, key concepts and beliefs are held together in its own particular time frame and without some consciousness of this, we are in danger of creating a mishmash of people, celebrations and beliefs totally separated from their conceptual context.

It can be no accident that numbers proliferate within religions. In essentially oral cultures such as those from which the religions sprang, numbers can assist the memory, enabling the believer to recall important events and commands, such as those to pray five times a day. But numbers can be much larger than 'five': there are ninety-nine Beautiful Names for Allah and more than three thousand aspects of the divine in Hinduism. All seem to suggest that the divine is greater than that which human beings can comfortably contain by definition. In textual terms, the Christian Bible includes many examples where certain numbers are repeated and raising questions about the possible symbolism of such repetitions can enliven the study of secondary pupils as well as encouraging insight into the texts. Examples might include the world being created in six days with God resting on the seventh, Moses being on Mount Sinai for six days when it was covered in cloud and God speaking on the seventh day; or, Moses remaining on the mountain for forty days and nights, while Jesus spends forty days in the wilderness. A further example might be that following the feast of the Passover, when the boy Jesus stayed in the Temple in Jerusalem until he was discovered by his parents after three days, a story which seems to echo Peter's three denials and Jesus's resurrection after three days following another Passover. Numbers are also significant in the Jewish tradition, each letter of the alphabet having a numerical value. At Rosh Hashanah, many Jews will not eat nuts as the Hebrew word *egoz* has the same numerical value as the Hebrew word for sin, *cheit*.

Of course there are opportunities to explore *rangoli* patterns at Divali, or Islamic patterns can contribute to the understanding of symmetry, and pupils could engage in surveys, graphs and charts. And for those teachers who are totally committed to the development of computational skills, a visit to a supermarket to purchase kosher or halal food for a festival offers opportunities to engage in calculation. But there would seem to be much better reasons for engaging in mathematical concepts in Religious Education, reasons related to developing a deeper understanding of religious time frames and therefore a deeper understanding of the spiritual impetus driving the members of faith communities in our midst.

Religious Education and ICT

> This is a new age of discovery, and ICT is the gateway.
> (Douglas Adams, quoted in DfEE/QCA 1999)

ICT has the potential to transform learning in Religious Education. However, while RE specialists have promoted the development of ICT skills and have capitalised on the power of the computer to gain greater access to information about religions, opportunities to harness the ICT revolution to promote a skills based approach to learning in RE have moved at a slower pace. Interpretation, reflection and analysis are just three of the skills which could be significantly developed by the use of ICT. They are also skills which might be employed to address some of the criticisms levelled at the use of ICT in RE, for its use does raise issues related to the capacity of ICT to provide a full and balanced experience of religion.

Without doubt, the internet has significantly extended access to information about religions. Both teachers and pupils can gather up to date information from sites prepared by faith communities and thus learn how the communities see themselves. Websites providing virtual tours of local places of worship offer opportunities to 'see' artefacts and sacred scriptures 'in situ' when time constraints or geography prevent an actual visit. Access to religious texts have traditionally been difficult to access yet now daily readings from the Guru Granth Sahab, the Sikh holy book, can be received by email and, with the correct technology, a class can hear the Qur'an read aloud. With the use of CD-ROMs, pupils can meet members of each faith tradition to learn about their festivals, places of worship and beliefs or explore the items on the Seder plate or a collection of classical religious art.

Information and communication technology also lends itself to significant changes in classroom methodology with the possibility of live interaction between pupils and faith communities. Pupils in essentially monocultural and monofaith communities can exchange emails and digital photographs with pupils in multicultural and multifaith communities and even leaders in those communities: one RE inspector recalls observing a group of Year 6 pupils interviewing Desmond Tutu. With pupils experienced in communicating via technology, this form of interaction breaks down barriers of age and gender and the sometimes embarrassing silences of face-to-face confrontations.

ICT can also prove a spur to the improvement of presentation skills with desktop publishing packages and scanners making the production of guide books for places of worship, newspaper reports on locally celebrated festivals or promotional literature on charities or power point presentations a regular part of classwork and homework assessment. However, this raises one of several questions which must be raised about the use of ICT in Religious Education and that is this: what is it that we are assessing? Is it a well-presented and illustrated guide book or a stunning power point presentation which demonstrate a high level of skill in the use of ICT, or is it a pupil's capacity to interpret, analyse, apply and express? BECTa (2000) highlights the need for ICT to be used only when it supports RE learning objectives and only when those learning objectives cannot be met more easily through an alternative methodology. For Religious Education, learning objectives must focus on the understanding of religious concepts, usually through the development of knowledge and will need to identify the skills by which the understanding of those concepts is demonstrated. So a description of a font in a guide book for a church without an interpretation of its use and meaning for Christians, or a 'cut-and-paste' section of sacred text without reference to its context and reflection on its meaning is not the best use of ICT. The danger of the unevaluated 'cut-and-paste' has always been present but with pupils' ICT skills more finely tuned than their RE based skills, the temptations are probably greater for an even wider audience! It is all too easy to 'log on and regurgitate'.

Another perhaps more important issue raised by the advent of ICT relates to the area of 'truth claims'. In the not too distant past, a scientific view of the world was considered to be based upon rational thought and was thereby 'true'. In contrast, a religious view of the world was considered of a lesser order. There has been a considerable shift in attitudes to science, in no small part due to scientific discourse setting itself in a broader, less rigid framework. However, its former place seems to be assumed by the new technologies which dominate the world's communications. Almost everything can be accessed, and accessed at speed. It is technology which has credibility both outside and inside the classroom. So where does this leave RE? Burridge (1999: 10) suggests that the use of ICT could bring about a 'shift in emphasis and value from wisdom to information', since ICT has problems with 'knowledge or wisdom that cannot be presented as information readily translated into computer language' (1999: 10). She considers that as ICT becomes more central to learning, then wisdom will be viewed as less important, with people becoming less interested in questions of truth and only interested in finding out different truths. A consequence of this, Burridge suggests, is that people will be seen as sources of information and that anyone seen as 'information-poor' will be marginalised. This is a highly significant issue for Religious Education, since encounters with religious believers are not focused primarily on people who are 'information rich' but those who are able to speak from personal experience about personal beliefs, often gained through a lifetime. This is not the stuff which can be acquired at the press of a button.

So while the use of ICT can make a significant and positive contribution to learning in Religious Education, there are some cautionary notes. While greater access and speed can considerably develop pupils' knowledge of religions, there is a danger that this remains surface knowledge rather than being modified through interpretation, evaluation and analysis to a deeper understanding of religious concepts. Or, even more, that while the use of ICT can contribute to the communication of knowledge and communication between individuals, it can also impede access to the type of communication which is the life-blood of Religious Education, the exchange of the personal and often subtle accounts of religious 'truths', the beliefs and experiences which can only be shared and explored face to face, when the speaker can read, and trust, the eyes and faces of the audience. ICT is of considerable value to the Religious Education teacher but its value and the values its use promotes should be debated long and hard.

The contribution of Religious Education to personal, social and health education and to citizenship education

> The school curriculum should pass on enduring values, develop pupils' integrity and autonomy and help them to be responsible and caring citizens capable of contributing to the development of a just society.
>
> (DfEE/QCA 1999: 11)

Beliefs which govern behaviour, both personal and social, and the concept of a just society are integral to the teaching of Religious Education and to the frameworks for personal, social and health education and citizenship education identified within the *National Curriculum Handbooks* (DfEE/QCA 1999). There are therefore natural links between the three areas which can be traced through both the content and methodologies. However, while commonalities can be explored, there are also sharp distinctions in terms of learning intentions and underlying values which must be addressed.

Current aims for teaching and learning in Religious Education include the intention that the subject should enable pupils to:

σ   develop an understanding of the influence of beliefs, values and traditions on individuals, communities, societies and cultures;

σ   develop the ability to make reasoned and informed judgements about religious and moral issues;

σ   enhance their spiritual, moral, cultural and social development by reflecting on their own beliefs, values and experiences;

σ   develop a positive attitude towards other people, respecting their right to hold beliefs different from their own, and towards living in a society of diverse religions.

(SCAA 1994)

These aims clearly identify the interface between Religious Education and pupils' personal development and a clear focus through Religious Education on local and national communities. It was Harold Loukes who, in the early 1960s, considered that Religious Education should be 'conducted in an atmosphere of realism and relevance' and should enable the adolescent pupil 'to make sense of his [sic] own human condition' (Loukes 1961:11). Loukes pre-figured current concern with thinking skills, believing that 'we are concerned in religious education, as in all education, with how to think' (1961: 46) and devised a 'problem approach' to the RE curriculum, based on problems of personal relations issues of authority, (friendship, sex and marriage), problems of personal responsibility (money, work, leisure and prayer) and problems of meaning (suffering, death and learning), with pupils encouraged to learn through thought and discussion. In many respects, both Loukes's basis for the study of religion at the secondary phase of schooling and his methodology can be traced within current Key Stage 4 examination syllabuses and in approaches utilised by the second of the two attainment targets for Religious Education, 'learning from religion', whereby pupils 'make informed, reflective and personal responses based on their own experiences and values and engage with and interpret the views of others' (QCA 2000: 16). This attainment target which seeks to develop pupils' skills of asking and responding to questions of identity and experience, meaning and purpose, values and commitment (QCA 2000: 4) and thus contributes to their personal development, counterbalances Attainment Target 1 which focuses on the development of pupils' knowledge and understanding.

This focus on personal and social issues also links closely with citizenship education, the guidance document for which acknowledges that 'learning from real life experience is central to citzenship' (QCA 2000: 34). Many concepts advocated for citizenship education reflect those identified within the Religious Education curriculum, for example, the individual and community, authority and rights and responsibilities, while the development of skills such as listening, accepting another point of view and distinguishing between fact and opinion, are necessary for Religious Education, citizenship and personal, social and health education. Furthermore, teachers working in the three areas will need to adopt strategies which will enable their pupils to recognise bias, evaluate evidence and identify different interpretations (QCA 2000: 35).

It was the Swann Report (DES 1985) which most publicly recognised the contribution that Religious Education might make to developing pupils' knowledge and understanding of the diverse beliefs and practices present within local and national communities. Religious Education is one of the few subjects in the school curriculum which literally takes pupils out into the local community to visit churches, mosques, synagogues and gurdwaras and to meet members of local faith communities. Furthermore, one aim for Religious Education, cited above, is the fostering of respect for difference, for the right of individuals and communities to hold diverse beliefs and practices within a multifaith and multicultural society. The Swann Report (DES 1985: 518) regarded such teaching as having potentially important implications both for pupils themselves and for society: 'Bringing about a greater understanding of the diversity of faiths present in Britain today can also therefore we believe play a major role in challenging and overcoming racism.' Now while the development of such knowledge and understanding through interactions with local communities is consonant with the concepts and enquiry approaches of citizenship education (DES 1985: 21), it is at this point that a clear distinction between the learning intentions of Religious Education and citizenship begins to arise, for while the intentions of Religious Education focus on the development of knowledge, understanding and skills, the three interrelated strands of citizenship education, namely social and moral responsibility, community involvement and political literacy, include an intention that pupils become 'actively engaged' in local and national community activities, so developing for society 'an active and politically literate citizenry' (DES 1985: 7). While one might concede that some outcomes of citizenship education might indeed be commendable, the fact that learning intentions can be behaviourally based, raises questions about the nature of the curriculum and the process of education itself. This is particularly true for Religious Education, which has long refuted any claim that it might be associated with forms of indoctrination or nurture and has assiduously directed its aims and learning intentions towards the development of knowledge, understanding and skills. The suspicion that programmes for personal, social and health education and citizenship education are governed by more than pure educational aims, could be further fuelled by the fact that the initial proposals for each area strongly identified a need to address social issues; the proposal recommending a stronger focus on personal, social and health education (DfEE 1999) noted a rise in teenage pregnancies and drug misuse, while the Crick Report (QCA/DfEE 1998) noted a need to counteract 'a further decline in the quality of our public life' (1998: 14). The links between these documents and their implications for Religious Education have been identified elsewhere (see the chapter by Broadbent in Bailey 2000).

There is some concern expressed by teachers of Religious Education that the inclusion of discrete lessons of personal, social and health education and citizenship education might severely encroach upon curriculum time hitherto allotted to RE. The issue raises one further and perhaps more significant matter for consideration. While there is a commonality between the concepts and values addressed by the three areas, there is within the religions, an identified historical and/or religious context within which these concepts and values are grounded. The historical events and the teachings of key religious figures give rise to the religious beliefs, practices and values of adherents today and constant reference back to the source of these beliefs and values both protects the teacher from accusations of indoctrination and contributes to an education about religious communities. Taught solely outside the context of Religious Education, these values become 'secularised'. This in itself would not be negative, were it not for the fact that in a multifaith society such as Britain, there are large numbers of people for whom their religion is their guiding principle for daily life and the source of their values. Not to acknowledge this through programmes of Religious Education would undermine the preparation of pupils for life in a multifaith society and, in the end, undermine respect for the multifaith society itself.

There are natural links between Religious Education, personal, social and health education and citizenship education through their subject matter, their concepts and through the skills which each area promotes. However, Religious Education needs to protect the integrity of its aims, firmly based as they are within an educational framework, namely the development of knowledge, understanding and skills, and guard against being jostled, or even subsumed, by additions to the curriculum which could have repercussions for the continuation of a harmonious multifaith democracy.

The contribution of Religious Education to pupils' spiritual, moral, social and cultural development

In 1992, the Education Act identified a school's provision for pupils' spiritual, moral, social and cultural development as one of four areas subject to inspection under the OFSTED Framework for the Inspection of Schools. While mention of the spiritual and moral were not new, for the Education Act of 1944 had made it incumbent upon every local authority to make provision for the spiritual, moral, mental and physical development of the community, it now became crucial for schools to seek definitions of these areas which could apply to educational provision. Most problematic was considered to be the term 'spiritual', with its strong quasi-religious associations, and in recent years the spiritual or spirituality has elicited a wealth of literature (see Hay 1998; Bigger and Brown 1999; Thatcher 1999; Wright 2000).

Initially, two documents were published, designed to support teachers' understanding of the terms themselves and their application to educational provision. The first, *Spiritual and Moral Development – A Discussion Paper*, was published in 1993 by the National Curriculum Council (NCC) and was later re-published in 1995 by its successor, the School Curriculum and Assessment Authority (SCAA). The paper identified spiritual development as 'applying to something fundamental in the human condition', open to all pupils irrespective of religious belief, or none. The 'spiritual' was described through eight interrelated aspects, namely the development of personal beliefs, a sense of awe, wonder and mystery, the experience of feelings of transcendence, the search for meaning and purpose and for self-knowledge, the valuing of relationships, the expression of creativity and the use of feelings and emotions as a source for growth (NCC 1993: 2–3). The second discussion paper, entitled *Spiritual, Moral, Social and Cultural Development*, was published by OFSTED in 1994, and this again distinguished the 'spiritual' from the 'religious' and focused on its essentially personal nature relating it to 'that aspect of inner life through which pupils acquire insights into their personal existence which are of enduring worth' (OFSTED 1994: 8). This association of the spiritual with the personal was frequently reflected in an activity popular on training courses in the 1980s, whereby groups brainstormed the word 'spiritual' and then, separately brainstormed the word 'religion' (see Hammond and Hay 1990). The exercise rarely failed to elicit positive and 'personal and enlivening' associations with the term 'spiritual', and frequently negative and 'collective' associations with the term 'religion', which was seen as rule-bound and oppressive. This makes for a difficulty in identifying the contribution which Religious Education might make to pupils' spiritual development if religion is regarded in such negative terms. The contribution of RE is almost invariably linked to 'secularised' interpretations of religious material through Attainment Target 2, yet Religious Education can have a role to play in exploring the spiritual in a distinctively religious as well as in a 'humanistic' context. Religions describe significant moments in the lives of key figures: for example, the call of Moses, the Enlightenment of the Buddha, Jesus's temptations in the desert, the revelation of the Qur'an to the Prophet Muhammad, the call of Guru Nanak. These are personal moments which bring dramatic changes in the lives of the individuals – but they are spiritual moments, experienced in private, and we can but wonder what the moment was like if the individual and the writer described it as they did. And pupils can wonder too if given sufficient chance to ponder and question these mysteries, but all too often we, as teachers, are swift to apply a traditional religious interpretation to the accounts. Adolescents with many questions about life and its experiences are perhaps more able to live with the uncertainty of not quite knowing the answer and may perhaps find them a more authentic reflection of their personal experience. Maybe what is required is for the eight interrelated aspects of the spiritual from the NCC *Discussion Paper*, which has provided valuable access to 'the spiritual' for other subject areas, to be re-interpreted in specifically religious terms to enable Religious Education to make a rich and full contribution to pupils' spiritual development.

The contribution of Religious Education to pupils' moral development is, in some respects, a more straightforward matter and takes us back to the work of Harold Loukes. Religious Education provides opportunities to learn about the ethical teachings of religions which, in the case of the Judeo-Christian tradition have become the basis for many common rules and laws in society. The Ten Commandments is a ready source for moral explorations in primary and secondary schools. Through stories and dilemmas pupils can explore the means by which religious women and men have applied religious teachings to daily life, whether in relationship issues or in rather more dramatic areas such as euthanasia or war. While these opportunities relate to the development of knowledge and understanding, through the use of case studies and role play, pupils at all Key Stages can practice and develop their skills of moral decision making. The relationship between religious and ethical issues is explored in detail elsewhere in this book. Suffice to say that it is often essentially through the raising of moral issues that pupils at Key Stage 4 retain an interest in religious perspectives but we sell pupils, and religion, short if we present a religious response as a slick or swift route out of a moral dilemma. A moral dilemma is still a moral dilemma with more than one possible course of action, even for most religious believers, and it is this which continues to make religion a challenging subject of study.

The contribution of Religious Education to social and cultural development through visits to places of worship and encounters with members of local communities has already been identified in relation to citizenship. Religious Education was perhaps one of the first subjects in the curriculum to willingly address cultural diversity in the early 1980s and it continues to do so today, through the marking of religious festivals and the use of a wide range of resources such as through examples of religious dress, the visual arts and music to support teaching. But perhaps the greatest contribution which Religious Education makes to pupils' cultural development lies not so much in the fact that it draws upon a range of culturally based resources but that it attempts to make pupils aware of the distinction between religion and culture, for it is the conflation of religion and culture that frequently gives rise to misunderstanding. Cultural accretions, for example in relation to attitudes to the position of women, if not explored and correctly attributed to cultural rather than religious practice can present a mistaken or one-sided view of a religion which leads to prejudice. Islam is but one religion which has, in recent years, been the subject of such misunderstanding. To disentangle religion from culture is crucial within a society highly susceptible to and dependent on media images. Here then is a vital role for Religious Education.

In conclusion

This chapter suggests that Religious Education can make a significant contribution to whole school initiatives without compromising its aims or its content. On the contrary, it could be argued that the process of addressing issues such as literacy, numeracy and citizenship positively enhances teaching and learning in Religious Education. Other subject areas too, when exploring their own contribution to whole school initiatives, might reach similar conclusions. And this begs the question: whether the education system exists primarily to support a rigidly structured subject based curriculum, or whether the subjects themselves should serve as a means of structuring learning about literacy, numeracy, ICT, personal, social and health education, citizenship and spiritual, moral, social and cultural development? Discussions about the structure of the curriculum have, in the past, focused upon the relationship and balance between the subjects and broader cross-curricular areas (DES 1977; HMSO 1992). The significant number of initiative introduced into the curriculum in recent years raises the issue once again. How we respond to such questions depends on our beliefs about the nature and purposes of the curriculum itself. It is an old debate which might well warrant a resurrection.

Questions

1 How far do you consider that the curriculum should be subject-based, and how far should it be concerned with developing cross-curricular initiatives?
2 What might be the differences rather than the similarities between personal and social education and Religious Education?
3 How might addressing the cross curricular initiatives add value to pupils' achievement in Religious Education, and how would such achievement be expressed?

14 Is Religious Education and ethical and moral debate a contradiction?

Peter Vardy

The assumption behind this title is that 'ethical and moral debate' must be open, wide-ranging and questioning and that Religious Education is incompatible with such an approach. The key issue in this assumption is, of course, what is meant by Religious Education. The question is less open than it might have been as it contrasts Religious Education with 'ethical and moral debate': the inclusion of the word 'debate' necessitates discussion and evaluation as part of the education process. If the question had been whether Religious Education and ethical and moral education was a contradiction, then the additional question would arise of what ethical and moral education involves as it need not involve debate. However the editors have restricted the discussion and so the focus of this chapter is on the possible tension between ethical and moral debate and Religious Education. Necessarily, much of this chapter will focus on the nature of Religious Education.

Up until the Second World War, in much of the Western world, Religious Education involved three pillars which mutually supported and reinforced each other. These three pillars were:

- Church
- family
- school

In Christian households children went to Church with the whole family on Sunday, often said grace before meals at home, prayed in the evenings and the children had this whole form of life reinforced by education at school. There was a relatively seamless interconnection between Church, family and school. This was the cornerstone of Catholic education in particular. Children were formed at home, Church and school and the pillars supported each other. The result was exceptionally powerful and it led to the saying often attributed to the Jesuits: 'give me a child to the age of seven and I will have them for life'.

In many countries, Religious Education took place even when there was no family background. In Britain, Religious Education was a compulsory part of the curriculum and it was assumed that everyone was educated at school into being a Christian. Indeed almost everyone would have said that they were Christian (or Catholic; the two terms were not regarded as synonymous). This would be the case even if they never went to Church: when soldiers in the First World War were asked their religion they usually replied 'Church of England'. There was a near universal assumption that if one did not belong to a particular church then one would be classed as 'Church of England'. After all, the Church was there at birth, marriage and death: it was part of the fabric of society. Being educated into Christianity was equivalent to being educated into being English. When the British Empire spread round the world, it took with it an education system that included Religious Education so there were young Africans singing very English hymns about good King Wenceslas plodding through the snow even though the equatorial temperatures at Christmas were in the nineties. Being Christian was part of culture and the legacy has been left in Christian Churches around the world. Indeed, any claim that the Anglican Church has to be a worldwide Church is based almost entirely on the legacy of British imperialism and the education system that went with it. The same applied to Catholicism, which was taken with the armies of the Roman Empire after Constantine; with the Conquistadors of Spain into South America; with the Portuguese into Angola, Mozambique and Macau; and with the French into their colonies in Africa. Of course, there were countries where this did not apply: for instance Australia, New Zealand and the United States where state education was entirely secular. Nevertheless, even in these countries the influence of Christian schools tended to be highly significant.

If Religious Education is cultural education, then the aim is to 'form' or mould young people into an acceptance of the prevailing culture. This may well be one reason why parents want their children to go to schools with a denominational background the same as, or similar to, their own. However this view of Religious Education can be challenged, and to understand the nature of the challenge a digression is needed.

Realism and anti-realism

Realism is the theory of truth which claims that a statement is true if it corresponds to the state of affairs that it attempts to describe. Thus:

(a) *The cat sat on the mat* is true iff (if and only if) there is a cat which is sitting on the mat.
(b) *his woman is beautiful* is true iff and only if this is a woman and she is beautiful (note this means being beautiful in some absolute, Platonic sense and not simply because in the culture in which we live this is the accepted view of what constitutes beauty).
(c) *Murder is wrong* is true iff murder is in an absolute sense wrong – if this statement corresponds to some absolute order of value, either one laid down by God or gods or to some transcendent order like Plato's Forms which existed timelessly and spacelessly and of which the world around us represents but pale shadows.

Realists affirm bivalence. This means that they maintain that a statement is either true or false depending on whether it does or does not correspond to the state of affairs it sets out to describe. This does not mean that we can necessarily *know* whether a given statement is either true or false, but this epistemological uncertainty does not undermine the claim that there is a truth to be known. Realists maintain that truth claims are verification transcendent; they do not depend on their ability to be verified. Thus 'The Holy Qur'an was dictated to the Prophet by the Archangel' or 'Jesus rose from the dead on the third day' would be true iff these statements corresponded to what actually happened.

Anti-realists, by contrast, reject correspondence and instead maintain that statements are true because they cohere with other true statements made within a particular form of life.[1] They reject all attempts to make language mirror reality, and instead maintain that truth is essentially a human construct. They reject bivalence and instead claim that truth claims are internal to the language game being played. Truth depends on what is agreed within the community who use language not on dispassionate enquiry. Fr Gareth Moore OP ends his book *Believing in God* with the sentence: 'People do not discover religious truths, they make them'. This idea that truth is something that human beings create is central to the anti-realist understanding.

Anti-realism holds to a different understanding of truth to realists but it still maintains that the statement 'God exists' is true. Realists maintain 'God exists' is true (or false) because this statement corresponds to (or fails to correspond to) the being or spirit called God who created and sustains the world. Anti-realists, by contrast, maintain that 'God exists' is true because it is accepted and endorsed by the rich Christian, Islamic and Judaic traditions. There are foundations for religious belief and, indeed, for the whole rich 'form of life' of the religious believer which includes prayer, worship, liturgy, morality, etc., but truth does not depend on reference but rather on what is accepted as true within a particular culture.

The anti-realists will reject the claims of natural theology to be able to prove the existence of God on the basis that none of the arguments for the existence of God succeed. They will further agree with the reformed epistemologist that the existence of God is obvious to and unquestioned by the believer and that the believer does not need any justification for this belief. Indeed they will hold that it is a characteristic of religious belief that it is not tentative and does not depend on probability.

Anti-realists will hold that statements are true because they cohere with other true statements within a particular form of life. For instance:

1   Within Islam, the statement, 'There is one God who is Allah and Muhammad is his prophet', is unquestionably true.
2   Within Islam the statement that, 'The Holy Qur'an was dictated by Allah to Muhammad', is unquestionably true.
3   Within Judaism, it is unquestionably true that God is the father of the Jewish nation and God promised the land of Israel (however this is defined,

and there is little agreement between different groups of Jews on the exact boundaries of the promised land) to the Jews in perpetuity.

4   Within Roman Catholicism the statement, 'The Pope, when speaking *ex cathedra*, can promulgate dogmas which, once they have been received by the Church must be accepted by the faithful', is true.

5   Within evangelical Christianity the statement, 'God has redeemed us through Christ Jesus who has died for our sins and has revealed God to us through the pages of Holy Scripture', is accepted without question.

None of these statements can be verified by any evidence that would stand up before neutral observers. There is no proof for any of them. To be sure, they seem more or less to be confirmed by the stories held fast by certain traditions, but these stories have been passed down and developed by an oral tradition over longer or shorter periods of time and one set of stories is, when viewed from outside the communities to which the stories belong, no more likely than another. Each group of believers will strongly maintain that, of course, their stories and claims are true because they can be independently verified, but none of them will accept the verifications proposed by other religious groups except in so far as they accord with their own.

Jews look to Abraham as the father of the Jewish nation and inheritors of God's promise to Isaac; Muslims look to Abraham as the first Muslim and see themselves as inheritors of God's promise through Ishmael while Christians look to Abraham as the 'father of faith'. Meanwhile Biblical scholars point out that the figure of Abraham probably never even existed. Abraham may well be a mythical figure based on oral stories handed down and built on over hundreds of years. There is not the slightest evidence outside the Biblical stories that there was such a man as Abraham and the only 'evidence' is that contained within the stories accepted within the different religious traditions.

The anti-realist maintains that the whole idea of a search for evidence is out of place. Religious truths are not subject to proof; in this, they consider that reformed epistemologists are right. Reformed epistemologists are found within the evangelical Christian tradition; these are realists who maintain that they know that their truth claims are correct (in a realist sense) because the truth of these claims is guaranteed by the revelation they have been granted. Thus evangelical Christians know that they have been given the grace to see the world correctly because of the revelation of Jesus Christ. They are so certain of the truth of their claims that they need no justification. The problem is, of course, that this appeal to revelation can be countered by other claims in other traditions to the 'rightness' of their own revelation. Anti-realists agree with reformed epistemologists that no justification for religious belief is required, but they differ in that they reject any idea of reference. Instead, anti-realists claim, people are educated into a form of life. As the Hegelian philosopher Bradley said, individuals are not born into a desert, they are inculcated into a tradition.

If, then, one is an anti-realist then the function of education is to 'form' young people into the truth claims of one's community. These truth claims are not validated by independent enquiry. 'Ethical and moral debate' (to go back to the title of this chapter) is likely to undermine the ethical system into which young people are being inculcated. Once one educates the young Muslim to consider whether the Qur'an was, in fact, made up by Muhammad or the young Orthodox Jew to consider whether the story of God's promise to Abraham was created by the scribes of David's court in order to legitimise the boundaries of his then kingdom, then there is every danger that the moral certainties of the child's community will fragment and the child may grow up in a moral vacuum. It is not surprising, therefore, that some religious people consider 'moral and ethical debate' to be unacceptable as part of their children's Religious Education.

However it is not only anti-realists who will maintain this. There will be many vehement realists who will also reject any form of moral and ethical debate because they will claim that their religion has the truth in a realist sense. Thus Muslims will claim that as God revealed the Qur'an to Muhammad, what the child needs is to learn God's will and to be obedient, not to debate the issues. Similarly many conservative Catholic bishops will insist that the emphasis of Religious Education should be catechetical: in other words, to teach children the truth proclaimed by the Catholic Magisterium. Questioning and debate will simply undermine the faith of the young. It is for this reason that the Magisterium has condemned the inclusion of situation ethics or proportionalism in school education, as these positions have been declared to be false and erroneous by the Pope and it should be no part of the Catholic education system to educate the young into error.

The second sentence of the last paragraph included the important word 'vehement'. The fact that a particular group are vehement advocates of the realist nature of their religious truth claims does not mean that the claims are true in a realist sense. Certainty and truth are not necessarily connected and this is a vital part of the question under review in this chapter. If parents are certain that they are right in their religious views, is it any part of the function of education to question these views? Many would say that it is not.

Liberal democracy is the ruling assumption of the Western world, and this involves tolerance of the views of others. To challenge or criticise the religious views of others is widely regarded as unacceptable. The great world religions are all considered to be equally deserving of respect and the 'live and let live' motto prevails. No-one would seriously suggest questioning the right of parents to bring their children up in their own religious tradition. However this very tolerance in fact implies an anti-realist position on truth, namely that all religious views are equally valid within their own communities of belief. The trouble is, of course, that most religions carry with them ethical and moral imperatives as well, which brings us back to the title of this chapter: how can one engage in genuine ethical and moral debate if one is committed to Religious Education?

Aims of Religious Education

There are various views on the point of Religious Education in schools and they can briefly be characterised under the following headings. Each heading gives rise to a different perspective on the realist/anti-realist debate.

1   To inculcate young people into the religious tradition of the school. This is the approach favoured by many Catholic bishops and also by Muslim, Jewish and many evangelical Christian schools. The assumption is that parents have sent their children to the school in order to be educated into the values of the religious tradition which the school affirms. Parents often like this approach because it confirms their own belief framework and also it is held to impart clear moral values which the children can live by.

This would be the approach favoured by anti-realists who maintain that their religious truth claims are right because these are the claims taught by the teaching authority of their religious group. The function of education is seen as to help young people accept these framework beliefs. However, this approach could also be favoured by realists who are convinced that they alone have a realist understanding of truth and, therefore, that the function of schools is to educate young people into these ultimate truths.

2   The Religious Studies approach, which aims to help young people to understand a wide variety of religious views and to have empathy for them. In Britain, Religious Studies now dominates most University departments concerned with these issues (my own College, Heythrop College of the University of London, is one of the few that has refused to take this route). This is effectively a sociological approach to religion and aims to stand outside any religious tradition and to view different religions from this supposedly independent perspective.

This is the non-committed approach which sees Religious Education as involving helping young people to understand different traditions. It is best represented by an anti-realist understanding of truth claims which see all such claims as worthy of respect and maintains that the task of education is to understand the 'depth grammar' (to use a phrase from Wittgenstein) or religious belief.

3   The general ethical and spiritual approach, which sees Religious Education as aiming to foster moral development (often in schools that adopt this approach Religious Education is combined with personal and social education) and a general sense of a spiritual (defined as non-material) attitude to life.

This approach sees religious truth claims as unimportant but nevertheless sees value in religion as pointing to a different perspective on life which is valuable for young people. This is usually an anti-realist approach although possibly with a realist understanding of human nature, maintaining that to be human involves more than a search for material wealth and that this alternative perspective can be fostered through an understanding of religious claims.

4   Religious Education as a search for truth and wisdom. This approach emphasises a critical examination of religious claims and which sets out to evaluate, challenge and understand the key intellectual issues arising from such truth claims. The aims include to help young people decide for themselves on the truth or otherwise of the claims being made and, where appropriate, to make decisions as to how life is to be lived. Part of the education process will be to get young people to challenge their own core beliefs and to question the moral values accepted by their parents and society in order to come to a fuller understanding of the basis for these claims. This is the approach taken by many schools in Britain where Religious Education is an academic subject and where philosophy and rational reflection on, for instance, key beliefs and texts will be a vital part of the education process.

This last approach will probably discuss realism and anti-realism with students and will help them to understand the difference between the two positions. The nature of relativism in religion and morality will be considered and the truth claims made by religious traditions and the ethical positions that flow from them will be closely examined.

The great advantage of the first of the above approaches is that young people grow up within a firm faith framework which is endorsed by their parents (who have chosen the school which reinforces this framework). They 'know where they are' and are 'formed' according to clear values of their community. The problems are, however, equally obvious as each such group grows up with a conviction of the rightness and superiority of their own perspective and with little realisation of the cultural relativity of many claims to truth.

The second approach seems to affirm open-mindedness, but in fact there is a relativist assumption lurking beneath it which is likely to undermine commitment to any religious tradition. When one attempts to study all forms of life from without, it is likely that one will not affirm any of them and, more seriously, the whole idea of a search for ultimate truth (if, of course, it exists which in a post-modern world is debatable) will be rejected.

The third approach has real value in opening up dimensions to what it is to be human that are often neglected in mainstream education. The spiritual side of human beings may well best be found in silence and solitariness. One is more likely to ask questions about who one is and about the nature of human existence while walking in the mountains than while in the disco bar or travelling on the tube, and finding space in the educational curriculum to open these windows into the soul is a worthy endeavour. However, as with the first two alternatives, the idea of a search for truth will again not be important to the educational enterprise.

The fourth approach is more complex.

Socrates was condemned to death on two counts. One was atheism because he did not believe in the state gods. The second charge was 'corrupting the young'. When people ask what I do at the University of London or when lecturing to young people, I frequently reply 'endeavouring to corrupt the young'. Socrates was accused of this corruption because he saw his task as to get people to think for themselves – not to automatically accept the views of their elders – and to be willing to probe and question. His young audience were delighted with this process, but it is not surprising that his older listeners were not. Socrates embarked on his educational mission because the Delphi Oracle had said that he was the wisest man in Athens and Socrates set out to prove the Oracle wrong as he simply could not believe this. Socrates felt that he knew nothing, so he set out to question those who were thought wise by many or who thought themselves wise. It rapidly became clear that they were far from wise, they had not thought deeply about any significant and moral issues and had little depth. The same applies today. When the fourth approach is taken seriously, it is embraced enthusiastically by young people and the numbers of pupils in Britain taking GCSE and 'A' level is rising rapidly. Their parents, unlike the parents of Socrates's day, are also generally keen and enthusiastic as they feel that they missed out on similar education at school. The only group who are not keen on this method is those who are sure they have the truth already and do not want their children's minds 'corrupted' by being allowed or forced to think for themselves. These parents are naturally concerned that the conclusions that young people come to may not be the conclusions to which they want them to come.

The fourth approach respects the autonomy of the individual student. However, this is not the 'rational autonomy' beloved of 1970s philosophers of education. All too often this concentration on rationality prevented broader perspectives of what it is to be human being opened up and developed. Religious Education, at its best, seeks to help young people to address the question of what it is to be human and the different ways in which this can be understood. It includes a major commitment to philosophy and ethical reflection, but is not exhausted by ethics and philosophy. It should also include the affective side, helping young people to develop an awareness of the importance of stillness and silence.

The ideal model of Religious Education today can be represented by a spiral curriculum running from pre-prep through to Year 12, in a carefully planned curriculum that involves deepening and developing understanding across five strands as the child moves through his or her school life.

The Five Strands approach to religious and values education

The Five Strands approach has been pioneered in Australia over the last six years but it lies, implicitly, behind the best Religious Education in Britain today. It consists of a spiral curriculum covering the following areas:

1   The Hebrew and Christian scriptures and the Christian tradition. The Hebrew and Christian tradition underlies Western culture and it is not possible to engage with great European art, literature or music without understanding the scriptures that have shaped European culture. More than this, to understand Judaism, Christianity or Islam requires an engagement with these stories at a level that goes beyond the superficial. Too often the level of understanding of the great stories of the scriptures remains the same at Year 1, Year 5 and Year 12. Jonah is regarded as a story of a great fish being ill and the creation stories in Genesis are taken literally. It is not surprising that young people fail to engage with the scriptures when the stories are treated in such a superficial and banal manner. Good Religious Education will help young people to wrestle with the problem of how stories can convey truth without being literally true.

2   Ethics: theoretical and applied. The ethical problems confronting young people have never been more complex. Every week, new challenges arise in the fields of genetics and medical ethics, and it is essential that young people should be equipped with the intellectual tools to be able to consider these issues in depth. This requires a detailed consideration of not only applied ethical issues but also the different ethical theories that inform the debate.

3   Philosophy of religion is the fastest growing area in British Religious Education. This is because it provides young people with the opportunity to think deeply and well about central areas of religious belief ranging from the nature and existence of God to religious language, prayer and miracles to the problem of evil and innocent suffering. Young people care deeply about these issues but they do not wish to be given the answers; they wish to be able to think for themselves, and this philosophy of religion enables them to.

4   World religions are increasingly important, but these have to be taught well. Too many schools still adopt a sociological approach, teaching, for instance, through festivals and outward practices. This completely fails to enable young people to empathises with the beliefs of a different form of life and is likely to increase prejudice rather than the reverse. By contrast, a spiral approach will enable young people to develop an increasing awareness of the depth and profundity of the great religious traditions, as well as their weaknesses.

5   The fifth strand may seem surprising but it may be the most important of the five: this is the affective approach which seeks to build into the school curriculum, through a child's school life, opportunities for stillness and focused silence to enable young people to realise the importance of the inner journey and to be freed from the tyranny of busyness and the hectic activity of an over-crowded curriculum. There are real cognitive benefits in stillness, and when a school embraces its importance it can have a transforming effect. The following parable was written by a 16 year-old girl after taking part in an affective RE exercise, and this may illustrate something of the effect it can have:

It began like this; a man began to walk, getting faster and faster and ignoring more and more of what was going on around him. Eventually he found himself in a tunnel. The tunnel was long and dark, there was not even a glimmer of light at the end. The man continued to walk. Had he stopped to discover, he would have found that the walls of the tunnel were transparent, so if he had stopped he would have seen the bright, light-filled world of variety around him. Still he continued to walk, getting faster and faster. Had he stopped to listen, he would have been told the way out and yet he continued to walk further and faster into darkness. Perhaps then we should remember that when we find ourselves in a tunnel long and dark, we should stop, look, listen and discover freedom from the narrowness of life in the tunnel (16 January 1999; Leanne Symes, age 16).

Naturally to implement such a curriculum throughout the school depends on the willingness of the head and the senior management team to see the vital importance of good religious and values education and to recruit and value trained specialists. Much will depend on the head's view of education. If the primary aim of the school (no matter what the prospectus says) is to top the performance league tables and to be outcome-dominated so that the production of economically effective workers is the real, if implicit, agenda of the school, then religious and values education will have a low priority. However many of the best heads have a broader view and consider that the education of the whole person is of vital importance. Once education is seen as being to help young people to become fully human and to realise their potential (as Aristotle would have understood this), then the above approach will be seen as central to effective education.

A former Lambeth Conference (the meeting of Anglican bishops every ten years from around the world) said that Anglican Christianity is dedicated to 'an open Bible and a fearless love of truth'. This is a proud banner under which to sail, and is fully compatible with the above approach. Catholic Christianity has always been committed to the equal importance of philosophy and theology in training of its priests. The Qur'an says that the decision to become a Muslim must be a free one and must not be coerced. Religion at its best will respect the freedom of young people to make their own decisions and to decide for themselves whether to commit their lives or not. However, there are still those who are frightened of such an open-minded approach and who do not trust young people. They will resist any idea of critical thinking. They will only seek to 'form' people into their own tradition and will endeavour to avoid their young being corrupted.

If the 'Five Strand' understanding of religious and values education is adopted, then there is no tension and certainly no contradiction between good religious and values education and ethical and moral debate: indeed, the two are necessarily complimentary. Not all, however, will share this vision of education, and in this case it may be worth their considering what view of truth they are committed to and what they see the aim of education as being.

Questions

1 Should it be part of the function of education to encourage pupils to challenge parental views?
2 If 'education is seen as being able to help young people to become fully human and to realise their potential', what is the distinctive contribution of Religious Education?
3 'Individuals are not born into a desert, they are inculcated into a tradition'. In what circumstances could Religious Education in schools be regarded as endorsing this statement?

Note

1   This is an expression introduced by Wittgenstein and it represents the whole rich life of, say, a religious believer including not just the words said in liturgy, prayer, creeds, etc. but behaviour, outlook and all that goes to make up the person's world. Language expresses a form of life and forms of life differ between cultures and within cultures.

15 Embodying the spirit

Realising RE's potential in the spiritual dimension of the curriculum

John Hammond

Religion is an important resource for spirituality. It is not the only source, but to omit religion in a spiritual search is to ignore a central and enduring strand in humanity's quest for meaning and right living. Religion is the place where spiritual energies, organised around ritual, symbol, narrative, doctrine and ethical code have been most systematically honed and shaped. Religious Education has, therefore, a major contribution to make to the spiritual dimension of the curriculum. Spiritual development, though, needs more than the study of religious and spiritual content. It requires a personal engagement with the material studied. It is much more than just learning about the facts of religion. The learner needs to confront and have an opinion on the truths of religion. This is a study which looks for resources and inspiration for one's own life way. The possibility of undertaking this engaged, personally involved kind of study is closely related to the nature of the learning experience. Some kinds of teaching and learning enhance it, others tend to obstruct.

Imagine: a group of experienced teachers from a range of disciplines, on a residential course to retrain as RE specialists. They are worked hard, there is so much religious content to cover as well as attainment targets, teaching and learning strategies, assessment and so on. The afternoon session is on worship in Christianity and they are relating the text of an African Eucharist to the major Christian doctrines. Energies are flagging.

They are invited to read aloud together from their copies of the text, and someone suggests that David takes the part of the celebrant. David, who was a Trappist monk for fifteen years, agrees. He comes to the front, stands, and with all the appropriate movements and gestures, chants the celebrant's part. The rest of us recite the responses. The atmosphere in the room begins to change. We are all drawn into the growing gravity of the event. Attention becomes increasingly focused, the recitation takes on a new seriousness and there is a growing solidarity between us. We are increasingly involved in an event which is tangibly 'spiritual', with distant but distinct echoes of the holy. The singing, the gestures and our own participation draw us into a level of affective engagement quite different from the kind of learning experienced earlier. We have shifted from an intellectual exercise comparing liturgical text with major doctrines to an affectively charged performance that, though it was not a

Eucharist – there was no bread or wine and no intention – got us nearer to one of the central activities of believing Christians.

The debrief was extensive. For everyone, the experience had been highly engaging and the learning significant. But not everyone felt at ease. Some did not know quite where they had been. They knew, intellectually, it was not a celebration of the Eucharist, but they felt the boundaries between learning about worship and participation in it had become blurred. They were at the same time both in and not in a religious event. Overall this experience had left us with a sense of involvement in something 'spiritual', and a feeling that we now better appreciated the central act of Christian worship.

The dramatic performance: presence to and participation in the actions, singing, and communal recitation had touched everyone personally at some depth and greatly enhanced the quality of the learning.

Let me offer one more example. A group of students are in a theatre studies class discussing the topic of human responsibility and environmental destruction. The exchange is a combination of self-conscious seriousness, platitudes, doom-laden prophecy (believed and doubted), black humour and glazed uninterest.

They are then taken through the process of the *Council of All Beings*. This event (returned to in more detail below) involves identification with some non-human being, mask-making and then assembling in the circle of the 'Council' to music, drumming and appropriate readings. The participants then speak as 'their' being through the masks, and hear and jointly respond to the words of others.

During the debrief the event is discussed and environmental issues revisited. But the nature of the exchange is now different. There is a high level of involvement throughout the group. There is little new information, but the heartfelt quality of the contributions is evident. The members of the group are now struggling with an issue the complexities and magnitude of which often encourages despair or denial. But they are speaking from the heart, giving tentative solutions or expressing personal hopes, fears and frustrations. The performance of the *Council*, the mask-making and wearing, the gathering in a circle, the drumming and speaking has changed the atmosphere and the nature of the exchange. It has brought the issue close to their own real beliefs and values and provided a context where they can speak.

The dramatic performance in both situations permitted and encouraged a considerable depth of personal involvement. The religious content of Religious Education lessons will only contribute to the spiritual dimension of the curriculum and students' lives in a significant way if RE's teaching and learning styles make possible this kind of engagement.

The aspiration of RE to contribute significantly to the spiritual development of young people is rooted in its subject matter and its two attainment targets, particularly the second. The two attainment targets in the QCA Model Syllabuses are well known and much used: *Attainment Target 1, Learning About Religion*, and *Attainment Target 2, Learning From Religion*. They frame a consensus of what RE professionals try to achieve with their students but they are not particularly new. The twin, linked, aims of acquiring knowledge about religion in order to enrich the learners' spiritual life appear in the Durham Report of 1970 which aimed to 'explore the place and significance of religion in human life and so to make a distinctive contribution to each pupil's search for a faith by which to live' (*The Fourth R* National Society and SPCK 1970). These twin aims are taken up in a rather different form in 1970 by the Schools' Council Working Paper 36 where it highlights the distinction and attempts to build bridges between religious phenomena and significant questions in the pupil's own experience in its talk of explicit and implicit religion. The present language of learning about and learning from religion was first introduced by Grimmit in 1973.

Learning about religion entails a working knowledge of the nature of the religious traditions in their origin, structure, principal beliefs and ethical systems. This is a school-sized scientific study of religion. Attention to the second attainment target, *Learning from Religion*, should ensure that this knowledge is acquired in such a way that the students' own self understanding and perceptions of life will be challenged, deepened and perhaps reshaped. An RE without Attainment Target 2 would be largely irrelevant to the development of student spirituality. Spirituality is about any or all of the great human questions that Derek Webster describes as 'questions whose answers are never fully given. What is my origin and end? What is my duty to my neighbour? How may people find justice? What are truth, freedom and beauty? Can my guilt ever be cleansed?' (Wright and Brandom 2000: 212). But without an engagement and self investment on the part of the learner, study of even these 'spiritual' topics will not develop spirituality. Spirituality is always first person. Where it remains third person the activity might be good scholarship (on someone's spiritual endeavours), but it will not be spirituality.

RE, particularly in secondary schools, is better at achieving AT1 than AT2. OFSTED notes our lack of success in AT2 (OFSTED 1997). This is a view shared by the QCA, which felt it necessary to publish guidance specifically designed to strengthen teacher effectiveness in *Learning from Religion* (QCA 1999). If you are or have been a teacher, think of your own successes in promoting students' spiritual development through the study of religion. There are no doubt some successes, but for many practitioners these are fairly rare, and often unforeseen. In spite of some forty years of professional literature concerned to span the gap between students' experience and the religious traditions, the spiritually rich subject matter of an RE syllabus still too often results in spiritually bland exchanges in the RE classroom.

Why is this? The lack of success is more about approach than content. Teachers have taught syllabuses dense with religious content and heavy with the great existential questions of humankind, but the methods used have not always secured a meaningful encounter between their students' experience and the available religious wisdom. Like most of schooling, the majority of the approaches surveyed in Michael Grimmitt's *Pedagogies of Religious Education* (Grimmitt 2000) are largely disembodied and essentially cognitive. The bridges that religious educators have sought to build between the experience of pupils and the world of religion are, for the most part, intellectual and imaginative. The language is of *dialogue* (SCWP

1971) between religion and experience; of *building conceptual bridges* (Grimmitt 1973) between the pupils' experience and the central concepts of religion; of *evaluating* religion in personal terms and self in religious terms (Grimmitt 1987); of *hermeneutical* activity where pupils are *active interpreters* of religious beliefs and practice (Everington and Jackson 1995); of *concept cracking* requiring the *discovery of parallels* between religious belief and pupil experience (Cooling 1994).

The emphasis on cognitive activities is perhaps most marked in the increasingly influential QCA model syllabuses. In the introduction to the models, nine skills and five attitudes are listed. These are to provide the intellectual tools for achieving the two attainment targets. The same list serves both ATs. These capacities (Investigation, Interpretation, Reflection, Analysis, Synthesis – even Reflection and Empathy) are set out in a way that fits well with an objectifying and scientific approach to religion, and the first Attainment Target's requirement to identify, name, describe and explain the religious material under consideration. But the same list of skills and attitudes also underpins the second Attainment Target. This needs a very different approach. It requires a more open, receptive and engaged encounter with the beliefs and practices of others. The objectifying mode appropriate to the scientific study of religion (and necessary for the achievement of AT1) may actually inhibit a receptive encounter with the faiths (as required by AT2).

Contrast the skills essential to RE as listed in the model syllabuses (Investigation, Interpretation, Analysis, Synthesis) with what people do in religion (celebrate, pray and meditate, wash, sing, eat and drink, walk – on pilgrimage). Contrast too the emphasis in RE on Learning About Religion, with the concern of the religions that the lives of their adherents be informed by their faith, that is, that they learn *from* it. RE favours Learning About and emphasises cognitive skills. Religions favour Learning From and emphasise bodily enactment. Could it be that spirituality requires embodied activity and so RE itself needs to learn from religion? Should RE students therefore do religious things as well as study them? When people religiously celebrate, pray or wash, they perform rituals. Should rituals be performed as well as studied in RE? Would the physical enactment of rituals in addition to their observation and analysis promote a more engaged and fruitful spiritual encounter between students and the world of religion?

To answer this question and to consider whether classroom enactment is educationally permissible, it is necessary to look more closely at the nature of ritual.

The *Encyclopedia of Religion* describes rituals as 'voluntary, repetitious and stylised bodily actions, centred on cosmic structures and/or sacred presences'. The social anthropologist Victor Turner fills out this definition when he speaks of ritual as 'a stereotyped sequence of activities involving gestures, words and objects, performed in a sequestered place to influence preternatural entities or forces on behalf of the actors' goals and interests' (Turner 1977: 183). Rituals, then, are essentially bodily. You cannot perform rituals in your head. They are enacted rather than witnessed, and the actions are stylised, theatrical, and made stronger, not diminished, by repetition. The actions are accompanied by words and objects and are performed in a special space, set apart for the purpose from everyday life. In religious ritual, the focus will be a sacred presence or extraordinary power that can meet the actors' needs. Barbara Meyerhof refers to this possibility of life transformation when she claims, quoting Clifford Geertz, 'that rituals have the effect of fusing the dreamed-of with the lived-in order' (Schechner and Appel 1990: 246). In the context of ritual the community's deepest longings and aspirations can enter the everyday reality of their lives and world. Turner refers to this power to change as 'transformance', rituals transform those who perform them. Following Van Genep, Turner saw ritual in three phases: *separation*, when the participants move from their ordinary world to a special, sacred, 'sequestered' place of performance; *liminality*, the place of 'limen' or threshold where, through the elements of the ritual, the transformation would be effected; and *reaggregation* the return, changed, to the everyday world. So in marriage two persons go, usually accompanied by family and friends, to a special place to exchange promises and rings, break glasses, walk round a fire, and return to the world they had left, changed into a couple with a new joint identity. Rituals, according to Tom Driver 'are the oldest, in many ways oddest members of the performance family. Their business in society is to effect transformations that cannot otherwise be brought about' (Driver *The Magic of Ritual*).

Ritual is not confined to religion. It is not even confined to humankind. Ritualised behaviour is evident in the mating and conflict of other primates and in the life cycles of many other species. It is arguable that humans are of their nature ritual making animals, the predisposition hard wired into their make up and genetic inheritance (see chapter by Turner in Schechner 1993). Our sporting and social occasions and political events have their own rituals. Participants separate to the place of the match, rally, party or rave. Here, in an atmosphere charged by the press of others, the decoration and lighting, the music, chanting, speeches, special symbols, gestures, food and drink, they participate in a transformation which will affirm or alter identity, strengthen bonds, change relationships or shift perception. Then they return, more or less changed, into the routines of ordinary life.

The member of the performance family closest to ritual is perhaps theatre. But while there are important areas of overlap there are also important differences. These are usefully set out by Richard Schechner in his 'Efficacy–Entertainment Braid' (Schechner 1988: 120).

Efficacy (Ritual)	**Entertainment (Theatre)**
results	fun
link to an absent Other	only for those here
symbolic time	emphasis now
performer possessed in trance	performer knows what s/he is doing
audience participates	audience watches
audience believes	audience appreciates
criticism discouraged	criticism flourishes
collective creativity	individual creativity

Schechner stresses that the efficacy of ritual and the entertainment of theatre are not so much in opposition as two poles on a continuum, and adds: 'no performance is pure efficacy or pure entertainment' (1988: 120). That there is drama in religious ritual was noted by Honorius of Autun in the twelfth century. He observed that like the gestures and actions used by actors the cele-brant at mass 'represents by his gestures in the theatre of the church before the Christian people the struggle of Christ and teaches to them the victory of his redemption' (quoted by Schechner 1988: 125). What makes a particular perfor-mance ritual or theatre depends not on the gestures or objects used, but on the context. So, Schechner again: 'Any ritual can be lifted from its original setting and performed as theatre. This is possible because context and function, not fundamental structure or process distinguish ritual, entertainment and ordinary life from each other' (1988: 138). The 'Eucharist' enacted by the teachers on the retraining course was therefore theatre rather than ritual. It was a piece of drama used effectively for educational ends.

The significance of this for RE is that elements of ritual structure and process which predispose the performer to a reflective and engaged attitude and so the possibility of new insights and understanding, can be performed in a context not predetermined by the beliefs and doctrines of a faith. This predisposition encouraged by the creation of a setting, the use of music, dress, words, objects and actions not only results in a certain openness and a willingness to engage seriously with the subject of the event, but also provides invaluable insight into what religious ritual does for those who perform it. The understanding gained by means of performance is of a different order to the information resulting from reading a description or watching a video.

The threefold structure of separation, liminality and reaggregation is common to rituals across cultures and across the sacred secular divide. Similarly, the elements of celebration which charge the liminal space and effect transformation are common to many peoples and across Schechner's efficacy/entertainment, ritual/theatre continuum. Other elements of ritual also span the sacred and the secular. These include the orchestration of designated space by the framing of circles or squares, the appropriate use of light and colour, and the symbols specific to the group. There is also music. Colin Turnbull described music as 'the royal road to the liminal' (Schechner and Appel 1990: 77), because of its power to transform mood, shift perceptions and bind together the members of a group. The performers, wearing special clothing or masks may dance, perform gestures and effect particular postures. They will proclaim, chant, sing, listen to their founding stories, and keep silence. They will eat, drink, greet and embrace. They will use symbols: earth (especially its fruits), air, fire, and water. Again, none of these elements or practices is specific to religious ritual. Rather, the elements and the actions are part of the repertoire of human ritual-making.

What makes a celebration religious is not the gestures, the chanting or the eating but the context of the activities and their function in the lives of the participants. This will become clearer if we situate the two examples we began with on Schechner's 'Efficacy–Entertainment Braid'.

Let us take first the Retrain teachers and the 'Eucharist' and examine the event against each of the braids of the efficacy–entertainment continuum. The asterisks mark the position on the braid as given by the context and function of the event.

Efficacy (Ritual)	Entertainment (Theatre)
results *	fun
link to an absent Other	* only for those here
symbolic time	* emphasis now
performer possessed in trance	* performer knows what s/he is doing
audience participates *	audience watches
audience believes	* audience appreciates
criticism discouraged *	criticism flourishes
collective creativity *	individual creativity

There are results rather than fun. The results are educational and possibly spiritual, rather than religious or cosmic. The event is essentially for those who participate and lacks a focus on the absent Other. The time, though embracing an ancient act, is the present. The performers are not in trance. However, any intensification of experience or attention contributes to a deepened awareness of the matter under consideration and further insight into themselves as persons. They participate rather than watch (though they could choose to watch), and although some might be Christian believers, at this event they, with others who do not share their beliefs, are deepening their appreciation of the origins and history of this central act of worship. Their appreciation means their attitude is one of respect rather than criticism, and the structure and the communal nature of the event makes the creativity collective rather than individual.

On the braids that would make an event religious (belief/appreciation; trance/awareness; symbolic/present time; absent Other/those here) the event was firmly at the 'theatre' end of the continuum. Where, however, it occupies the 'ritual' end of the spectrum (collective creativity, audience participation) these are characteristics which enhance the effectiveness of the learning experience.

If we situate on the braids the other example we began with, *The Council of All Beings*, then the profile is similar, though in important respects different.

The emphasis is again toward educational results rather than fun, though the whole process of mask making and gathering in a circle is playful as well as serious. Like the 'eucharist' the emphasis is for those there, in the present, and again, though the use of masks, the drumming and the gathering in a circle create a heightening of experience, the participants know who they are and what they are doing. As with the earlier example the audience extensively participates rather than watches.

It is with the believe/appreciate braid that there is an important difference from the teachers at the 'Eucharist'. The students performing the *Council* obviously do not believe that they have become the beings represented by their masks. But the use of the masks and the suspension of disbelief is a dramatic means for exploring and expressing their own beliefs about the natural world and the nature of their relationship with other species. It is what they themselves believe that is at stake here, not just the 'appreciation' of what someone else may hold. The enactment is not a religious ritual, but it is an efficacious event in the sense that it creates a context where deeply held beliefs on a highly significant and complex subject can be clarified, shared and transformed.

On the remaining two braids (criticism discouraged/flourishes and collective creativity/individual), the pattern is similar to the other example with the emphasis towards the efficacy end of the spectrum.

What I think we have in these two examples is, first, a case for performing, respectfully, the rituals of religion. This is because, though they can provide an invaluable means for understanding religion when performed in the classroom, they are not religious rituals. Second, we have an illustration of how the performance of a ritual process, which is not directly related to a specific religion, can enable students to engage at depth with their own beliefs and so make a significant contribution to the spiritual dimension of the curriculum.

Elements of ritual process in the form of experiential learning strategies are already fairly widespread in Religious Education classrooms. Often these strategies are a kind of mini-ritual, in that they entail bodily enactment and active participation, and can be seen as elements of more elaborate ritual processes. Many teachers, for example, will build into their programmes of study exercises involving the use of *silence*, work with *symbol* and the exploration of *story*.

The structured use of silence will involve a range of stilling and meditative exercises that attend to sitting posture, breathing and the use of the imagination (see for example Beesley 1990, Erricker and Erricker 2001, Fontana and Slack 1997, Hammond and Hay 1990).

In working with symbol students explore the richness in objects of multiple and near universal meanings. The great symbols of earth, air, fire and water, of light and darkness, of the tree and animal forms are central elements of religious discourse and of all language. In choosing and interpreting symbols of themselves or responding to symbols in the art and architecture of religious traditions students can appreciate the nature of religious discourse which while rooted in the objects of the present looks toward a further reality. Paul Ricoeur's statement, 'The symbol gives rise to thought', depicts this quality and the related need for interpretation. It is the importance of symbol in religion and the need for interpretation that has been effectively developed into a teaching method and course of study in the Birmingham research project, *Religion in the Service of the Child* (RISC 1989–92).

Story is the primary mode of communication in religion. It is important that students have the opportunity to read, listen to and explore stories from many ages and places as well as the great founding narratives of the world's faiths.

Methods to lead them into the narratives are numerous and might include the motif of the quest, and draw on Auden's six characteristics of *Hero/Heroine*, the *Journey* undertaken, the *Obstacles* encountered, the *Hinderers* who obstruct, the *Helpers* who support and guide, and finally, the *Goal* or *Treasure* which lies at the end of the quest. Students can then apply these to their own life to open up their own quest, and also to the lives of religious founders and the history of a tradition.

Like ritual, the disciplined use of silence, the encounter with symbol, the telling and hearing of narrative are within and outside of religion and can act as bridges between the world of religion and the experience of the student. Because they predispose the learner to that open, engaged and subjective involvement in the content of the study they are strategies that are gateways to the spiritual dimension of the curriculum.

Though silence, symbol and story can be considered separately, in practice, in the classroom and in religion, there is often substantial overlap between these three and with other elements of ritual process. So, stilling exercises and the practice of silence usually involve ritual posture and the use of particular symbols. Narrative may be told in a ritual context and will contain important symbols that are themselves central elements in the enactment of ritual. Many rituals include silent reflection on their key symbols and shared story.

These experiential methods are also 'religious', or, perhaps, 'spiritual' exercises. But this is not because of their religious content, and certainly not because they require commitment to a particular belief or founder. They are religious or spiritual because they are practices or modes of apprehension that are firmly, though not exclusively, rooted in religion. They are what religious people do.

The more elaborated performance of ritual is perhaps less common though not unknown in RE classrooms. It is appropriate to use both religious and non-religious ritual forms, depending on the circumstances and aims. In the religious category, for example, teachers organise the performance of rites of passage: initiation rites, marriages, and funerals. Because enactment tends to hook in to the experience of the performers, funerals need to be handled with particular sensitivity. Given appropriate preparation the rites result in excitement, involvement and significant learning. At the classroom wedding the atmosphere engendered by a decorated space, the gathering, the music and the costumes, and the experience of the exchange of promises and joining of hands leaves a lasting impression – and everyone knows it is not a marriage. Pupils 'baptised' by full immersion (no water) by letting themselves fall slowly back into the receiving hands of their peers learn more about risk and trust as well as something of the dying and rising to the new life of the catechumen.

Enacting a Passover takes time in preparation, performance and debriefing. But the experience of the candles, cups and items of food on the set table, and then the recitation and eating and drinking gives students a memorable and important learning experience. They can encounter a model of suffering transformed in hope while growing in understanding of the origins, practices and hopes of the Jewish people.

Sue Phillips (1999: 39) describes the enactment of Yom Kippur with a group of Year 10 students. The classroom 'synagogue' was draped in white and the group, clad in white sheets, remove shoes and jewellery and stand in silence to hear the readings. Then, identifying with the festival's spirit of repentance, the students think of their own regrets and put these into a chosen stone that, at the end, is placed in a bowl of water for symbolic cleansing. 'It is alright for the Jews', one student remarked at the debriefing, 'they do it every year. I had so much to regret in a whole lifetime'.

In Church schools during Lenten services of reconciliation, chosen stones are used to embody regrets and failures, or statements of regret are written in secret on slips of paper. In a reflective context of music and readings the stones as burdens are released or the papers burnt, in a dramatic expression of the need and possibility of setting aside the past to begin again.

Built into the floor of the thirteenth-century Chartres Cathedral is a labyrinth, thirteen metres in diameter with its pathway winding two hundred and sixty metres from entrance to centre. This was a pilgrimage, a journey to the holy city, Jerusalem. The labyrinth is a microcosm of religious pilgrimage and life journey. It is a ritual of transformation where pilgrims leave the security of their homes for the hazards of a journey to the holy place, from which they later return, changed and renewed to take up again their life in the world. The labyrinth painted full size on a school playground excites interest, and invites participation. Students, aware of its origin and ancient purpose, are invited to make their own journey, in silence, to the centre and back. As they enter the labyrinth they are given a question, put to generations of pilgrims to carry with them: 'What do you seek?' The act of walking combined with the dynamics of the labyrinth encourages reflection on present experience and future hopes and provides a measured space to consider where life is going.

Whereas the above are drawn from religions, non religious rituals can also be used, or created. An example used effectively by numbers of teachers and already referred to is *The Council of All Beings* (Seed *et al.* 1988). This could accompany work on religions and environmentalism or be part of a consideration of the nature of religious ritual.

In preparation for *The Council of All Beings*, participants consider situations in the natural world that bring them joy, and those that bring sadness. There is the opportunity to talk with others about their experiences, then they are asked to leave the room in silence to identify a being in nature for which they feel a particular attraction. This could be an animal, a tree or plant, or an inanimate object like a mountain or river. When they return they are provided with materials to make a mask that they will wear to represent their chosen being at the Council.

The masked participants then assemble to music or drumming in the decorated space of the council circle. After the opening and appropriate readings, one by one the participants speak as their chosen beings of their life and its struggles, and leave a message for the 'two-legged ones'. The rest, as a group, acknowledge what has been heard. When all have spoken there is another short reading and words of closure. The masks are removed and laid in the circle, the group stands and before leaving is reminded, now as the 'two-legged ones', to carry what they have heard back into their everyday lives.

All the examples need situating in a syllabus. All need careful preparation, performance and debriefing. But all can deeply involve the pupils' own personal experience while forming an effective bridge between their experience and the practices and beliefs of the religions. All the examples are performance and rituals in the broader sense, and all are appropriate for use in school provided the context and function is essentially educational.

To conclude, if RE is to make a more significant contribution to the spiritual development of young people it needs to incorporate into its largely cognitive and cerebral repertoire of teaching strategies the wider enactment of ritual process. Because it is of the nature of ritual in human life to provide a safe passage at testing times of loss and transition, it can provide a supportive context to address and reflect on those areas of my life that are deepest and most significant to me. The performance of ritual can provide pupils with the opportunity of a more open, engaged and personally involved attitude to matters of moment and spiritual concern, and build an effective (and affective) bridge to the practices, convictions and wisdom of the religions. Participation in ritual is a 'royal road' to *Learning from Religion*. If Religious Education uses ritual, and so religious process as it teaches the content of the world's religions, then its contribution to the spiritual dimension of the curriculum will be truly significant. The enactment of more ritual in classrooms is therefore desirable. It is also permissible, and educationally sound, in that while performance of ritual in the classroom brings certain clear learning advantages, it does not presuppose religious commitment. Where the function and context are educational, ritual process can contribute powerfully to educational goals. The processes of ritual are indeed powerful, and require considerable sensitivity and skill on the part of the teacher. This will also mean that the teacher has first hand experience of the processes; that they have themselves performed and reflected upon the activities they offer to their students.

Turner used the term *communitas* to describe the interpersonal experience of the liminal phase of ritual. 'The bonds of communitas', he claimed, 'are anti-structural...They are undifferentiated, egalitarian, direct, extant, non-rational, existential, I–thou, relations. Communitas is spontaneous, immediate, concrete, it is not shaped by norms, it is not institutionalised, it represents the desire for a total, unmediated relationship between person and person' (Turner 1969).

Schools contain many rituals and, in a number of ways, are themselves the liminal space between the morning separation and the afternoon reaggregation in pupils' family lives. The effect of many school rituals is to promote a stratified and competitive mindset in which pupils, largely without thinking, are deferential to some while they compete with and subjugate others. If Turner is right about communitas, it is important in the interests of community, tolerance, equality and compassion – spiritual qualities prized within and beyond religion

– that the conscious awareness and widespread enactment of ritual process are a common feature of school life. Religious educators, out of their specialist understanding of ritual in religion, can provide the understanding and encourage the enactment of classroom and whole school rituals that meaningfully address issues of growth and transformation and help to strengthen the bonds of community and mutual respect.

Questions

1 Is it really easier to achieve AT1 than AT2? Why is this?
2 Think of some successes you have had where RE has really contributed to the spiritual dimension of the curriculum and the lives of your students. What was significant about the strategies you used? Did these strategies relate to or draw on the processes of ritual?
3 What do you see as the advantages and problems of incorporating the enactment of ritual in an RE syllabus?
4 Where in your syllabus could the enactment of ritual extend and enrich learning in RE and make a real contribution to the spiritual dimension of the curriculum?

16 Religious Education and Collective Worship

Bedfellows or just good friends?

Geoff Marshall-Taylor

Not too many waking hours are spent in schools by staff or governors weighing up the difference between Religious Education and Collective Worship. Mention the matter among most teachers and you are likely to get a glazed look and a distinct impression that the discussion is best left to anoraks, who like to pick over the minutiae of legislation and school policy.

And yet, looking into these two school activities, and giving rigorous thought to them, has to be an essential part of a school's policy-making and provision-assessment processes. Although RE is, like any subject, chiefly the preserve of the subject department, Collective Worship impinges on everyone in a school: even those staff who do not end up preparing or leading it, are, along with the pupils, consumers and participants, and they will have views, often definite views, about whether a particular assembly worked or not. Collective Worship provides one of the few occasions when teachers regularly see other colleagues in teaching mode, doing a presentation for a group, mainly made up of young people, but including adults as well.

There is a strong chance that, in any school, a teacher will at some time be drawn into planning or leading Collective Worship, maybe willingly, maybe reluctantly. If you are an RE specialist, there is an even stronger chance that senior management will look in your direction for help with Collective Worship. Maybe that is not unreasonable; after all, they do have elements in common. But often it reveals an unhelpful blurring in many people's minds about the two activities. They can seem like bedfellows, so why not leave them to the same people?

Collective Worship can be rewarding and at times can provide key inspirational moments for individuals and for a school community. Many of those who lead it see it as important and worthwhile; but, for some, it is a chore which they would rather do without. Some teachers would go further and, particularly in secondary schools, see it as counter-productive, even destructive for spiritual development. For some it is an inappropriate activity, given the diversity of belief positions – religious and non-religious – which are represented in any school community.

There is no doubt that leading Collective Worship is a challenging experience. The most nerve-jangling moment during my own PGCE course was when, on a school placement, the head asked me to take an assembly the next morning, because he and the deputy were called away and no one else was available. The request contained a piece of curious logic which illustrates the confusion about the activity. It went like this: 'You go to church, you'll know what to do.' True, I could find a story, a song and a prayer: that is what they had every day. But a school community is not a Church community, and I had given no thought to asking what sort of event Collective Worship ought to be and what expectations would be reasonable. Add to this uncertainty the reality that Collective Worship has as much to do with theatre as teaching, and the nerves set me up for a sleepless night. The theatrical element can be daunting – less so if the 'vision' is nothing more than a daily diet of blessed, or maybe not-so-blessed thoughts, passed on in a perfunctory way. What can be daunting is getting up in front of a large group of pupils and staff – in my case as scared as a stand-up on a first night – and attempting to turn on the school tribe, planning and presenting something that will engage; that will, for some, be memorable or even, on rare occasions, provide a pin-dropping moment that actually takes people further or in new directions on their intellectual and spiritual journeys.

So, it is worth giving some thought as a teacher to what Collective Worship is and what it can attempt to achieve. It is a different creature from Religious Education and needs to be understood and treated as such, in spite of some common elements which can be found in both. They are overlapping circles. Each is separate and needs to be seen as distinctive, particularly in the under-lying educational objectives. But there is common ground that needs to be acknowledged and seen as beneficial for individuals and the school community.

'Bedfellows' is not a word I'd choose to describe RE and Collective Worship. They are more like people in separate rooms which have inter-connecting doors. For the sake of clarity in policy and planning, it is easier to shut the doors between them and think of them separately. But then, when the identity of each is clear, it may well be worth opening up the connections and, who knows, it might be the beginning of a great relationship.

In England and Wales, RE and daily Collective Worship are statutory requirements. Schools are required to teach RE and provide daily Collective Worship. Although the main focus of this article is on those two countries, many of the principles and issues have a bearing on school worship in Northern Ireland and school 'Religious Observance' in Scotland.

The content of RE in England and Wales, which has to draw on Christianity and the other principal religions in the United Kingdom, is determined not by a national curriculum, but by locally agreed syllabuses. In the case of voluntary aided schools, most of which are Church of England or Roman Catholic foundations, the school draws up its own syllabus in keeping with its identity.

Recent years have seen RE taking significant strides in establishing its academic credentials as a subject, with great attention being paid to the content of syllabuses and schemes of work. Thorough in-service training, coupled with more rigorous inspection, has led to an improvement in standards and greater academic expectations. This has fed through from the primary to the secondary phase and, together with the new Short Course GCSEs, has led to an extraordinary increase in the numbers taking RE and RS at GCSE level.

There is a consensus throughout the UK that RE is about more than acquiring knowledge or information about religion. It is, in addition, about exploring ultimate questions such as the nature of suffering or the origins of the universe, about what it means to be part of a religious community and about engaging personally with the moral and religious perspectives which can inform important life issues and choices. In the past some RE teachers, feeling uncertain about stepping into, as they saw it, the quicksands by encouraging personal responses, retreated into the safety zone provided by knowledge-based RE content. This meant exploring predominantly the phenomena, the external certainties of religion such as key beliefs, festivals or sacred texts. In some classrooms this became no more riveting than a conducted tour of a valley of dry bones.

Of course, there are facts about religion and religious experience to be acquired, just as there is a language of religion to be understood: as with any subject this is about being equipped with some basic tools and ideas to enable young people to enter fully into the more dynamic, creative elements of personal enquiry and discovery that RE offers. As with any subject there are things to be learned, understood and explored. The nature of the material is such that, at times, it is likely to make an impact on pupils' own spiritual journeys. It is hard, for example, to hear the late Gordon Wilson's words of reconciliation, following his daughter's death in the Enniskillen bombing in Northern Ireland, without having to think hard about our own attitudes to people who have wronged us.

His words, tested literally in the fire, will probably have been introduced into an RE lesson in the context of finding out about Forgiveness, one of the key teachings of Christianity. It is a theme which cannot be investigated just by looking at the life and teachings of Jesus in the biblical narratives and by summarising the relevant doctrines and services of the Christian Church, although all those are likely to be part of class activity from Key Stage 2 upwards. It has also to be looked at in the light of the experience and commitment of Christians down the centuries, including Christians today. The theme will take on contemporary impact when seen through the lives of individuals, but also through societies or nations. For example, a class may consider the responses and attitudes of Christians in the black community in South Africa following the demise of apartheid, or the reasons why the majority of Christians, who believe in forgiveness as a reaction to wrong, support the punishment of offenders and the concept of a just war.

Such class activities may well be part of the RE syllabus adopted by a school. In addition, the teaching will be as capable of scrutiny as the teaching of any other subject in terms of objectives, schemes of work and assessment. The syllabus is likely to reflect the two attainment targets which formed part of the QCA (then SCAA) model RE syllabuses. These were 'learning about religion' and 'learning from religion'. 'Learning about religion' describes the knowledge based areas: the cognitive domain; 'learning from religion' relates to the experiential and responsive areas: the affective domain.

This is not the stuff of which Collective Worship is made. Planning is required, but not a syllabus. The word 'collective' indicates that this is an activity which is designed to make an impact on a group, not just on individuals: that might be a class, a tutor or year group, or a much larger gathering such as the whole school. The challenge is to present a theme in a way which will enable the whole group, whatever their belief backgrounds, to celebrate together, to be challenged together and to reflect together. This is why most head teachers see Collective Worship as providing key occasions in establishing the ethos of the school community and as a significant contributory factor in the spiritual development of pupils. It is often at times of sorrow that the bonding potential of Collective Worship can be most clearly seen. I recall powerful, pin-dropping moments in assemblies, which followed the death of a pupil or major news stories, such as the Hillsborough football disaster or the terrorist attacks on New York and Washington on 11 September 2001. Well-chosen prayers and moments of quiet reflection gave scope for acknowledging and, importantly, sharing grief and bewilderment, in addition to allowing opportunities for supportive prayer.

If Gordon Wilson's story were told as part of Collective Worship, it would give opportunities for the assembly group to reflect on the theme of forgiveness and make connections between his actions and their own life situations. The inclusion of this theme and story, as a model for personal choice and action, makes a statement that it is an ethical model, which the school community endorses on behalf of the wider community. But there is more to Gordon Wilson's words than an ethical reaction to wrong-doing. His motivation stemmed from a profoundly held Christian faith, which informed and influenced his life in all its aspects. Any retelling of his story should reflect this. Not everyone in the assembly will share in this faith, but the story is incomplete without it. Because of the different belief positions held by the pupils and staff, the responses to the story will be varied. For some, Gordon Wilson's faith will have a personal resonance, deriving from their own religious beliefs. For others it will not. Nevertheless, all present will potentially be able to respond to issues relating to forgiveness in the face of wrong-doing: therefore this will probably be the main focus of the assembly and the unifying concept for reflection.

Because of the diversity of any school community, Collective Worship has to be planned to allow for a variety of personal responses. Most schools are not faith communities: the same assumptions about belief consensus cannot be made as are made for gatherings of people in churches, mosques, gurdwaras, synagogues or temples. DfES *Circular 1/94*, which offers guidance on Collective Worship policy in England, underlines this:

> Worship in schools will necessarily be of a different character from worship amongst a group with beliefs in common.
>
> (DES 1/94 Para. 57)

Collective Worship assumes that the worship of God is involved, although the relevant legislation does not define worship. *Circular 1/94* says that it:

Should be concerned with reverence or veneration paid to a divine being or power.

(DES 1/94 Para. 57)

The aim of Collective Worship is stated in Paragraph 50 as:

> To provide opportunities for pupils to worship God, to consider spiritual and moral issues and to explore their own beliefs; to encourage participation and response.

The first part of the aim underlines the key distinction between RE and Collective Worship. Whilst exploring worship in Christianity and other religions is a part of all RE syllabuses, in Collective Worship everyone in the assembly, pupils and staff, is expected to have the opportunity actually to worship God for themselves individually and as a gathered group, as far as they are able.

'Opportunity' is a key word in this. My experience in preparing acts of worship, both in schools and for the BBC's widely used school Collective Worship series, is that it is possible to devise occasions which allow for different layers of response: the worship of God for those who have a religious faith and also, for everyone, engagement with a spiritual and ethical/moral dimension. Most schools see such inclusiveness as essential for Collective Worship, when, they would hope, occasions are provided which unite the school community. To achieve this, the wording used to present Collective Worship is as important as the material being used in allowing such layered responses. For example, there are a number of ways of introducing a prayer, which can acknowledge the range of possible levels at which different people can connect with it. One may be along these lines:

> Now let's be still for our reflection – a chance to pray or think about the words.

Or:

> I'm going to read a prayer now – just listen to the words if you like, or make them your own prayer.

Or:

> I'm going to read a Christian/Sikh/Jewish/etc., prayer about...let's think about the words.

I have found that, when asking pupils to write and read their own thoughts on a theme for Collective Worship, it works well to include in the presentation a mixture of prayers and non-religious reflections.

The well-known Prayer of St Francis illustrates how a specifically religious item can itself be inclusive. Although the opening line addresses God, the ideas in the body of the prayer are sentiments with which everyone present, whatever their beliefs, can identify or aspire to.

> Lord, make me an instrument of your peace.
> Where there is hatred, let me sow love;
> Where there is injury, pardon;
> Where there is discord, union;
> Where there is doubt, faith;
> Where there is despair, hope;
> Where there is darkness, light;
> Where there is sadness, joy.

A similar inclusiveness is the hallmark of most of the songs used in Collective Worship. Although singing is not a common feature in secondary schools, in primary school Collective Worship it plays a prominent part. The most widely used primary school anthology is the BBC's *Come and Praise* book (Marshall-Taylor 2000). Although it contains a selection of traditional hymns, those most sung are items, like the Prayer of St Francis, which are based in the Christian tradition but allow a range of responses, one of which is worship. There are, for example, several narrative songs about the life of Jesus, which achieve inclusiveness.

I have visited schools where, for a variety of reasons, they prefer not to invite everyone to sing: they have sometimes played a recording of a song or asked a choir to sing, in order to encourage reflective listening. Everyone participates, but in listening, not singing.

So many teachers have themselves been brought up on ' a story, a hymn and a prayer' that they assume that singing is a necessary ingredient. Appropriate songs, well sung, can be enjoyable, celebratory and unifying. More often than not, in primary schools they are. However, I've sat through too many secondary assemblies when the singing was both embarrassing and counterproductive, even alienating, for many pupils. In small tutor-group or year-group gatherings it is simply out of the question. Far better in those contexts to aim for short, pithy occasions which allow the sort of open, inclusive reflectiveness which can convey a sense of value for all present.

The choice of Collective Worship themes and material contributes as much to creating a climate of inclusiveness as the wording and manner of the presentation. *Circular 1/94* allows for considerable diversity in both. How can this be so if the Education Reform Act requires that Collective Worship in a community school is to be 'wholly or mainly of a broadly Christian character?'

In Paragraph 62 of 1/94 it makes it clear that:

> It is open to a school to have acts of worship that are wholly of a broadly Christian character, acts of worship that are broadly in the tradition of another religion, and acts of worship which contain elements drawn from a number of different faiths.

This is further emphasised in Paragraph 63, where it says that:

> Provided that, taken as a whole, *an act of worship*, which is broadly Christian, reflects the traditions of Christian belief, it *need not contain only Christian material* (my emphasis).

How might this work for a school's policy? First it means that a school can choose whether to have all its acts of worship broadly based on the Christian tradition; they would be 'wholly...of a broadly Christian character'. Alternatively they could base acts of worship on other traditions so long as the majority in, say, a term were based on the Christian tradition; they would then be 'mainly of a broadly Christian character'. It's worth underlining that this does not apply to Voluntary Aided or Controlled schools, which may well want all their Collective Worship to reflect the religious and denominational foundation of the school, whether that is Christian, Jewish, Muslim, Sikh or any other tradition.

In practice, how might a school include a diversity of material in Collective Worship? Let us take the example of a primary school which decides that it will have a week on the theme of water. They meet in varied groupings: whole school assemblies on three days, one class assembly day and one day when they meet as separate infant and junior gatherings. On the days when they are not meeting as the whole school, the Collective Worship co-ordinator provides a story and suggested reflection/prayer for the staff who are leading the classes or other groups. The variety of content is along these lines:

Day One: Whole school. *The importance of water in daily life*: what we use it for, statistics of the amounts we consume for different domestic, leisure and industrial purposes. Thanksgiving is the dominant note, coupled with reports about a Water Aid project the school is supporting. The song 'Think of a world without any flowers' would work well.

Day Two: Infant/Junior. *Water as a symbol of home and family*: the account in the Hebrew Bible (the Old Testament) when, during a campaign against the Philistines, three of King David's soldiers risked their lives to bring him well water from Bethlehem, his home village (2 Samuel 23). It was not because he was thirsty, but because it represented all the things about home for which he longed.

Day Three: Whole school. *A Muslim story, sometimes called* 'The Caliph's Reward' (from *The Paragon Parrot*) A. Scholey, in which a ruler hears that a Bedouin couple is coming to give him an offering of a cup of brackish water they have found in the desert. He asks that they be brought into the palace by a side door, so that they would not see the great river, which ran along the opposite side, lest they might feel that their gift was of little consequence. The theme is about the value we place on things in our lives.

Day Four: Class groups. *The story about Jesus and the great catch of fish* (Luke 5). This gives opportunity to consider how water provides a harvest of fish and our need to conserve this, even though the story is predominantly about the disciples' faith and trust in Jesus. Schools in fishing towns might be able invite a fisherman to talk briefly about his life and its dangers. This may lead to a prayer/reflection about people who work in the fishing industry. The prayer of the Breton fisherman would work well.

Day Five: Whole school. *A 'sharing assembly' with parents present.* Classes which have been doing work on *water in Science* (especially plant growth) show and talk about what they have found. This is a celebration, using a great deal of non-religious material, developing a sense of wonder at the properties of water.

Stories in Collective Worship need not be drawn only from religious sources. What makes them appropriate is the context they are placed in and the connections which are made between their themes and those present in the assembly. This was the basis of Jesus's own storytelling technique. He, in common with other Middle Eastern teachers, told anecdotes drawn from everyday life; he then used them to make a theological or moral point, or, at times, to leave his hearers with a cliff hanger question.

A great deal of material which is appropriate for Collective Worship also has a place in RE, as with the example of Gordon Wilson's story. What makes the difference are the objectives and the context provided by the presentation of the material. The use of the story of Esther, celebrated at the Jewish festival of Purim, illustrates this further. I have told it in Collective Worship with a variety of age groups, ranging from 4 to 13. In this biblical story, a young queen called Esther hears that a courtier called Haman is planning to destroy the Jewish community. Unknown to King Ahasueras, Esther herself is Jewish. She realises that only she can save her people, so, putting her life at risk, she approaches the king uninvited and, as a result of a sequence of events set in motion by her, the Jewish people are spared and Haman is killed.

When Jews celebrate Purim, this story is told in a pantomimic way, with children listening in fancy dress, booing, hissing and stamping whenever Haman's name is mentioned. There are special foods and some communities hold Purim fairs. In both RE and Collective Worship, the story can be told in this pantomimic way with loud and enthusiastic audience participation. In RE, the aim is to find out what happens at the festival and what it means to Jews today: there may be a chance to make some special Hamantashen cakes or have a visit from someone in a local Jewish community. It would be appropriate to link the story to the Holocaust and to wider Jewish history, which has given rise to the Jewish belief that God has been with them even in the most difficult situations. It may be profitable to explore the ways in which religious faith can make a difference in such circumstances. In RE, pupils would be 'learning about' Jewish life and beliefs through the festival and 'learning from' the celebrations through developing an understanding of what it means to be Jewish at Purim and when confronted with suffering. This is likely to lead to pupils considering their own responses to difficult situations.

In Collective Worship, the same story would be told, but it would be necessary to identify a theme in which everyone could share, as a focus for celebration and challenge. This theme might well be that of the courage to stand up for what is right, even when faced with difficult situations, using Esther's decision as the exemplum. There could also be a related assembly on bullying (with Haman as the starting point) and, on the other side of the same coin, respect for others. In these sorts of ways a specifically Jewish event can become the inspiration for a celebration, which has meaning and value for everyone present, staff and children alike. The prayer/reflection would provide an opportunity for those with a personal religious faith to relate their own beliefs to difficulties they may be facing; those without a faith background would be able to reflect on the need to make the right choices in all situations.

Can these Collective Worship ideas, based on Purim, be 'broadly Christian'? Apart from the fact that the story is in the Hebrew part of the Christian biblical canon, the themes which emerge from it – of making a stand against injustice and placing value on other people – are at the heart of the teachings of Jesus, who directed his followers to maintain the ancient Jewish precept to 'Love your neighbour as yourself'. In fact these are unifying principles common to most belief systems, religious and non-religious. Unquestioningly, they can be said to be 'broadly Christian'.

RE and Collective Worship do have much in common. Before the Education Reform Act, many schools saw Collective Worship as their means of teaching RE. The distinction which now exists in the legislation, in Circular 1/94 and in school policies and practices, has had a beneficial effect on RE: there are signs that it is now being approached with that sort of academic rigour which has been brought to other subjects. For many teachers, Collective Worship remains a difficult area both to plan and to present, although many feel relief when they find that a much greater variety of content and presentation is possible than, perhaps, a first reading of the legislation might indicate.

RE and Collective Worship may not be bedfellows. They are, however, definitely under the same roof. When you wander into their rooms at Spirituality Mansions, the furniture looks much the same. In fact they often swap it around and borrow bits and pieces from each other. But something is different. Then it dawns on you what it is; it is not the furniture itself. What is different is what they do with it. And that can sometimes be a world apart.

Questions

1 What are some of the distinctive characteristics of Religious Education and Collective Worship?
2 What is the value of Collective Worship for individuals and a school community?
3 What makes Collective Worship challenging to plan and present?
4 What guidelines and objectives would you devise for someone taking on the role of Collective Worship co-ordinator?
5 Given the diversity of beliefs among those present at school Collective Worship, what range of responses would you reasonably expect to achieve if you were leading it? What sorts of items would you want to include to encourage the responses?

17 World religions

The boundaries of belief and unbelief

John Bowker

Editors' introduction

There is no easy way to paint a picture of the importance and significance of Religious Education across the world. It means so many different things. Approaches differ within a European context and even within the British Isles, in fact, between Scotland and England. However, over the last thirty years John Bowker has been drawing attention to one highly pragmatic reason why RE matters so much: most of the long-running and intransigent disputes in the world have deep religious roots. Think only of Northern Ireland, the Middle East, the Balkans, Cyprus, the Sudan, Kashmir, Afghanistan, Sri Lanka, the Philippines, Indonesia, with others, like Nigeria, not far away. It is not that religions *cause* these conflicts, but religious beliefs certainly contribute to them. From *Licensed Insanities: Religions and Belief in God in the Contemporary World* (1987) to *Is God a Virus? Genes, Culture and Religion* (1995) and the article on Religion in *The Oxford Dictionary of World Religions* (1999) he has been warning that conflicts once conducted with swords and clubs will inevitably be conducted in the future with nuclear, biological and chemical weapons. The process has already begun.

Can we do anything about it? Clearly not, if those who make political and economic decisions have at best only a rudimentary understanding of religions. As he wrote in *Licensed Insanities*, 'Education is no panacea. As the saying has it, when you have educated the devil, what you have at the end is a clever devil. But education contributes to understanding and wisdom; and if I have appendicitis I would rather be treated by someone who has been medically educated than by one who proceeds by intuition and bedside reading' (Bowker 1987: 31ff.).

The remarkable feature of this chapter is its freshness and contemporary relevance: it could have been written in 2002. We believe John Bowker sets out the importance of Religious Education in a global context in a startling, almost frighteningly relevant way. His insight into religion carries a warning, that complacency is dangerous, and that students, politicians and teachers ignore religion at their peril.

World religions: the boundaries of belief and unbelief

In an interview for the programme *Sunday*, shortly after the introduction of the 1988 Education Reform Act for England and Wales, the then Secretary of State for Education defended the absence of Religious Studies from the new National Curriculum on the grounds that the study of religion was not an academic subject.

The defence clearly rests on an error: not only has the study of religion been an academic subject, at all levels of education, for many years, but provision for it as such is made in the Act. The error presumably arose because of the way in which, both in this and in the previous 1944 Education Act, RE was provided in conjunction with acts of worship. By linking the two to each other, and both to the local community, an emphasis has clearly been on respecting the wishes of parents (and of others, such as Church leaders) to initiate children into communities of faith – or not; hence the conscience clauses.

But the price to be paid for denying that the study of religion is an academic subject, in the sense that it should have belonged to the National Curriculum as first conceived, will always be extremely high. The subject was, by definition, marginalised, despite the fact that the legal safeguards were stronger than they had been. Since then, the situation has changed in that a minimum norm of 5 per cent RE curriculum time for all pupils in maintained schools has been approved by central government, and the School Curriculum and Assessment Authority has published national model syllabuses for RE that cover six religions during the course of both primary and secondary years of schooling. However, all this has done little to address the problem of how to guarantee that good-quality RE teaching is actually provided by schools, when specialist teachers are in short supply, and not all head teachers appreciate the significance of the subject.

Why is it then that RE is an academic subject of any importance? One reason undoubtedly stands out. On pragmatic grounds alone, the study of religions is necessary, since without it, it is impossible to understand the nature of so many bitter conflicts in the world today. For years I have been pointing out that religions are likely to destroy human life as we know it now on this planet.

Religions contribute to virtually all the intransigent and seemingly insoluble conflicts in the world. They are rarely the sole cause of those conflicts. There are always other contingent and contributing factors. But equally, it is false to say, as many do, that it is not the religions which cause the conflicts, but rather the misuse of religions for political or ideological ends. The truth is that religions cannot easily be disentangled from the politics and the ideologies in which they are immersed.

So it comes about that it is particularly easy to predict future conflicts of a serious kind: take a map of the world and draw on it the boundaries where religions (or sub-systems within a religion) meet; or where they are advancing towards each other, since the religious map is always on the move. There is nothing new in this. What is new is the scale and extent of the weapons with which these conflicts can be conducted. Yet far from realising, at a moment when this country is a great deal more pluralistic religiously than it has been in the past, that we need to understand the nature and dynamics of religions dispassionately and academically, we have kept the subject tied to the commitments in very subtle ways. Paradoxically, we are often too polite about religions for fear of appearing intolerant. As I put it in 1987:

> Religions are extremely dangerous animals; and one might well put up on their boundary the notice I saw once in a game reserve in Africa, 'Advance and be bitten'. And yet, despite the obvious involvement of religious beliefs and ideology in so many of the dangerous and destructive problems in the world, it is virtually impossible to find any politician or economist (let alone people who make the operative decisions in the worlds of commerce or industry) who has any serious knowledge of what religions are or why. As I put it in an article on this theme: 'One of the most obvious reasons why we seem to drift from one disastrous ineptitude to another is, ironically, that far too few politicians have read Religious Studies in Higher Education. As a result, they literally do not know what they are talking about on almost any of the major international issues. They simply cannot.'
>
> (Bowker 1987, p. 2)

It was no satisfaction – it was a frustrating misery – to see and hear this demonstrated in the Gulf crisis and war and again in the former Yugoslavia.

In the first chapter of the same book, and now in more detail in *Is God a Virus? Genes, Culture and Religion* (1995), I have tried to show why religions are so dangerous, and why we need a more extensive understanding of them. In brief, religions are bad news because they are good news. Religions are extremely long-running and strong systems, which protect information. They are the oldest cultural systems, to which we have access through evidence, for the protection of gene-replication and the nurture of children; hence the preoccupation of religions with food and sex. But manifestly, religions protect the transmission of information (from life to life and from generation to generation) of a far more extensive kind than that. Religions are the resource of virtually every kind of human creativity and achievement, even to the point where they became the context in which humans discovered that they were themselves discovered and created by God.

Fundamentally, therefore, religions are systems in which symbols are generated and sustained through which individuals and groups can maintain their lives coherently (both in terms of meaning and in terms of social reality), and through which also the structured properties of the human brain (the 'preparedness' from the genes of biogenetic structuralism) can be given adequate, and often new, expression.

It is here that we can see why issues of authority can be tense, though they are not always so. Religions must necessarily be conservative as systems: they must conserve the symbol system which has, up to that point, been life-giving. Yet equally, the incorporation of symbols may be powerfully innovative and creative. So a religious system (that is to say, the operators of, and participants in, a religious system) may give conservation such high priority that maintaining the system and the transmission of information becomes an end in itself; or it may be highly innovative, seeing the maintenance of the system as a means to some other end, which may range from personal enlightenment to the coming of *the* End. Systems are by no means identical to each other, simply by virtue of being systems. To understand the conversation of any religion with the world around it, one needs to understand what the priorities are which are set within the system itself. That is an academic subject, which requires great attention to detail, and which has enormous political implications.

This can be seen through the example referred to allusively above, 'the coming of the End'. But what 'end'? Religions differ greatly in their answer to that question. But at the same time, all the major and continuing religions portray, or at least point to, both proximate and ultimate futures which constrain their present behaviours. This is what I have called 'cultural prolepsis' (in contrast to what anthropologists call 'cultural lag'). Religions live towards immediate futures, in which appropriate behaviours are mapped and described; and they live also towards eschatological futures, which can also be mapped and described; and in both cases (immediate and eschatological) the consequences are causative on present behaviour.

This is a dramatic example, therefore, of what is known as 'downward causation'. In biological terms, this means that in an evolutionary advance of exploration into new environments, in which successful mutations are encoded for subsequent generations, the conditions of success are set by the environmental circumstances into which the mutation (and its organism) are projected. In that sense the future causes the present. That is to say (using the language of 'constraint' rather than 'cause', for reasons developed at greater length in *Licensed Insanities* (1987) and *Is God a Virus?* (1995)), conditions which lie in the future, from the point in time of the organism, are a part of the network of constraint which delimits the range of possibility into its eventuality – into its being that which comes to pass. Thus in hierarchically organised biological systems, the conditions of each of the higher (more complex) orders determine in part the distribution of lower-level events and substances. The organisational levels of molecule, cell, tissue, organ, organism, breeding population, species, ecosystem, social system, are not arbitrary. At each level, the processes at the lower levels are constrained by, and act in conformity with, the requirements and laws of the higher levels.

This means that in the organisation of available energy, the higher levels of organisation, including the macrosocial phenomena of contemporary human life, are as real and causal as the atoms and molecules on which they depend. While this means that it is not possible to reduce higher-level behaviours to the chemistry and physics on which they nevertheless depend, it also means, the other way around, that the futures which humans construct act as powerful constraints on their present behaviours. We can trivialise this at the level of horoscopes and tea-leaves, or we can ennoble it by the promises we make and try to keep: 'Will you take this woman to be your wedded wife? Will you love her, comfort her, honour and protect her, and, forsaking all others, be faithful to her as long as you both shall live?'

In the case of religions, the future constraint can be even more decisive in the forming of present behaviours, particularly when it relates the believer to eternal reward or punishment. That is why, despite a politician's surprise at the fact, it was possible for *both* sides to win the Gulf war, even though one of them is left in a derelict condition. Religions live towards futures which are encoded in strong symbols. These allow religious believers to decode present circumstances in ways which do not necessarily conform to other kinds of analysis. The complex codes of religious symbol systems need to be learned – and that is a task far beyond the impressive linguistic competence which such institutions as a state department and Foreign Office already and undoubtedly require if we are to have some chance of understanding the politics of the contemporary world.

The key to such understanding lies in recognising the dynamics of continuity in the case of religious systems, since clearly the dilemma of any religion is how to sustain the system in the face of threats to it. The threats may be physical and literal, or they may be conceptual. Thus secularisation is often described as a competing ideology – as what Don Cupitt calls 'the shift from myths to maths'. But in fact displacement theories of secularisation are proving increasingly barren. Nevertheless, in so far as secularisation is a word which describes the consequences arising from the proliferation of choices, of which choice among ideas, including religious ideas, is a part, it clearly creates strategic problems for religious systems. Secularisation is not a 'thing', prowling about and seeking what religions it may devour. It is a term which summarises the preferential option for options which characterizes Western styles of democracy. For religions (immersed in such democracies) whose own style, particularly in relation to political decision making, does not allow for such openness of choice, the problem is extreme. David O'Brien (1987) has traced the painful process through which Roman Catholics in the USA had to come to terms with the fact that the separation of Church and state in the Constitution would not allow them to implement a European style of Catholic control, not even indirectly through the 'Catholicisation' of US institutions. So he concluded:

> If American Catholicism is to survive, even more if it is to make a substantial contribution to public life, it will have to engage directly the reality of voluntarism, the evangelical imperatives, and the reliance on popular support which are the inevitable by-products of religious pluralism in a democratic society.
>
> (O'Brien 1987, p. 25)

But all this can represent a profound threat to those who see it as their responsibility to protect and transmit non-negotiable information (information, of course, means much more than verbal items) to subsequent generations. One predictable response is to mark the boundaries more securely and more defensively; or offensively, if that is regarded as the better form of defence. And where boundaries exist, border incidents will always occur.

Such incidents are not always incidents of conflict. They may be explorations of the conditions of coexistence, for all religions have voices of inclusion as well as exclusion. But this again only emphasises how important it is to bring the study of religion much more centrally (and academically) into the curriculum. Religions are not going to go away or be eroded by a new world-view (the wrong understanding of secularisation). They are long-running systems which have given meaning and value, vision and truth, to virtually the whole human population for millennia – as to most people they still do. It is all the more important, therefore, to reinforce the voices of inclusion and coexistence, so that the incipient schisms in the human communities of knowledge and understanding are not rent open even more widely than they already have been.

The study of religion, then, seeks to understand the kind of stories which people tell through their lives, and how the components of those stories are sustained and made available in particular societies or families, or schools. It is here that religious authority is located, because it arises from the nature of the resource which supplies a particular story into life. The various '*Guides, Gurus and Gods*' (to quote the title of a BBC series) may be very different, and what they offer may be extremely different. But they have authority because they become, at least to some extent, authors or joint authors of those other lives. In the Latin dictionary of Lewis and Short, *auctor* is defined as he who brings about the existence of any object, or promotes the increase of prosperity of it, whether he first originates it, or by his efforts gives greater permanence or continuance to it. It is an excellent definition of religious understandings of creation; and from it flows the meaning of *auctoritas*: basically, it has to do with bringing something into being, an invention. So it also means an opinion, or advice, or encouragement. It means weight, or importance, and hence power and our sense of authority: to have the power to bring something into being, and to do so, is to be the author of its being.

In all religions, authorship and authority may be exercised in a dictatorial manner, a literal 'dictation' of the stories that ought to be told: Vatican Catholicism under the present Pope is a spectacular, albeit tragic, example of a religious system discerning threats to its boundaries and reacting defensively. The tragedy arises because it creates a radical dissonance between the stories that Catholics tell through their lives and the stories the Vatican is attempting to tell through them. All religions have the means within themselves to act in a comparable way. But since secularisation means the proliferation of choices, there would be a far greater wisdom in religions (at least if they are looking to their own future) integrating the religious choice as being of paramount worth within the multiplicity of options, rather than setting it against the world as though all the world's options are inimical. Thus (to give just one example), the notion of *taqlid* in Islam could well be seen as a warrant for an aggressive imposition of authority. In Schacht's succinct definition, *taqlid* means 'clothing with authority' in matters of religion, the 'adoption of the utterances or the actions of another as authoritative with faith in their correctness without investigating his reasons'. And certainly the meaning of the verb *qallada* reinforces that impression of blind obedience: 'to put a rope around the neck of an animal in order to lead it along'. But while *taqlid* undoubtedly means accepting the authority of earlier generations in interpreting *fiqh*, it does not imply unquestioning conformity to their decisions with no further reflection. If that appears to be happening in Islam, then there would be a greater wisdom in establishing dispassionately (and academically) why it is a contradiction of Islam. Blind reliance on authority is rejected in Islam, whatever the impressions to the contrary; and that is why at the head of al-Bukhari's collection of *ahādith* stands a tradition which states: 'Surely actions will be judged *biniyya* [by intention], and a person will have what he intends'.

The issue of authority in religion, therefore, is always the issue of constraint: how is the transference to be effected (if it is effected) from external authority to the internalisation of the constraints which are the necessary condition of attainment and of freedom? We are familiar, in biology, with the observation that the greater the network of constraints, the greater the resulting degrees of freedom for the organism concerned. We are equally familiar with this in all other aspects of learning, whether of physics, French or the flute. In the last case, it requires the internalisation of the constraints of notation, fingering and scales, as well as the limitation on options in spare time, before you are eventually brought into the far greater freedom of playing your own music. The same applies, *mutatis mutandis*, to religious life. The crisis of religions at the present time is brought about by, on the one side, those outside religions who refuse to acknowledge the profound place that religious symbol systems still play in the construction of human lives (e.g. the nineteenth-century attitudes which seem to prevail amongst civil servants responsible for education), and on the other, those inside religions who refuse to allow the internalisation of constraints to lead to imaginative and creative freedom.

Putting the two extremes together, religion is written off by the one extreme as fundamentalist fanaticism, which the other extreme then promptly confirms by its behaviours.

Mediating between the extremes is RE as it has been unfolding in the postwar years, against great odds, but with nevertheless enormous achievements on which to build. Shap[1] initiatives constitute but one voice within this appeal, that to understand the destructive and intransigent problems of the world, we need immensely better (and much more widespread) understanding of religions. Religions are only bad news because they are such good news. We have to appreciate all that religions have meant to people in constructing through their lives virtually all the memorable achievements of what we now call civilisation. Because religions matter so much, those who belong to them become 'edgy' (to say the least) when they perceive the necessary boundaries of the system coming under threat. The study of all this, and in particular of the dynamics of religious systems, is manifestly an academic subject. When will this or any other government take it seriously as such?

Note

This chapter was originally published in *Freedom and Authority in Religions and Religious Education* edited by Brian Gates (Cassel Education 1996). It is re-produced here with permission from the publisher and the author.

1 The Shap Working Party in World Religions in Education.

Bibliography

Adams, C. (ed.) (1986a) *Primary Matters: Some Approaches to Equal Opportunities in Primary Schools*, London: ILEA.
—— (ed.) (1986b) *Secondary Issues: Some Approaches to Equal Opportunities in Primary Schools*, London: ILEA.

Alexander, R., Rose, J. and Woodhead, C. (1992) *Curriculum Organisation and Classroom Practice*, London: HMSO.

Altena, P., Hermans, C.A.M. and Van Der Ven, J. (2000) 'Towards a Narrative Theory of Religious Education: A Study of Teachers' Aims in Catholic Primary Schools', *International Journal of Education and Religion* 1(2): 217–47.

Anthony, S. (1998) *Discovery of Death in Childhood and After*, London: John Bowlby.

Arnot, M. and Miles, S. (eds) (1996) *Promoting Equality Awareness: Women as Citizens, A Pedagogic Handbook for Initial Teacher Education for Secondary Schools* (94-00-EGA-0194-00, EEC).

Arthur, C. (1990) *Biting the Bullet: Some Personal Reflections on Religious Education*, Edinburgh: The Saint Andrew Press.

Assessment and Qualifications Alliance (AQA) (1999) *General Certificate of Education: Religious Studies Specification 2000/2001 Advanced Subsidiary and Advanced*, London: AQA.

Asteley, F. and Francis, L. (1996) *Christian Theology and Religous Education*, SPCK, pp. 165–83

Bailey, R. (2000) *Teaching Values and Citizenship Across the Curriculum*, London: Kogan Page.

Ballard, R. (1994) *Desh Pardesh: The South Asian Presence in Britain*, London: Hurst.
—— (1999) 'Panth, Kismet, Dharm te Qaum: Continuity and Change in Four Dimensions of Punjabi Religion' in Pritam Singh and S.S. Thandi (eds), *Punjabi Identity in a Global Context*, New Delhi: Oxford University Press, 7–37.

Barratt, M. (1994a) *An Egg for Babcha*, Oxford: Heinemann.
—— (1994b) *Lucy's Sunday*, Oxford: Heinemann.
—— (1994c) *The Seventh Day is Shabbat*, Oxford: Heinemann.
—— (1994d) *Something to Share*, Oxford: Heinemann.
—— (1994e) *The Buddha's Birthday*, Oxford: Heinemann.

Barratt, M. and Price, J. (1996a) *Meeting Christians*, Book One, Oxford: Heinemann.
—— (1996b) *Meeting Christians*, Book Two, Oxford: Heinemann.
—— (1996c) *Meeting Christians*, Book One, Teacher's Resource Book, Oxford: Heinemann.

Baumann, G. (1999) *The Multicultural Riddle: Rethinking National, Ethnic and Religious Identities*, London: Routledge.

BECTa (2000) *Using ICT in RE: Supporting a Pupil's Entitlement*, London: BECTa.

Beesley, M. (1990) *Stilling*, Salisbury: Salisbury Diocesan Board of Education.

Beier, U. (ed.) (1966) *Origins of Life and Death: African Creation Stories*, Oxford: Heinemann.

Berger, P.L. (1999) *The Desecularization of the World*, Grand Rapids, MI: Eerdmans.

Bigger, S. and Brown, E. (1999) *Spiritual, Moral, Social and Cultural Education*, London: David Fulton.

Bildungsdirektion des Kantons Zuerich (2000) Weiterentwicklung des Konfessionellkooperativen Religionsunterrichts an der Oberstufe der Volksschule in das Fach "Religion und Kultur", paper (Zuerich).

Bishop's Conference of England and Wales (1996) *Religious Education, Curriculum Directory for Catholic Schools*, London: Catholic Education Service.

Bowker, J. (1987) *Licensed Insanities: Religions and Belief in God in the Contemporary World*, London: Darton, Longman & Todd.

—— (1995) *Is God a Virus? Genes, Culture and Religion*, London: SPCK.

Brannen, J. (ed.) (1992) *Mixing Methods: Qualitative and Quantitative Research*, Aldershot: Avebury.

Brown, A. and Brown, E. (1996) *Religious Education in the Primary School*, London: The National Society.

Brown, E. (1996) *Religious Education for All*, London: David Fulton.

—— (1998) *Signposts and Milestones: Implementing the Agreed Syllabus in Special Schools*, Westminster College Worcestershire C.C.

—— (2001) *Enabling Access*, London: David Fulton.

Burghart, R. (1987) *Hinduism in Great Britain: The Perpetuation of Religion in an Alien Milieu*, London: Tavistock.

Burridge, S. (1999) *To Surf or Not to Surf? That is the Question* Resource 22, Derby: PcfRE.

Byrne, A., Malone, C. and White, A. (2000) *Here I Am, A Religious Education Programme for Primary Schools*, London: Collins.

Cam, P. (ed) *Thinking Stories 1 and 2* (1993/1994) Hale and Iremonger.

Carpenter, B., Ashdown, R. and Bovair, K. (2001) *Ennabling Access*, 2nd edn, London: David Fulton.

Chief Inspector of Schools (1995) *Religious Education: A Review of Inspection Findings 1993–4*, London: HMSO.

Christ, C. and Plaskow, J. (eds) (1985) *Womanspirit Rising: A Feminist Reader in Religion*, New York: Harper and Row.

Church Schools Review Group (2001) *The Way Ahead: Church of England Schools in the New Millennium*, London: Church House Publishing.

Clarricoates, K. (1981) 'All in a Day's Work', in D. Spender and E. Sarah (eds), *Learning to Lose*, London: The Women's Press.

Cole, D., Hill, D. and Shan, S. (1997) (eds) *Promoting Equality in Primary Schools*, London: Cassell.

Copley, T. (1997) *Teaching Religion*, Exeter: Exeter University Press.

Cooling, T. (1994) *A Christian Vision for State Education*, London: SPCK.

—— (1996) *Education is the Point of RE – not Religion?*, London: SPCK.

Cox, E. (1983) *Problems and Possibilities for Religious Education*, London: Hodder & Stoughton.

Cox, E. and Cairns, J. (1989) *Reforming Religious Education: The Religious Clauses of the Education Reform Act*, London: Kogan Page.

Daly, M. (1974) *Beyond God the Father: Toward a Philosophy of Women's Liberation*, Boston: Beacon Press.

Davie, G. (1994) *Religion in Britain since 1945*, Oxford: Blackwell.

—— (1999) 'Europe: The Exception That Proves the Rule?', in P.L. Berger (ed.), *The Desecularization of the World*, Grand Rapids, MI: Eerdmans, 65–83.

Dearing, R. (1996) *Review of Qualifications for 16–19 year olds*, London: SCAA.

Deem, R. (1978) *Women and Schooling*, London: Routledge & Kegan Paul.

—— (ed.) (1980) *Schooling for Women's Work*, London: Routledge & Kegan Paul.

Delamont, S. (1980) *Sex Roles and the School*, London: Methuen.

DES (1977) *Curriculum 11–16*, London: HMSO.

—— (1985) *Education for All: The Report of the Committee of Inquiry into the Education of Children from Ethnic Minority Groups* (The Swann Report), London: HMSO.

—— (1988) *Education Reform Act 1988: Religious Education and Collective Worship* (Circular 3/89), London: HMSO.

DfEE (1996) *National Literacy Project*, London: DfEE.

—— (1997) *National Literacy Strategy*, London: DfEE.

—— (1999) *Preparing Young People for Adult Life: A Report by the National Advisory Group on Personal, Social and Health Education*, London: DfEE.

—— (1999) *The National Curriculum: Handbook for Primary Teachers in England*, London: DfEE.

DfEE/QCA (2001) *Planning, Teaching and Assessing the Curriculum for pupils with Learning Difficulties: Religious Education*, London: DfEE/QCA.

—— (2001) *Key Stage 3: National Strategy: Language at Work in Lessons*, London: DfEE/QCA.

Deflem, M. (1991) 'Ritual, Anti-Structure and Religion', *Journal for the SSR* 30:1.

Durham Commission (1970) *The Fourth R*, London: SPCK.

Durham Diocesan Board of Education (1993) *Durham Diocesan Syllabus for Religious Education in Church Aided Primary Schools*, Durham: Diocesan Board of Education.

Durkin, K. (1996) *Developmental Social Psychology* Blackwell.

Edexcel (2000) *Edexcel Advanced Subsidiary GCE in Religious Studies, Edexcel Advanced GCE in Religious Studies*, London: Edexcel Foundation.

Eggenburger, H. (2000) in Schreiner, P. *Religious Education in Europe*, Müns Cr pp. 165–70.

Erikson, E. (1956/1977) *Childhood and Society*, St. Albans: Triad/Paladin.

Erricker, C. (1998) 'Spiritual Confusion: A Critique of Current Education Policy in England and Wales', *International Journal of Children's Spirituality* 3(1): 51–63.

Erricker, C. and Barnett, V. (1988) *World Religions in Education: Women and Religion*, Chichester: SHAP/CRE.

Erricker, C. and Erricker, J. (2001) *Meditation in Schools*, London: Continuum.

Everington, J. (1996a) 'A Question of Authenticity: The Relationship between Educators and Practitioners in the Representation of Religious Traditions', *British Journal of Religious Education* 18(2): 69–78.

—— (1996b) *Meeting Christians*, Book Two, Teacher's Resource Book, Oxford: Heinemann.

Everington, J. and Jackson, R. (1995) *Bridges to Religions: Teacher's Resource Book*, The Warwick RE Project, Oxford: Heinemann.

—— (1995) *Interpreting Religions* series, Oxford: Heinemann.

Fontana, D. and Slack, I (1997) *Teaching Meditation to Children*, Element.

Francis, L.J. (2000) 'The Domestic and the General Function of Anglican Schools in England and Wales', *International Journal of Education and Religion* 1(1): 100–121.

Garcia, J. and Maitland, S. (1983) *Walking on the Water: Women Talk about Spirituality*, London: Virago.

Gates, B. (1996) *Freedom and Authority in Religions and Religous Education*, Cassel Education.

Geaves, R. (1998) 'The Borders between Religions: A Challenge to the World Religions Approach to Religious Education', *British Journal of Religious Education* 21(1): 20-31.

Geertz, C. (1973) *The Interpretation of Cultures*, New York: Basic Books.

Gilborn, D. and Mirza, H.S. (2000) *Educational Inequality: Mapping Race, Class and Gender*, London: HMSO.

Goldman, R. (1964) *Religious Thinking from Childhood to Adolescence*, London: Routledge & Kegan Paul.

Gower, R. (1986) 'Equal Opportunities in Religious Education', *RE News and Views* 3(2): 14.

Grimmitt, M. and Read, G. T. (1977) *Teaching Christianity in R.E.*, Kevin Mayhew, Leigh-on Sea, Essex.

Grimmitt, M. (1973) *What Can I Do in RE*, Great Wakering: Mayhew-McCrimmon.

—— (1987) *Religious Education and Human Development: The Relationship Between Studying Religions and Personal, Social and Moral Education*, Great Wakering: McCrimmon.

—— (ed.) (2000) *Pedagogies of Religious Education*, London: McCrimmon.

Groothuis, D. (2000) *Truth Decay*, Leicester: IVP.

Guimeli, A. (1983) 'The Problem is the Image', *RE News and Views* 3(2): 14.

Hall, J. and Waters, J. (eds) *Dialogue: A Journal of Religion & Philosophy*.

Hammersley, M. and Atkinson, P. (1995) *Ethnography: Principles in Practice*, 2nd edn, London: Routledge.

Hammond, J. and Hay, D. (1990) *New Methods in Teaching RE: An Experiential Approach*, Essex: Oliver & Boyd.

Hampshire Education Authority (1980) *Paths to Understanding*, Winchester: Hampshire Education Authority.

Hanlon, D. (1986) 'Identify Sexism, Create Opportunities and Bring about Change in the Classroom', *RE News and Views* 3(2): 14.

—— (2001) 'Struggling, Stumbling or Surviving? Some Reflections on Initial Teacher Training for Religious Education', *Education Today* 51(1): 25–30.

Hay, D. (1982, 1987) *Exploring Inner Space: Is God Still Possible in the Twentieth Century?*, Oxford: Mowbray.

—— (1998) *The Spirit of the Child*, London: HarperCollins.

Heimbrock, H.G., Scheilke, C.T. and Schreiner, P. (2001) *Towards Religious Competence*, Münster, LIT-Verlag.

Heyward, C. (1979) 'Reuther and Daly: Theologians Speaking and Sparking, Building and Burning', *Christianity and Crisis* 39(5): 66–72.

Hick, J. (1986) 'Theology and Verification' Chap 3 in Mitchell, B., (ed) *The Philosophy of Religion*, OUP..

Hill, B. (1982) *Faith at the Blackboard*, Grand Rapids, MI: Eerdmans.

—— (1985) 'Values Education in a Secular Democracy', *Journal of the Indian Council for Philosophical Research* 3: 65–79.

—— (1986) 'The Educational Needs of the Children of Expatriates', *Missiology: An International Review* 14(3): 325–46.

—— (1990) 'Will and Should the Religious Studies Appropriate to Schools Foster Religious Relativism?', *British Journal of Religious Education* 12(3): 126–36.

—— (1999a) 'Can Religious Education be Theologically Neutral?', *Journal of Christian Education* 42(1): 9–24.

—— (1999b) 'Should the Fourth R for Generation X be S?', *Journal of Education and Christian Belief* 3(1): 9–22.

Hill, D. and Cole, D. (1997) 'Introduction', in D. Cole, D. Hill and S. Shan (eds), *Promoting Equality in Primary Schools*, London: Cassell.

Hirst, P. (1974) *Knowledge and the Curriculum*, London: Routledge & Kegan Paul.

Hobson, P. and Edwards, J. (1999) *Religious Education in a Pluralist Society*, London: Woburn Press.

Holm, J. and Bowker, J. (eds) (1994) *Picturing God*, London: Pinter Publishers Philosophy for Children.

Hull, J. (1998) *Utopian Whispers*, Norwich: RMEP.

—— (2001) *'Religious Education in Western Pluralistic Societies: Some General Considerations'*, unpublished paper, Istanbul, 28 March 2001.

Hull, J.M. (1989) *'The Act Unpacked: The Meaning of the 1988 Education Reform Act for Religious Education'*, Birmingham Papers in Religious Education (University of Birmingham and the Christian Education Movement).

Inner London Education Authority (1987) *Sexism and Religious Education*, Policy Sub-Committee Equal Opportunities Section, London: ILEA.

Ipgrave, J. (1998) *Religious Education and Muslim Students*, London: Teacher Training Agency.

—— (1999) 'Issues in the Delivery of Religious Education to Muslim Pupils: Perspectives from the Classroom', *British Journal of Religious Education* 21(3): 146–57.

—— (2001) *Pupil-to-Pupil Dialogue in the Classroom as a Tool for Religious Education*, Occasional Papers 2, Coventry: Warwick Religions and Education Research Unit, University of Warwick.

Isaacs, N. (1930) 'Children's 'Why' Questions' in Isaacs, S. *Intellectual Growth of Young Children*, London: Routledge & Kegan Paul.

Jackson, R. (1989) *Religions through Festivals: Hinduism*, London: Longman.

—— (1997) *Religious Education: An Interpretive Approach*, London: Hodder & Stoughton.

Jackson, R. and Nesbitt, E. (1993) *Hindu Children in Britain*, Stoke-on-Trent: Trentham.

Johnson, C. (1996) *Christian Teachers and World Faiths*, Derby: CEM.

Kaempf, B. (2000) 'France' in P. Schreiner (ed.), *Religious Education in Europe*, Münster, 43–8.

Katalushi, C. (1998) 'Teaching Traditional African Religions and Gender Issues in Religious Education in Zambia', *The British Journal of Religious Education* 21(2): 101–20.

King, U. (1987) *Women in the World's Religions, Past and Present*, New York: Paragon House.

—— (1988) *Some Reflections on Women and World Religions*, New York: Paragon House.

—— (1990) 'Religion and Gender', in U. King (ed.), *Turning Points in Religious Education*, Edinburgh: T & T Clark, 275–86.

—— (ed.) (1995) *Religion and Gender*, Oxford: Blackwell.

Krisman, A. (2001/02) 'The Yin and Yang of RE and Special Needs in 'Living Community', in Brown, A. and Hayward, M. (eds) *Journal of the SHAP Working Party on World Religions in Education*, 83–5.

Kung, H. (1978) *On Being a Christian*, London: Collins.

Lall, S. (1999) *I Know Who God Is*, Oxford: Farmington Institute for Christian Studies.

Lambert, R. (2000) *Resources for Teaching Sikhism at Key Stage 1*, Oxford: Farmington Institute for Christian Studies.

Lincolnshire County Council (2000) *Lincolnshire Agreed Syllabus for RE*, Lincoln: Lincolnshire County Council.

Longhorn, F. (1993) *Religious Education for Very Special Children*, London: ORCA Publications.

Louden, L. and Urwin, D. (1992) *Mission, Management and Appraisal*, London: The National Society.

Loukes, H. (1961) *Teenage Religion*, London: SCM Press.

Macpherson, W. (1999) *The Stephen Lawrence Inquiry: Report of an Inquiry by Sir William Macpherson of Cluny*, The Stationery Office.

Manchester Diocesan Board of Education (1995) *Syllabus for Religious Education*, Manchester: Diocesan Board of Education.

Mantin, R. (1997) *Religious Education*, in D. Cole, D. Hill and S. Shan (eds), *Promoting Equality in Primary Schools*, London: Cassell, 331–48.

Mantin, R., Cole, M., Hill, D. and Shan, S. (1997) *Promoting Equality in Primary Schools*, London: Cassell.

Marshall-Taylor, G. (2000) *Come and Praise*, London: BBC.

Martin, J. (1999) 'Gender in Education', in D. Matheson and I. Grosvenor (eds), *An Introduction to the Study of Education*, London: David Fulton, 103–15.

Martin, M.J., White, A., Brook, A., Gray, P., May, Y. and Walmsley, D. (2000) *Icons, A Religious Education Programme for 11–14*, London: Collins.

Methodist Church Division of Education and Youth (1996) *Student Entitlement to Spiritual, Moral and Personal Values in the FE Curriculum: A Compilation of Examples*, London.

Ministerium für Schule und Weiterbildung, Wissenschaft und Forschung des Landes, NRW (1999) *Sekundarstufe II Gymnasium/Gesamtschule: Richtlinien und Lehrpläne, Evangelische Religion*, Dusseldorf.

Morgan, S. (1999) 'Feminist Approaches', in P. Connolly and N. Smart (eds), *Approaches to the Study of Religion*, London: Cassell, 42–72.

Mukta, P. (1997) '"New Hinduism": Teaching Intolerance, Practising Aggression', *Resource* 20(1): 9–13.

Murray, D. (1985) *Worlds Apart: Segregated Schools in Northern Ireland*, London: Appletree Press.

Myers, K. (1992) *Genderwatch: After the Reform Act*, Cambridge: Cambridge University Press.

NCC (1991) *RE: A Local Curriculum Framework*, National Curriculum Council.

NCC (1993) *Spiritual and Moral Development – A Discussion Paper*, York: National Curriculum Council.

Nielsen, N. C. (1993) *Fundamentalism, Myths and World Religions*, State of New York University Press.

Nesbitt, E. (1991) 'My Dad's Hindu, My Mum's Side are Sikhs', Issues in Religious Identity, Arts, Culture, Education Research and Curriculum Papers, Charlbury: National Foundation for Arts Education (Available from author).

—— (1993) 'Children and the World to Come: The Views of Children Aged Eight to Fourteen on Life after Death', *Religion Today* 8(3): 10–13.

—— (1997) '"We Are All Equal": Young British Punjabis' and Gujaratis' Perceptions of Caste', *International Journal of Punjab Studies* 4(2): 201–18.

—— (1998a) 'Bridging the Gap between Young People's Experience of their Religious Traditions at Home and at School: The Contribution of Ethnographic Research', *British Journal of Religious Education* 20(2): 102–14.

—— (1998b) 'British, Asian and Hindu: Identity, Self-Narration and the Ethnographic Interview', *Journal of Beliefs and Values* 19(2): 189–200.

—— (1999a) 'Friend in the Field: A Reflexive Approach to Being a Quaker Ethnographer', *Quaker Studies* 4(2): 82–112.

—— (1999b) '"Being Religious Shows in Your Food": Young British Hindus and Vegetarianism', in T. S. Rukmani (ed.), *Hindu Diaspora: Global Perspectives*, Montreal: Concordia University Press, 397–425.

—— (1999c) 'The Impact of Morari Bapu's Kathas on Young British Hindus', *Scottish Journal of Religious Studies* 22(1): 95–118.

—— (2000) *The Religious Lives of Sikh Children: A Coventry Based Study*, Leeds: Community Religions Project, Department of Theology and Religious Studies, University of Leeds.

—— (2001) 'Ethnographic Research at Warwick: Some Methodological Issues', *British Journal of Religious Education* 23(3): 144–55.

—— (2001) 'What Young British Hindus Believe: Some Issues for the Researcher and the RE Teacher', in H.-G. Heimbrock, C. Scheilke and P. Schreiner (eds), *Towards Religious Competence*, Münster, Lit-Verlag, 150–64.

Oberoi, H. (1994) *The Construction of Religious Boundaries: Culture, Identity and Diversity in the Sikh Tradition*, New Delhi: Oxford University Press.

O'Brien, D.D. (1987) *Public Theology, Civil Religion and American Catholicism*, Philadelphia: University of Pennsylvania Press.

OFSTED (1994) *Spiritual, Moral, Social and Cultural Development: An OFSTED Discussion Paper*, London: OFSTED.

—— (1997) *The Impact of the New Agreed Syllabuses on Teaching and Learning in RE*, London: OFSTED.

—— (2000a) *Standards and Quality in Education 1998/1999: The Annual Report of Her Majesty's Chief Inspector of Schools*, London: HMSO.

—— (2000b) *National Summary Data Report for Secondary Maintained Schools*, London: HMSO.

Ogden, V. (2000) *Establishing and Enriching Religious Education at 16-plus*, in Wright, A. and Brandon, A. M. 2000 *Learning to Teach Religious Education in the Secondary School*, Part III, ch. 9, London: RoutledgeFalmer.

Oliner, Samuel P. and Pearl, M. (1988) *The Altruistic Personality. Rescuers of Jews in Nazi Europe*, Macmillan.

Opie, I. and P. (1959) *The Lore and Language of Schoolchildren*, O.U.P.

Østberg, S. (2002) *Pakistani Children in Oslo: Islamic Nurture in a Secular Context*, Leeds: Community Religions Project, Department of Theology and Religious Studies, University of Leeds.

Ouseley, H. (2001) *Community Pride not Prejudice. Making Diversity Work in Bradford*, Bradford: Bradford Vision.

Oxford, Cambridge and RSA Examinations (OCR) (2000) *OCR Advanced Subsidiary GCE in Religious Studies, OCR Advanced GCE in Religious Studies*, Oxford: OCR.

Phenix, P. (1964) *Realms of Meaning*, New York: McGraw-Hill.

Piaget, J. and Weil, A. (1951) 'The Development of the Idea of the Homeland and of Relations With Other Countries', in *International Social Science Bulletin 3*.

Pocock, D. (1976) 'Preservation of the Religious Life: Hindu Immigrants in England', *Contributions to Indian Sociology* 10(2): 341–65.

Preston, N.S. (1997) '*Becoming a Copt*' in *Between the Desert and the City*, Oslo: Novus Institute for Comparative Research in Human Culture.

—— (1998) 'Multiple Choice? Language-Usage and the Transmission of Religious Tradition within the Coptic Orthodox Community in London', *British Journal of Religious Education* 20(2): 90–101.

Prinja, N.K. (1996) *Explaining Hindu Dharma: A Guide for Teachers*, Norwich: Religious and Moral Education Press.

QCA (1998) *Religious Education and the Use of Language*, London: QCA.
—— (1999) *Guidance on Learning from Religion*, London: QCA.
—— (2000) *Non Statutory Guidance on Religious Education*, London: QCA.
—— (2000) *Citizenship at Key Stages 3 and 4: Initial Guidance for Schools*, London: QCA.
—— (2000) *Personal, Social and Health Education at Key Stages 3 and 4: Initial Guidance for Schools*, London: QCA.
—— (2000) *Religious Education: Non Statutory Guidance on RE*, London: QCA.
QCA/DfEE (1998) *Education for Citizenship and the Teaching of Democracy in Schools*, London: QCA.
—— (2000) *A Scheme of Work for Key Stages 1 and 2: Religious Education Teacher's Guide*, London: QCA.
QCA (2001) *Planning, Teaching and Assessing the Curriculum for Pupils with Learning Difficulties*: RE QCA.
Radford-Reuther, R. (1983) *Sexism and God-Talk: Towards a Feminist Theology*, London: SCM.
Read, G., Rudge, J. and Teece, G. (1992) *How Do I Teach RE?*, 2nd edn, Cheltenham: Stanley Thornes.
Robinson. E, (1977), *The Original Vision* The Religious Experience Unit, Manchester College, Oxford.
Runzo, J. and Martin, N.M. (2000) *The MEANING of Life*, London: One World Publications.
Said, E. (1978) *Orientalism*, London: Routledge & Kegan Paul.
SCAA (1994) *Model Syllabuses for Religious Education*, London: SCAA.
—— (1994) *Model Syllabuses for Religious Education: Model 1, Living Faiths Today*, London: SCAA.
—— (1994) *Model Syllabuses for Religious Education: Model 2, Questions and Teachings*, London: SCAA.
—— (1994) *Model 1: Living Faiths Today*, London: SCAA.
—— (1994) *Model 2: Questions and Teaching*, London: SCAA.
Schechner, R. (1988) *Performance Theory*, London: Routledge.
—— (ed.) (1993) *The Future of Ritual*, London: Routledge.
Schechner, R. and Appel, W. (eds) (1990) *By Means of Performance*, Cambridge: Cambridge University Press.
Schools' Council (1971) *Religious Education in Secondary Schools*, Working Paper 36, London: Evans Brothers and Methuen Education.
Scholey, A. (2002) *The Paragon Parrot (Tales of Rumi)*, London: Watkins Publishing.
Schreiner, P. (1999) 'Different Approaches to RE/RS in European Schools: The Scandinavian Approach in a European Context', in N.-Å. Tidman (ed.), *Into the Third Millennium...EFTRE Conference August 1998 in Copenhagen*, 111–29.
—— (ed.) (2000) *Religious Education in Europe*, Münster: ICCS/Comenius-Institut.
Schwartz, J. (1998) 'Christians Teaching in the Public Schools: What Are Some Options?', *Journal of Education and Christian Belief* 2(1): 53–64.
Schweitzer, F. (2000) *Das Recht des Kindes auf Religion*, Gutersloh.
Scott, J. (1986) 'Are Equal Opportunities Possible in RE?', *RE News and Views* 3(2): 13–14.
Searle-Chatterjee, M. (2000) '"World Religions" and "Ethnic Groups": Do these Paradigms Lend Themselves to the Cause of Hindu Nationalism?', *Ethnic and Racial Studies* 23 (3): 497-515
Seed, J., Macy, J. and Naess, A. (1988) *Thinking Like a Mountain*, New York: Heretic Books.

Shap (1999/2000) *The Journal of the Shap Working Party on World Religions in Education: Can I Teach Your Religion*, ed. A. Seaman.

Shaw, A. (2000) *Kinship and Continuity: Pakistani Families in Britain*, Amsterdam: Harwood Academic Publishers.

Skinner, G. (1993) 'Religious Education: Equal but Different?', in Pumfrey, P. and Varma, G. (eds) *Cultural Diversity and the Curriculum: The Foundation Subjects and RE in Secondary Schools*, Vol 1 Falmer

Slee, N. (2000) 'A Subject in Her Own Right: The Religious Education of Women and Girls', The Hockerill Lecture, London: 2000.

Smart, N. *The World's Religions*, 2nd edn (1998) C.U.P.

Smart N. (1999) *Dimensions of the Sacred*, Fontana Press.

Smith, W.C. (1978) *The Meaning and End of Religion*, London: SPCK.

Spender, D. (1980) *Man-Made Language*, London: Routledge & Kegan Paul.

Spender, D. and Sarah, E. (eds) (1981) *Learning to Lose*, London: The Women's Press.

Stanworth, M. (1983) *Gender and Schooling: A Study of Sexual Divisions in the Classroom*, London: Hutchinson.

Stringer, M. (1999) *On the Perception of Worship: The Ethnography of Worship in Four Christian Congregations in Manchester*, Birmingham: University of Birmingham Press.

Swann, M. (1985) *Education for All: Final Report of the Committee of Inquiry into the Education of Children from Ethnic Minority Groups*, cmnd.9453: HMSO, London.

Thatcher, A. (1999) *Spirituality and the Curriculum*, London: Cassell.

Theissen, E. J. (1993) *Teaching for Committment: Liberal Education, Indoctrination and Christian Nurture*, Gracewing: Leominster.

Thompson, P. (1996) 'Some Thoughts on the Problem of Pluralism', *Spectrum* 28(1): 3–44.

—— (2000) 'Sunday At Farmington', *The Farmington Institute Bulletin*, 5–8.

Tillich, P. (1959) 'A Theology of Education', in P. Tillich, *Theology of Culture*, Oxford: Oxford University Press.

Trevett, C. (1983), *The Lady Vanishes: Sexism by Omission in Religous Education*, British Journal of Religous Education, 5(2) pp. 81–3.

Turner, V. (1969) *The Ritual Process*, Chicago: University of Illinois Press.

—— (1974) *Dramas, Fields and Metaphors*, Ithaca, NY: Cornell University Press.

Turner, V. (1977) 'Symbols in African Religion' in *Symbolic Anthropology: A reader in the study of symbols and meanings*. Eds Dolgin, J. L., Kemnitzer, D.S., and Schneider, D.M., Columbia University Press: New York

—— (1986) *The Anthropology of Performance*, New York: PAJ.

—— (1992) *The Magic of Ritual*, Harper.

Verma, G. (ed.) (1998) *Cultural Diversity and the Curriculum: The Foundation Subjects and Religious Education in Secondary Schools*, Vol. 1, London: The Falmer Press.

Wadman, D. and Coddington, V. (1991) Forms of Assessment in Religious Education, Exeter University.

Walden, R. and Walkerdine, V. (1985) *Girls and Mathematics: From Primary to Secondary Schooling*, London: University of London Institute of Education.

Wardekker, W. and Miedema, S. (2001) 'Religious Identity Formation between Participation and Distantiation' in Heimbrock, H.G., Scheilke, C.T. and Schreiner P. (eds), *Towards Religious Competence*, Münster: 23–33.

Watton, V. (1996) *Religion and Life*, London: Hodder & Stoughton.

Wayne, E. and Everington, J. with Kadodwala, D. and Nesbitt, E. (1996) *Hindus*, Interpreting Religions series, Oxford: Heinemann.

Weatherley, L. and Hallis, S. (1996) *Inspire, Guidelines for Religious Education at Key Stages 1 and 2*, Salisbury: Salisbury and Winchester Diocesan Boards of Education.

Webb, S. (2000) *Taking Religion to School*, Grand Rapids, MI: Brazos Press.

Weiner, G. (ed.) (1985) *Just a Bunch of Girls: Feminist Approaches to Schooling*, Milton Keynes: Open University Press.

Whyte, J. (1986) *Girls into Science and Technology*, London: Routledge & Kegan Paul.

—— (1986) *Beyond the Wendy House: Sex Role Stereotyping in Primary Schools*, York: Longman.

World Council of Churches (2000) *Concepts on Teaching and Learning in Religions*, in EEF-Net 6–2000, 10–11.

Wright, A. (1993) *Religious Education in the Secondary School*, London: David Fulton.

—— (2000) *Spirituality and Education*, London: Routledge/Falmer.

Wright, A. and Brandom, A. (2000) *Learning to Teach Religious Education in the Secondary School*, London: Routledge/Falmer.

Young, F. (ed.) (1997) *Encounter with Mystery: Reflections on L' Arche and Living with Disability*, London: D.L.T.

Zimbardo, R. (1968) *Tolkien and the Critics*, Notre Dame: University of Notre Dame Press.

Internet references

www.farmington.ac.uk, details of the Farmington Institute for Christian Studies, 5 February 2002.

www.qca.org.uk, up-to-date information about RS in the 16–19 sector, 5 February 2002.

www.qca.org.uk/nq/framework/managing/c2k_reading.asp. Further reading can be found in *Managing Curriculum 2000 for 16–19 students*, 5 February 2002.

www.warwick/wie/wreru, details of the Warwick RE Project, 5 February 2002.

www.standards.dfee.gov.uk/genderandachievement/data_1.2.1.html, DfEE 2001, 'Gender and Achievement', 5 February 2002.

There are many interesting and useful articles in the 1994 Spring edition of *RE Today* on how primary teachers can practically begin to 'write women back' into primary curriculum.

Strategies for assisting primary, secondary and special schools and teachers to reflect on the hidden, as well as overt curriculum were promoted, in 'Genderwatch after the Education Reform Act'. The chapters on RE and Collective Worship contain 'assessment schedules' that direct teachers who 'want to do something but are not sure what' to where women's contributions in world religions can be found and highlights how these might be promoted in multi-faith RE.

The *British Journal of Religious Education* 1988 special edition on Gender and Religion published in 1998, Nicola Slee's Hockerill Lecture 2000 and the 1988 edition of the annual SHAP publication (Erricker and Barnett 1988) all contain a range of views, articles written by women from within faith traditions and remains an excellent source of information and insights into the current debates on women, religion and Religious Education.

Index

Abraham 181
Adams, D. 169
Advanced (A2) 156, 157
Advanced Extension Award (AEA), post-
    16 Religious Studies 160–1
Advanced Subsidiary (AS) 152, 156, 157
affective approach 186
affective aspect 140–1
Agreed Syllabuses 131; Church of England
    aided schools 34–5; Circular 1/94 6
altruism 104
Anglican *see* Church of England
answers, right and wrong 52
anti-realism: aims of Religious Education
    183–5; and realism 179–82
anti-religionist approach 50
AQA (Assessment and Qualifications
    Alliance) 155–7
Aquinas, St Thomas 127
Arthur, C. 23
assessment 13–14; assessing achievement
    56–70; GCSE Religious Studies 57–8;
    impact of National Curriculum 60–4;
    National Expectations for RE 64–7;
    post-16 Religious Studies 157–9; qual-
    ifications framework 68
Association of RE Inspectors Advisors and
    Consultants (AREAIC) 61, 66
attainment targets 62–3, 172, 175, 190,
    191, 192; AT1 and AT2 11–12, 62;
    National Expectations for RE 64; and
    special educational needs 140
auctoritas 215
Auden, W. H. 197
authority 215–16
autonomy 185
awareness 137–8

Bailey, J., Church schools 27–40

Baker, K. 4
Ballard, R. 114, 116
Bapu, M. 113
bar-mitzvah 141
Barratt, M. 118
Baumann, G. 114
Baxter, A. 113
BBC 21
being, and sensing finitude 109–10
belief, Key Stages 39–40
Bennett, D. 121
Bible, Key Stages 37
Birmingham LEA 8–9
birth, and death, cycle 168
Bishops' Conference (Roman Catholic)
    27, 28
Blunkett, D. 42
Bosnia-Herzegovina, Culture of Religions
    91–3
Bowker, J., world religions 210–17
Bradford 63; riots 20, 104
Bradley, F. H. 181
Broadbent, L.: rationale for religious
    education 16–26; special educational
    needs 136–49; whole school initiatives
    165–77
Brown, A. 36; special educational needs
    136–49; statutory requirements 3–15
Brown, E. 36, 148
Buddhism: Buddhists 105; communal roots
    139
Burghart, R. 114
Burnley, riots 20
Burridge, S. 171

catechesis 28
Catholic Certificate in Religious Studies 30
Catholicism: Bishops' Conference 27, 28;
    community   base   138;   European

context 87; realism and anti-realism 182; Roman Catholic schools 27–30; Roman Catholic schools, and Church of England schools compared 42; Roman Catholic Voluntary Aided schools 34; Roman Catholics 21; USA 214

Celebration 29

celebration, and change 140–2

Chosen People 105

Christianity: biblical knowledge 7–8; Christian festivals, Key Stages 1–2 38–9; Christian worship, Key Stages 1–2 39; and Circular 3/89 5–6; internecine warfare, liberals and conservatives 8–9; syllabuses and Circular 1/94 6–7, *see also* Catholicism; Church of England; Orthodox Church; Protestant RE

Church of England: aided schools 30–5; Board of Education 152; schools 27; schools, and Roman Catholic schools compared 42; Voluntary Controlled schools 35–40

Church schools 27–43

Church (the) 28; Key Stages 38

Circulars: Circular 1/94 6–7; Circular 3/89 5–6, *see also* legislation

citizenship, and Values Forum 10–11

Clarke, K. 6

Clarricoates, K. M. 125

Coddington, V. 62

cognitive development: critical thinking 107–8; developmental psychology 106

Cole, D. 123

Collective Worship 201–9; Circular 1/94 6–7; Education Reform Act 4–5; and Religious Education 7

Come and Praise (BBC) 206

commitment, and indoctrination 48–55

communitas 199

communities, and religion 138–40

community based education, realignment 41–3

community schools, Church of England Voluntary Aided schools 34

concrete thinking, child development 106

confessional approach 58; Europe 88; pupils with SLD 145–6; Roman Catholic schools 29

conservatism, and controversy 14

continued professional development (CPD) 67

controversy: and conservatism 14; and relativism 52

conventions, challenging of 143

Cooling, T., stories, commitment and indoctrination 44–55

Copley, T. 62

Coptic Orthodox Christians 113

corrupting the young, as education 185

Council of All Beings, The 190, 195, 198

Council for the Curriculum, Examinations and Assessment (CCEA), Northern Ireland 155

Cox, E. 17, 18, 137, 138, 141

creation story 134

Crick, B. 10–11

Crick Report 10–11, 174

culture: barriers, Europe 96; cultural development, whole school initiatives 176; cultural relativism 154, *see also* ethnography

Cupitt, D. 214

Curriculum Guidelines for Pupils with Learning Difficulties 66–7

cycle, birth and death 168

Daly, M. 127

dating, Christian calendar 168

Davie, G. 20, 21, 26

Dayton Peace Treaty 92

Dearing Report 34, 40, 41, 63, 150–1, 160

death 109; and birth, cycle 168

Deem, R. 125

Delamont, S. 125

denominational approach, Europe 88, 90

denominational education 42–3

Department for Education and Skills (DfES), Collective Worship 204–7

development: child development 101–2, 106; cognitive development, critical thinking 107–8; personal development, whole school initiatives 171–4; social and psychological development 101–10; spiritual, moral, social and cultural development 174–6

dialogical approach 128

Diana, Princess of Wales 21–2

Diocesan Board of Education (Church of England) 30

Divali, use of story 144

diversity 20; inclusive gender strategy 133, *see also* multi-faith

divine intervention 45

Driver, T. 193
Durham Diocesan Syllabus (1993) 30, 31
Durham Report 191

Early Years, assessment 67
Edexcel Foundation 155, 156, 157
education: liberal education 17; process of 18
Education Acts *see under* legislation
'Efficacy-Entertainment Braid' 193–5
egalitarian message (lost), feminists rejection of concept 127–8
'Eight Ages of Man' (Erikson) 23
empathy 104
Enlightenment, individualism 138
equality of opportunity, gender 123–4
Erikson, E. 23
ethics 186; aims of Religious Education 183–5; ethical debate, and moral debate 178–88; learning right from wrong 142–3; realism, and anti-realism 179–82
ethnic cleansing: Bosnia-Herzegovina 92, *see also* racism
ethnography 111–22; identity 113; pedagogy 120–1; research 111–14, *see also* culture
European context 86–98; Bosnia-Herzegovina, Culture of Religions 91–3; Germany, Protestant RE 91, 95–6; Switzerland, Religion and Culture 91, 93–4
European Forum for Teachers of Religious Education (EFTRE) 97
evangelisation 28
Everington, J. 118
Exploring Inner Space (Hay) 22

faith, Roman Catholic schools 29
Farmington Fellowship 117
Farmington Institute for Christian Studies 118
feminism: critique of religions 127–8; definition 124, *see also* gender
finitude 109–10
fiqh 216
Five Strands approach 185–7
forgiveness 203
Forms of Assessment in RE (FARE) 62
Fowler, R. B. 60
France 87
Freire, P. 97
fundamentalism, and terrorism 21

Future is Female, The 125

Ganesh 107
Gates, B., social and psychological development of pupils 101–10
GCSE (General Certificate of Secondary Education) 13, 40; gender 132; and *National Expectations for RE* 65, 66; Religious Studies 57–8
Geaves, R. 114, 115, 116
Geertz, C. 193
gender: aims and concerns of RE 129–30; definition 124; equal opportunities 123–4; feminist critique of RE 129; gendered nature of RE 131–2; inclusive gender strategy 123–35; pedagogy 132–5, *see also* feminism
Genderwatch Project 125
Gere, R. 21
Germany, Protestant RE 91, 95–6
gifts, pleasure of giving 103
Gilborn, D. 123, 126
Giles, A., Religious Studies at post-16 150–62
Goldman, R. 8, 23
Granth Sahib, Guru 120
Grimmitt, M. 47, 49–50, 97, 191
Gumpati 107

Hammond, J., spiritual dimension 189–200
Hampshire Education Authority 24
Handbook for the Inspection of Schools (OFSTED) 72–3
Hanlon, D., inclusive gender strategy 123–35
Hansard 4, *see also* legislation
Hay, D. 22
healing, and community 139
Here I am: A Religious Education Programme for Primary Schools 29
Hick, J. 45–6, 47, 49, 50, 51, 154
Hill, B. 46–7
Hill, D. 123
Hillsborough stadium disaster 21, 204
Hinduism: aspects of the divine 169; community activity 139; Divali, use of story 144; and ethnographic evidence 117; festival of Kumbh Mela 21; Gujarati 113, 115; Hindu tradition 105; Hindus 117; symbolic thinking 107; tradition, ethnographic research 113

Hirst, P. 17, 18–19
Hong Kong, RS at 'A' level 150
Honorius of Autun 194
horizons, extending, and stereotypes 104–5
Hull, J. 49
human sciences, child development 101–2
humanists, human development 102

Icons 29, 29–30
ICT (Information and Communication Technology), whole school initiatives 169–71
identity: ethnographic research 113; problematising 'religions' 114–17
inclusivity: gender 123–35; pupils with SEN 147–8
individualism 138
indoctrination 60; and commitment 48–55
information, and meaning 26
Inspecting Schools (OFSTED) 73
inspections *see* OFSTED; Section 23 inspections
Inspire 30, 32
instrumental view 50
Intereuropean Commission on Church and School (ICCS) 97
internet 170
Ipgrave, J. 113, 118, 121
Is God a Virus? Genes, Culture and Religion (Bowker) 212
Islam: BBC documentary 21; France 87; gender 135; Muslim calendar 168; names for Allah 169; realism and anti-realism 182; ritual and disability 142; sense of community 139
Isle of Wight 19

Jackson, R. 113, 114–15, 117, 118, 120
Jesus: Key Stages 1–2 37–8; story of walking on water 106
Jews 19
Jonah, story of 106
Joseph, K. 4
Judaism: approach to in Roman Catholic schools 30; bar-mitzvah 141; gender 135; Jewish calendar 168; Passover 197; Purim, use of story 144, 208; Rosh Hashanah 169; sense of community 139; Yom Kippur 198

Katalushi, C. 129

Keast, J. assessing achievement 56–70
Kent 63
Key Stages: critical thinking 107–8; Key Stage 1, Church of England aided schools 32–4; Key Stage 1, Church of England Voluntary Controlled schools 35–6; Key Stage 1, sense of belonging 104; Key Stage 2, Church of England Voluntary Aided schools 33, 34; Key Stage 2, Church of England Voluntary Controlled schools 36; Key Stages 1–2, Church of England Voluntary Controlled schools 37–40; Key Stages 1–3 12; Key Stages 1–3, assessment 67; Key Stage 4 172; moral development 176 pupils with SEN 146; weaknesses in RE 131, *see also* syllabuses
King, U. 128, 130, 134
knowledge: facts and understanding 58–9; forms of 17; limitations of internet 171; and meaning 18–19
Krisman, A. 148
KUE (Knowledge, Understanding and Evaluation) 57, 59
Kung, H. 24

labyrinth 198
Lall, S. 117
Lancaster 59
language barriers, Europe 96
language skills, whole school initiatives 165–7
L'Arche community 139
Lawrence, S. 20
learning: about religion and from religion 65–6; development of 167; learning right from wrong, SEN 142–4; and teaching 56
legislation: Education Act (1944) 9, 20, 174, 211; Education Act (1993) 62, 138; Education Act (1996) 138; Education Reform Act (1988) 3, 4–5, 16, 43, 59, 105, 124, 211; Schools Inspection Act (1992) 9, 71, *see also* Circulars; Hansard
Leicester, Roman Catholic schools 27
Leonard, Dr G. (Bishop of London) 4, 9
liberal democracy 182
Licensed Insanities (Bowker) 213
liminality 193, 194
Lincolnshire Agreed Syllabus 35–6
literacy, whole school initiatives 165–7

Local Education Authorities (LEAs):
Agreed Syllabus, Church of England
aided schools 34–5; Agreed Syllabus,
Church of England Voluntary
Controlled schools 40; agreed
syllabuses and OFSTED 74;
Education Reform Act 5, 16; gender
125; model syllabuses 12, 25; and
National Curriculum 12–13;
OFSTED reports 84
Loukes, H. 8, 172, 176

Macpherson Report 20
Madonna 21
Maintained Schools 132, 150
Manchester Diocesan Syllabus (1995) 30,
33, 36
Mantin, R. 134
Martin, J. 126
masks 198–9
meaning 24; and information 26; and
knowledge 18–19
media 20–5
meta-narrative, and stories 44–7, 50–1
Methodist Division of Education and
Youth 152
Mirza, H. S. 123, 126
Mission, Management, Appraisal (National
Society) 27
Mitchell, B. 50
Model Syllabuses for RE (SCAA) 49, 62
Moore, G. 180
moral debate, and ethical debate 178–88
moral development 176
Morgan, S. 127, 128
Morris, E. 42
Mukta, P. 119
multi-faith and multi-cultural society 9,
11, 19–20, 42; and denominational
education 42–3
music, pupils with SEN 143
Muslims 19, 58
Myerhof, B. 193
Myers, K. 124

Nanak, Guru 134
National Association of SACREs
(NASACRE) 66
National Board for Religious Inspectors
and Advisers (NBRIA) 76
National Curriculum 10, 16, 41; assess-
ment, influence on RE 60–2; RE as

part of 12–14; spirituality 48, *see also*
syllabuses
National Curriculum Council (NCC) 11;
agreed syllabuses 62; assessment 63
National Curriculum Handbooks 172
National Expectations for RE 64–7
National Qualifications Framework 68
National Society 75, 77
National Society's Inspection Handbook, The
75
Nesbitt, E., ethnography 111–22
Netherlands 87
neutrality approach, commitment and
indoctrination 49
New Year, calendars of different religions
168
Non-statutory guidance in RE 64
Northern Ireland 104; RS at 'A' level 150
numeracy, whole school initiatives 167–9

Oberoi, H. 115
objectivity 3
O'Brien, D. 214
OCR (Oxford, Cambridge and RSA
Examinations) 155, 156
OFSTED (Office for Standards in
Education) 9, 12, 13, 25, 40, 64;
feedback 82–3; inspections compared
to Section 23 inspections 75–8;
interview with subject leader 79–80;
lesson observation 80–2; preparing
for inspection 78; role of 71–4, 83–5;
spiritual, moral, social and cultural
development 174; spirituality 191;
subject report 83; weaknesses in RE
131; work scrutiny 82
Ogden, V. 151–2
ordination, gender 135
Orientalism 114
Orthodox churches, community base
138–9
Østberg, S. 113, 116
Ouseley Report 104

P levels 67
parallel play 103
parents, interest in religious schools 41
Pascal, B. 169
Passover 197
patriarchy 124, 133–4; and the creation
story 134
Pedagogies of Religious Education
(Grimmitt) 191

pedagogy 97; ethnography 120–1; inclusive gender strategy 132–5
Phenix, P. H. 18–19, 26
phenomenological approach 5, 18, 59
Phillips, S. 198
philosophy of religion 186
PHSE 12
Piaget, J. 23, 104
play, parallel play 103
pluralism 49
post-16 Religious Studies 150–62; Advanced Extension Award 160–1; awarding bodies, specifications 155–7; key skills 159–60; legal context 150–1; literature review 151–2; subject criteria 152–5; synoptic assessment 157–9
Prayer of St Francis 206
Preston, N. S. 113
Price, J. 118
Priestly, J. 62
primary schools, subject leaders 79
Prinja, N. K. 119
private schools, relationship with public schools in Europe 87–8
Professional Council for RE (PCfRE) 66
Protestant RE 91, 95–6
psychological development, and social development of pupils 101–10
public schools, relationship with private schools in Europe 87–8
Purim, use of story 144, 208

qallada 215–16
QCA (Qualifications and Curriculum Authority) 5, 12, 13, 16, 25, 64; and AREAIC 66; *Curriculum Guidelines for Pupils with Learning Difficulties* 66–7; Graduation Certificate 152; post-16 studies 153, 154–5, 156; special educational needs 138, 140, 144–6; spirituality 191; subject leaders 79, *see also* Model Syllabuses
qualifications framework, assessment 68

racism 20; ethnic cleansing, Bosnia-Herzegovina 92; little Englanders 105
Radford-Reuther, R. 127
Read, G. 191
reaggregation 193, 194
realism: aims of Religious Education 183–5; and anti-realism 179–82

recall 58
reciprocity, pleasure of giving gifts 103–4
Reformation, individualism 138
relativism, and controversy 52
relevance 8
Religion in the Service of the Child 196
Religious Education: An Interpretive Approach (Jackson) 114
Religious Education Curriculum Directory for Catholic Schools 28, 29
Religious Education in the Primary School (Brown and Brown) 36
Religious Education (RE) 3–4; Circular 1/94 6–7; Circular 3/89 5–6; and Collective Worship 7; Education Reform Act 4; Spiritual, Moral, Social and Cultural Development 9–10
Religious Education Teacher's Guide (QCA) 74–5
Religious Education and the Use of Language (QCA) 165
Religious Instruction (RI) 3, 59
Religious Studies (RS) 3–4, 8; aims of 183; AS and A level 68; and denominational approach 88, 90; post-16 level 13, 150–62
research: ethnography 111–14; spiritual experience 22
Revelation 28
Ricoeur, P. 196
right, from wrong 142–4
ritual 141–2, 192–7
Roman Catholic *see* Catholicism
Rudge, J. 61

Said, E. 114
SCAA (School Curriculum and Assessment Authority) 10–11, 211; Model Syllabuses 49, 62, 140
Schechner, R. 193–4
Schemes of Work in RE 13
Schools: Building on Success (Green Paper) 41, 68
schools, Church schools 27–43
Schools Council 59
Schools' Council Working Paper 4
Schreiner, P., European context 86–98
Searle-Chatterjee, M. 115
Section 23 inspections 74–8, 84
secularisation 214; neutrality approach 49
secularisation theory 90
self 109

SEN (special educational needs) 136–49;
  change and celebration 140–2;
  communities 138–40; Key Stages
  146; learning right from wrong
  142–4; QCA 138, 140, 143–6;
  syllabuses 146–8
sensitivities 137–8
sensory materials, use, pupils with SEN
  144–5
separation 193, 194
Shap Working Party on World Religions
  in Education 4
shared goals 53–4
Sikhism 19, 58, 117, 119–20, 134;
  communal roots 139
silence 184, 196, 197
skills 26, 53; post-16 Religious Studies
  159–60; pupils with SEN 145
Skinner, G. 130
Slee, N. 130
Smart, N. 4, 18, 60; re-feel the universe
  140, 141
Smith, W. C. 114–15
social development 176; and psychological
  development of pupils 101–10
social education, whole school initiatives
  171–4
sociological approach 186
Socrates 185
solitariness 184
'Son of God' (documentary) 21
Songs of Praise 21
Spiritual, Moral, Social and Cultural
  Development (SMSC) 9–10
spiritual experiences, research 22
*Spiritual and Moral Development – A
  Discussion Paper* (NCC) 175
*Spiritual, Moral, Social and Cultural
  Development* (OFSTED) 175
spirituality 175, 189–200; problem of definition 9–10, 48
Srpska, Republic of 92
Standing Advisory Council on RE
  (SACRE) 5, 84, 130
Stanworth, M. 125
statutory requirements 3–14
stories 196–7, 215; Collective Worship
  208; gender inclusive strategy 133–4;
  pupils with SEN 144; and religious
  education 44–7, 50–1
subject leader, interview with OFSTED
  inspectors 79
subversive, religion as 14
Swann Report 20, 173

Switzerland: Religion and Culture 91,
  93–4; sense of belonging 104
Syllabus Conference 5, 7, 13
syllabuses: Agreed Syllabuses 6, 34–5, 131;
  and Circular 1/94 6–7; Durham
  Diocesan Syllabus (1993) 30, 31;
  Manchester Diocesan Syllabus
  (1995) 30, 33, 36; Model Syllabuses
  11–12, 49; pupils with SEN 146–8;
  SCAA, Model Syllabuses 49, 62,
  140; West Riding syllabus 8, *see also*
  Key Stages; National Curriculum
symbolism 105–7, 196, 197, 212
syncretism 116
synoptic assessment, post-16 Religious
  Studies 157–9

Taliban, literalised understanding 107
taqlid 215–16
Taylor, G. M., Collective Worship 201–9
Teacher Training Agency (TTA) 79
teaching: grading in OFSTED inspections
  81–2; and learning 56
Temptation 32–3
terminology, European context 96
terrorism, and fundamentalism 21
thematic approach, Switzerland 94
'thick description' 112
thinking: critical thinking 107–8; literal
  and symbolic 105–7
Thompson, J., inspecting RE 71–85
Thompson, P. 50
Tillich, P. 106
Tomlinson, M. 71, 72, 83
transmission approach 97
Trevett, C. 133
truth 50, 171; realism and anti-realism
  179–82; and religious education 184
Turnbull, C. 194
Turner, V. 192, 193, 199
Tutu, D. 170

understanding 58

Values Forum, and citizenship 10–11
Vanier, J. 139
Vardy, P., ethical and moral debate 178–88
violence 8
Voluntary Aided schools 27; Section 23
  inspections 74–8
Voluntary Controlled schools 27; Church
  of England 35–40; Section 23 inspections 74–8

Wadman, D. 62
Walden, R. 125
Walkerdine, V. 125
Warwick Religions and Education
    Research Unit (WRERU) 113, 116
Watton, V. 118
'Way ahead: Church of England Schools
    in the New Millenium' (Dearing
    Report) 34, 40, 41, 63, 150–1, 160
Wayne, E. 118
Webster, D. 191
Weiner, G. 125
West Riding, syllabus 8
Westhill Project 54, 61
Whyte, J. 125
will of God 143

Wilson, G. 203, 204, 208
Winchester and Salisbury guidelines
    (Church of England) 30, 32
withdrawal clause, impact on teaching of
    RE 131
Wittgenstein, L. 153–4
Woodhead, C. 72
World Council of Churches (WCC) 90
world religions 8, 9, 210–17; approach to
    in Roman Catholic schools 30
World Trade Centre, bombing of 21
wrong, learning right from wrong 142–4

Yom Kippur 198
Young, F. 139
Yugoslavia *see* Bosnia-Herzegovina